COMPASS ENERGETICS

LEARN TO HEAL
YOUR ENERGY BODY

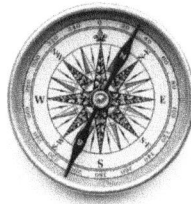

Book One

JEFFREY MIRAFLOR

ARNICA PRESS

Published by ARNICA PRESS
www.ArnicaPress.com

ISBN: 978-1-7352446-1-7

The material contained in this book has been written for informational purposes
and is not intended as a substitute for medical advice, nor is it intended to diagnose,
treat, cure, or prevent disease. If you have a medical issue or illness, consult a qualified
physician. The treatments and protocols described in this book are for reference only
and not intended to teach any technique, but rather to encourage further investigation
of those techniques. The author and the publisher disclaim any liability arising directly
or indirectly from the use of this book.

COMPASS ENERGETICS

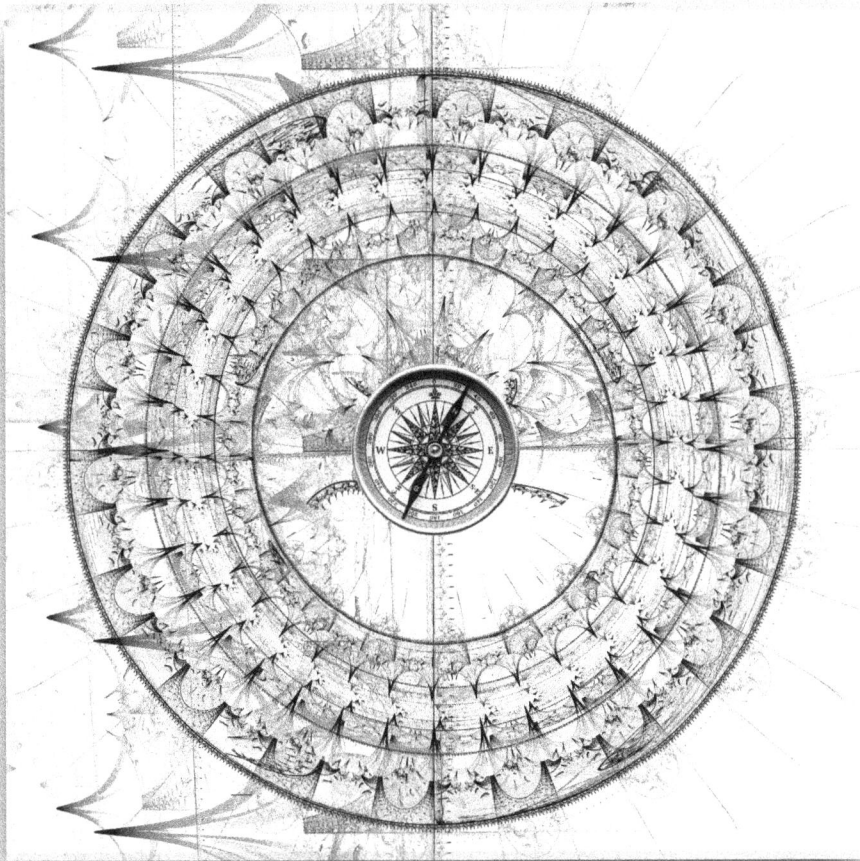

JEFFREY MIRAFLOR

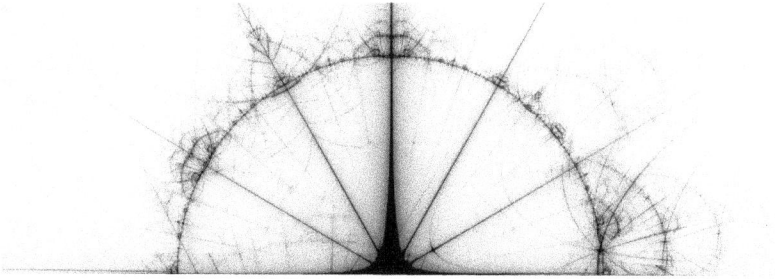

To My Parents,
Alberto and Consorcia

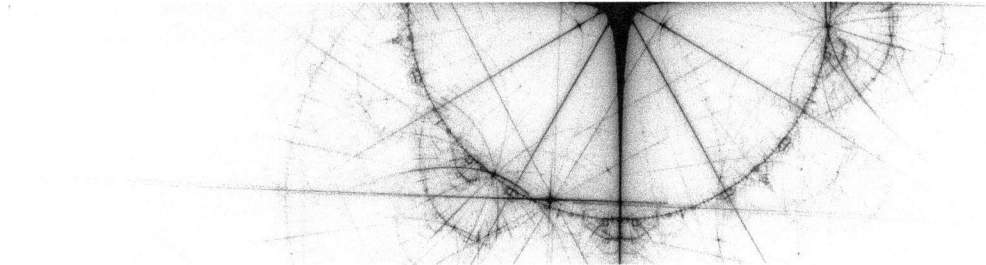

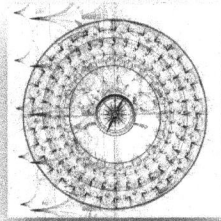

TABLE OF CONTENTS

Introduction   13

PART ONE ~ THE BIRTH OF A HEALER   17
I.   Knowledge is power   19
II. Father's love   25
III. The vow   30
IV. Uncharted territory   36
V. The big test   40
VI. The Master appears   46
VII. My mother's keeper   51
VIII. A true healer's heart   61

PART TWO ~ COMPASS ENERGETICS   71
IX. THE PRINCIPLES OF COMPASS ENERGETICS   73

X. THREE MOTIVATIONS   82

XI. SEVEN DIVINE INTELLIGENCES   90
      Information gatherers   91
      Social network people   93

Wordsmith people   95
Eggheads   97
Musical people   99
Sport Heroes   102
Visuals   103

XII. SUBTLE ENERGY AND THE BRAIN   106
Brain Spots   107
Genius Points   109
Hemispheres   112
Flip your brain   118
Brain Plaque and the Hippocampus   119
Reprogramming the Brain   119

PART THREE ~ THE HEALING PROCESS   123
XIII. CLEARING EMOTIONAL TRAUMA   125
Self-help Books   126
Belief systems   127
Energetic Clearings   129
Cords, Environment, and Chakras   130
Breathing Patterns   132

XIV. SCANNING , INTENTION, IMAGINATION   136
How I Perform My Clearings and Healing   137
Honey Bee   141
Wasabi   142
Dragon's Breath   143
Harvest Moon   145

XV. HEALING MODALITIES   148
Cleansing   148
Energizing   148

Energizing, and then Cleansing 149
How can I make you happy? 150
Let Nature take its course 150
Balloons 152
Vortex healing 153

PART FOUR ~ MAPPING 159
XVI. BRAIN MAPPING 161
Intrapersonal 162
Interpersonal 163
Linguistic 163
Logical 164
Musical 165
Kinesthetic 165
Visual 166
Left hemisphere 167
Right hemisphere 168

XVII. BODY MAPPING 170
The Face and Neck 174
Eyes 174
Ears 175
Nose 176
Tongue 177
Neck 177
Upper chest 178
Arms 179
Hands and fingers 180
Lower mid-section both front and back 180
Pelvis or genitalia 180
Hips and Legs 181
Feet and toes 182

PART FIVE ~ INNOVATIVE REMEDYING 185

XVIII. SUPER CHI 187
    Basics of Chi 187
    What is real health? 188
    Twelve primary channels and two vessels 189

XIX. THE YIN YANG PARADOX 193
    Ears 193
    Eyes 194
    Nose 195
    Arms 196
    Hips and Legs 197
    The Yin Yang Paradox 198
    The Yin yang of the seven intelligences 199

XX. EFFERENT AND AFFERENT NERVES 203
    Efferent nerves 206
    Afferent nerves 207
    Refference points 209

XXI. THE A, B AND C'S 214
    A ~ C Type people 217
    B type people 220
    A ~ C and B type 221
    Uniting A ~ C and B 221

PART SIX ~ OUR SUBTLE PATTERNS 225

XXII. BEHAVIORAL PATTERNS AND TRIGGERS 227
    Reptilian brain 234
    The subconscious 235
    Fear or insecurity masking another fear or insecurity 236

XXIII. BLOCKAGES   238
    Memory   241
    Ego   242
    Illogic   243

PART SEVEN ~ THE MULTIPLE- SELVES SYSTEM   251
XIV. PRINCIPLES OF THE MULTIPLE- SELVES
HEALING SYSTEM   253

XV. THE FIVE PRINCIPLE MOTIVATIONS   269

XXVI. AURA VARIATIONS   269
    Loving Aura   273
    Victim Aura   275
    Angry Auras   280
    Six signs to watch for   281
    It's about control – not love   282

XXVII. YOUR EARLIEST TRAUMA   286
    Expansion vs. Contraction   286
    Logical vs. Illogical thinking 287
    Chakra Map   289
    Clearing Your Blocks   292

Conclusion   293
About the Author   295

INTRODUCTION

The Chinese have a proverb stating *"A journey of 1000 miles starts with a single step"*. Writing this book has been my journey of a thousand steps, and I almost feel sorry that it is completed.

A year ago, my editor and mentor, Sabrina Mesko, encouraged me to write a book about my healing techniques and philosophy. At first I wasn't sure if I could pull it off, since I've never written a book before. But I went along with her advice, and with her encouragement and support continued.

It started out like any journey. Exciting at first, and then reality set in and the novelty quickly wore off. At times I wanted to turn back and return to my ordinary life. Now, I look back over the past year and am surprised how much I accomplished. If I had not finished or ever gotten started, I would have looked back on my life and be full of regrets.

The inspiration to write this book was a dedication to both my parents. They came to this country as immigrants, and worked very hard to give me the best possible life. I miss them dearly.

Writing a book truly forces you to think about what you know and what you're doing. Because of that, it has really honed my skills and made me a better healer.

The Multiple-Self Healing System was the first modality I developed and channeled. I had returned from a recent workshop where I learned Past-Life regression while using crystals. Back then, I never had any experiences with my past lives.

Before our session was conducted we were told that whatever talents, gifts, or abilities we had in the past life, could be downloaded. But for example, if we didn't learn to play the piano in the far past, then we couldn't download that skill today, because we never developed it in the first place.

As my session began, I was instantly transported back to the time of ancient Egypt. I was an Egyptian healer or Magi. It was like being in a movie, but I recalled clearly how it felt to be this individual. Remembering what my regression teacher said, I commanded to be downloaded. I saw geometric lines and symbols surround me. I felt as small as a drop of water in an infinite ocean floating and insignificant. The experience was powerful and difficult to describe. During this time my body was convulsing, because the download was too much for me to handle. The teacher had to be called in to slow down the process. I was told I was downloading at least seven lifetimes during which I was also a healer.

For several moments afterwards I was disoriented and mumbling outlandish predictions about myself. I don't remember half of what I said, except I knew in my heart of hearts, that I was destined to be an energy healer.

It hasn't been easy over the years. There are more times than I can recount, when I really wanted to quit. I thought the journey was going to be smooth and flowing. I would characterize it more like: something kept me going no matter how hard it was. And each day for more than two decades, I worked as hard as I could. If there's such a thing as talent, it would be my ability to do hard work.

What I've written is the culmination of over twenty years of experience investigating, researching, and disputing subtle energy teachings that I've been taught. I've tested every theory and idea presented to me on both myself and my clients. Many of my ideas are original and cannot be found anywhere else.

But that's the whole point. My purpose was to either re-interpret old-standing teachings for the modern age, or add new information. In ancient times teachings were limited to only a few selected students over a long stretch of time. Nowadays ancient teachings that were once kept secret are being revealed in unprecedented forms of media and books. We can now learn multiple healing modalities with less expense and trouble.

With the loving support of my family and my mission to take care of my mother, I devoted myself full-time to discover what works and what doesn't. I learned from every teacher and every workshop that I ever attended. Slowly, bits and pieces added to larger portions of the puzzle, until I developed my own system, Compass Energetics.

Whether you're a healer or just someone interested in the healing field, I hope to be a part of your journey.

May you be enlightened!

Jeffrey

PART ONE

THE BIRTH
OF A HEALER

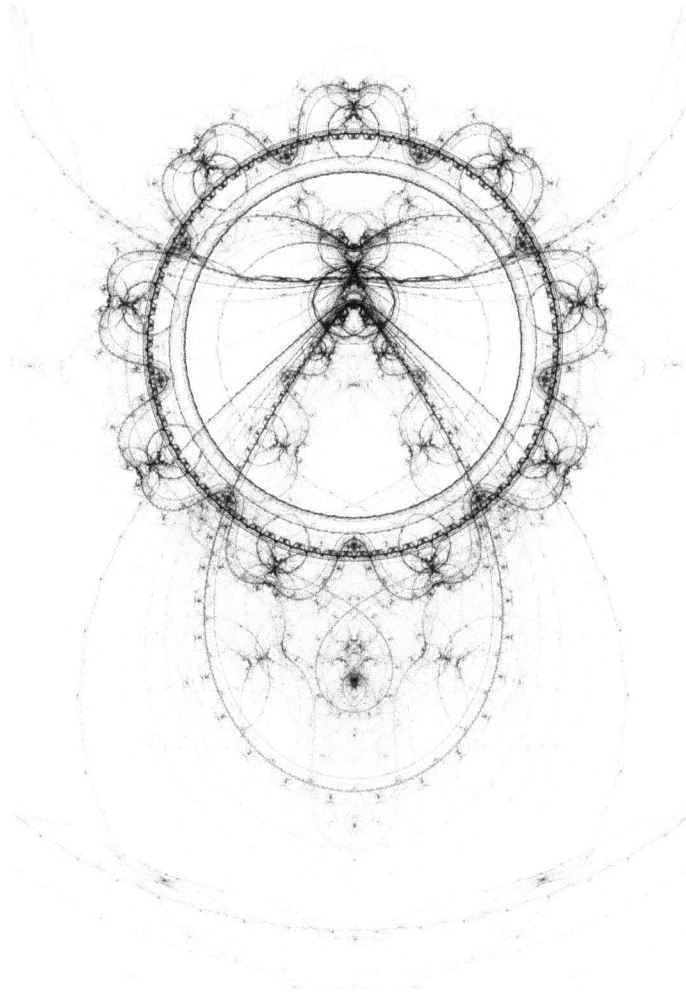

Chapter I.

KNOWLEDGE IS POWER

I was born an only child. My mother bore me at a late age soon after marrying my father. She was also in poor health, and had a defective heart condition. This was going to be her first and last child to bear – her last chance at being a mother. I remember her telling me that the doctors advised her, that it was best to get an abortion as this could result in a difficult pregnancy and her life could be endangered. She repeated this same story to me how she fought her doctors advise almost as a bedtime story. For the rest of her life she continuously reminded me how she risked her life for me, and that I should be grateful for being alive. Perhaps this played a role in me repaying a debt that I felt I owed to my mom, by becoming and being her healer. Either way, it set the stage that would play itself out in the years to come.

Guilt and shame were the first breaths I took in, the moment I was born and they plagued my entire life. Perhaps the delivery doctor who held me upside down by the legs was disappointed that my mom went against their wishes. Perhaps it was a difficult birth as I made my way into this world through a caesarean. Later on as a young child, I remember lying by my mom in the morning hours while waking up. I recall observing the strange scars I saw on her tummy and wondering where they came from. My mom would repeat the story that I was delivered this way.   Not understanding anything about birth, I thought it strange and weird to be brought into this world in such a way.   It added to my sense of responsibility I could not explain nor understand, but it was an awful feeling, nonetheless.

Many years later, as I grew older and was exploring different healing modalities, I came across *Rebirthing*. *Rebirthing* was a modality developed by Leonard Orr, to help him release traumatic childhood experience he had suppressed. Leonard Orr had a difficult childhood losing both his parents at a young age. He surmised that if he could recreate his time in the womb, he could heal many of his traumas by consciously releasing them.

The experiment he performed was both simple and genius at the same time. He laid in a bathtub where the bathwater was at the temperature of his body, at 97 degrees. He laid there and imagined he was back in the womb, while at the same time doing deep breathing exercises. Later the modality shifted from lying in water to laying on the floor while covered with blankets and performing breathing exercises. It seemed innocuous at first, but then deep emotions that I never knew surfaced and spontaneously burst out.

I've had designed rebirthing sessions and spontaneous rebirthing sessions during my many healing retreats. Spontaneous rebirthing experiences were more dramatic as they were unexpected and I felt unprepared. Suddenly I was funneled to this deep dark hole where I could not see anything. Everything felt dark. I could hear voices in the distance, but they were neither my mom's nor my father's voice. They seem loud and threatening. I could not understand the words, but I felt the intention.

I was going to die.

I felt fear grip me down to my spine. I could feel myself protesting that I wanted to live – I wanted to live! But no one heard me. I felt trapped. My legs squirming underneath me as I tried to get away. Both my legs felt numb and cold. It felt like two snakes slithering up my thighs and as they rose higher up my legs, I could feel the cold clamminess like streaks of lightning.

I felt alone and scared.

They say a developing fetus has no consciousness and therefore no soul. Therefore abortion is not a sin. That's why abortions are performed during the first trimester of pregnancy, and as early as possible. So basically I was a tadpole. My mom's pregnancy was quickly determined, and the doctors must have been debating considering my mom's heart condition as being risky.

The debate whether a fetus is aware is controversial. Ultra-sound machines placed on the wombs of pregnant mothers clearly show the fetus responding to their mother's voice and even to their environment. Whether it's true or not all I can say is that I never felt so much fear in my life. Until that moment I never knew that such a memory existed nor was I aware of how much I wanted to live. But it was the feeling of being trapped that was the worst. I could not escape no matter how hard I tried. It must have scarred me because as early as I can remember the world was a frightening place. The need to hide and not be seen became my main theme for most of my life.

Growing up as an only child is a lonely existence. I didn't have many playmates or friends to talk with. Because I was my mother's investment into motherhood, I was constantly under her watchful eye. Wherever I went or did, she was always watching me. And where she went, I had to follow. Handcuffed to her side I remembered being surrounded mostly by adults who became my secondary mothers and fathers. Being a small and well-behaved child, I was showered with praise and affection. Later in life I realized how this had such a profound effect on me and the direction I would pursue in life.

I was a quiet child who stayed with my aunts and uncles for protection. I was attached to them like a third arm. I was still and docile, mainly because it was the best strategy while being next to them. But I did love them dearly as they did me.

My fondest memory was my Aunt Elena. She was a single mother who divorced early in her life, but not before delivering her only child, Joel. Me and Joel grew up as brothers. Although we were close in age distanced by only a few months, we could not have been any more different. He was a rambunctious kid who always liked to get into trouble, while I stayed glued to his mother. I was so close to my Aunt Elena that my nickname for her became "Momma", and I was her little baby. I never left her side, not even to play.

My mom used to tell me that I loved my Momma so much, that I would plant kisses from her wrist all the way up her shoulder and cascade more kisses as I worked myself down. And when she had to leave to go home, I would strap myself to her leg protesting and crying all the way to the door.

I didn't know it at the time, that later in my life, events connected with her would have profound effects on my life. It would be the first of many turning points that would influence me to become a healer. But before that, if you had asked me what I wanted to be when I grew up, being a healer was the furthest thing from my mind. I had no clue how the events of the future would shape me, because as I later learned, you need to go through certain life experiences. And these experiences as painful as they may be, are necessary to opening up your gifts.

My father was the kindest man I ever knew. My parents met when one day he stopped over at my Aunt Rossi's house where my mom was staying. My mom was in the kitchen cutting up some vegetables, when she caught my dad's eye. She was still in her nightgown with rollers in her hair and no make-up. But my mom's natural beauty simply captivated my dad.

Soon afterwards they were married. My father was in my late thirties when he married my mom and over forty when he had me. He didn't expect to be a father, but unexpectedly my mom was pregnant with me. I wasn't planned, yes, I was an accident. My father was very nervous being a first-time dad, because he grew up without a father. And maybe that meant raising me was extra special for him, because he got to relive a childhood he never experienced. But it also added to his anxiety as he had no role model. I don't think that parenthood is something you can prepare for. It's just something that you learn and adjust to, and my dad did a terrific job. But my dad did a great job, and as a child I adored my dad.

At night as an infant he would lay me on his tummy and rock me to sleep. Later as I grew he would stretch out his arm and I would rest my head on it. And that's how I slept in my early childhood – between the warmth of both my parents. I did transfer to my own bed as I grew older but it's a tradition for many Asian families to have their children sleep with them.   It makes them more loving, and as our parents get old we take care of them.

I was told that in the Philippines we never put our elderly in resting homes, no matter how senile they become. The whole family takes care of them, and the children play with them as these grandparents act as little children again. These became the core values I grew up. Even now in my family we take care of our aunts and uncles by providing them with meals, transportation to the doctor, and even trips to the casino. And when they eventually passed on we mourn their memory through church services and prayers.

My dad was also the most generous man I knew.   Whenever I needed money, he always gave what I needed and never refused me.   And he always cooked for me whatever I wanted. It was his way of showing his love for me.

My father worked hard. He worked at the post office at night and always did overtime. As a young kid I could never understand why he was always sleeping, and didn't have time to play with me. More than anything I craved my father's attention.

One summer I got my wish. We went out every day fishing at a local pier. It was unusual because my dad worked nights, and so slept during the day. It was the first time that I can recall that my father spent quality time with me. Fishing was his favorite hobby, and we would spend hours waiting for the fish to bite. It didn't matter that we didn't talk much – just that he was with me. From then on, I learned an important lesson – more than the special treats he gave me or even the money, was the attention and time that I cherished the most.

As I got older I was allowed to accompany my Dad when he went and picked up my mom at work. My mom worked as a medical librarian at a large hospital. It was a sight to see my mom dressed very presentable and formal each time. I thought she was the most beautiful woman in the world. The library became my playground where I would often hide underneath wooden tables, roam the labyrinth of shelves, and peruse through magazine covers pretending I was in faraway places.

Just before we left and went home, I would help my dad pick up medical books left by the doctors and put them back on their shelves. I didn't know anything about the library system and how books were put in a certain order and selection. And so whenever I saw an opening on the shelves, I would just put the books there. I was always proud of my efficiency to clear as many books as possible.

One day I was at my mom's library when I came across this unusual book. Unlike the others it seemed to be leather-bound with gold lettering. I knew it was a special book, but I don't remember the title or the subject. Only that it was different and that it piqued my curiosity. As I opened to the first page there was a drawn outline of a Greek temple with the words, "Knowledge is Power". Silently I repeated those words to myself over and over – "Knowledge is Power!" And with that, my feelings of loneliness and despair seemed to dissolve away. Here was a world I could escape into – a world of information. Reading a book was like listening to an old friend who would not judge or condemn me. He would simply teach me, and as a result I would improve. I would grow in knowledge and be important. And the knowledge I gained, no one could take away from me, because it was locked in my mind forever. Like a library that I could go to whenever I wished.

My books became my friends and they filled the world of a lonely boy, so that I wasn't alone anymore. I was distracted, because my mind was filled with information and opening a book was like entering another world, whether it was fiction or non-fiction. And I became obsessed. Books were magical portals to another world. Each book was like a treasure chest filled with gold and precious gems.

Chapter II.

FATHER'S LOVE

My Aunt Elena, whom I fondly called Momma, was a single parent. Soon after her son was born, she was divorced. Momma worked as a cashier in the cafeteria at the same hospital as my mom. This is where my mom and she had met. Both being Filipino and my mom not having any family or relatives, they quickly bonded as friends.

My mom crossed over to America by ship. She was in her late twenties and as beautiful as any movie star of that time. But she was unlucky in love. She had several suitors who pursued her and even proposed to her, but none carried through. I remember growing up she would repeat the story that she had been jilted at the altar five times. As a young child I didn't know what those words meant. Marriage and proposal were foreign words to me, and at that time I was too young to be interested in girls.

And so not finding much success in the Philippines, she traveled to America by ship. It was a thirty days long trip during those days. I wondered how my mom ever survived such a voyage alone, while being stuck at sea for all that time, especially being a woman and with all those men onboard. But my mom was very strong and very fierce. She also had a temper. Because she was a singer in her youth, she knew how to use those high notes in her singing. It was like a lion's roar, frightening enough to scare away the most persistent admirers.

After arriving here in America, my mom stayed with a friend who was also Filipino. She was my Aunt Rossi who became my other mother. Aunt Rossi was voted Ms. University of the Philippines. She was beautiful! I would describe her as having the heart of an angel. She was absolutely the nicest and most generous person in the world! She raised me with her two other kids, Arthur and Rosalyn who were a few years older than me. Even though I wasn't her child, I spent more time with my Aunt Rossi then her own kids, because my mom and here were the best of friends and always hanged out. I truly had the most cherished and spoiled childhood.

My Aunt Elena - Momma, being a single parent, raised both me and her son Joel together. Joel was born only seven months after me and so we shared the same playpen, celebrated our birthdays together, and fought a lot, like brothers. My father became his surrogate father. My father was the nicest, kindest man in the world. He was a great father to both of us.

Growing up, Momma treated me very special. I was the baby of the entire clan. Because I was the "good boy" I was protected and even spoiled. I never spoke up, caused problems, or any type of trouble. In a way, I was the perfect child, because I was always obedient which made me more manageable. I was rewarded for good behavior and that made me seem as an ideal child.

As time goes on, even little boys grow up. I and Joel became teenagers and soon we were interested in girls. We both entered serious relationships, and so our priorities became our girlfriends and school. Being in love for the first time, I never knew anything so intoxicating. I still loved my mom and my maternal aunts with all my heart, but having a girlfriend was something else. And so I transferred my love and devotion from my mother and aunts to my girlfriend. I didn't know anything else, and they had been great role models.

I could see the pain in both my mom and my Aunt Elena's eyes. Their little boys had grown up and were now more interested in their girlfriends than them. Both I and Joel spent every waking moment with our girlfriends, and it was as if our mothers felt forgotten. We both still loved them dearly, but romance is an exciting journey – an adventure we've never experienced before.

I know that Aunt Elena - Momma, felt lonely. Joel was going off to college, and suddenly she was left alone by herself. In her loneliness she remarried a relative of my mom – my uncle. Getting married for the second time seemed like a good decision for her, and it was. She was no longer alone. Joel could concentrate on his studies, while knowing that his mother was taken care of.

Momma soon endured open heart surgery, similarly as my mom. Joel and I focused on our careers and between our studies and girlfriends, we saw our parents even less. We were building our new lives.

I'll never forget one afternoon getting a call from Momma. She had also called Joel the same day, and asked if both of us could come and visit her. We were both so busy that we both declined. I'll never forget her response while saying goodbye. She told me "I love you! And God Bless you!" Never in all my years of knowing her have I heard her say, "God Bless You!" These were the last words she ever spoke to me.

Momma was a smoker. During those days, smoking was looked upon as being very chic and was glamorized in the movies. All the major movie stars especially in the 1950's smoked. And so the stigma of smoking wasn't as strong as it is now. I remember being in the kitchen with Momma and asking her to please stop smoking. She rebuked me by saying that if she was going to die, then she was going to die, and to mind my own business. Even my dad smoked. I almost got in trouble because I took a carton of his cigarettes and threw them in the trashcan. My mom was more amused then anything and prevented my dad from punishing me.

Smoking caused my Momma's heart disease. I wasn't a healer at that time, so I couldn't give her any relief. I saw how much she suffered, and it really pained me. It wasn't long after the surgery that Momma was experiencing chest pains again. Her husband wanted to bring her to emergency, but she declined. She was tired of doctors and didn't want to go to the hospital. Somewhere during the night she never woke up,

She didn't die right away. For a while she was on life-support. All of us gathered around her to say our final good-byes, but for me that was extremely difficult. I couldn't say good-bye. I wanted to turn back the clock and revisit her, just like she requested. I was pleading with God to turn back the clock, but it was too late. I was numb on the outside still not believing that I was losing my Momma. I couldn't lose her – not her. I was in a haze walking the hallways of the hospital, unaware of where I was going or bumping into. I could hear people's voices around me, but I didn't respond. I wasn't sure of anything, but that I just needed to keep walking.

I was overcome by flashback memories of Momma bathing me, feeding me, and wiping away my tears. A silent scream emerged, but it wasn't my own. I didn't know where this scream was coming from, but it grew louder and louder. What is that sound, I wondered? My chest felt tight and I couldn't breathe. Panic set in, and suddenly I was engulfed in the flames of sorrow and loss.

There will be no tomorrow. Today was just a dream that I will never wake up from. Like a flash it was all gone in a blink of an eye. One moment Momma was alive, and the next moment she was gone. Still, there was a part of me that didn't accept this fate. How could she be taken away from me? Who would babysit my children? Take them to the playground or the zoo to see the animals. Or most of all, how could I continue to live without my Momma? A desperate void existed in me echoing such questions, but I had no answers.

As a child I could never imagine living without my Mommas. In my magical thinking world, I believed that they would live forever, and always be with me. In the deepest part of me was that little boy who planted kisses up and down her arms as if they were candy, and cried clutching her leg screaming "Don't Go!" It was that moment that I realized the fragility of life.

My mother talked to me after the funeral, and explained that this was why it was important to show the people you loved how much you loved them, while they were still alive. Because once they're gone, you can't show your appreciation. And I've seen this example played over and over with my cousins. You don't think that one day you'll lose the ones you love. You take it for granted that because they seem healthy and alive, there's nothing to worry about. Life moves fast and before you know it you're swept in it's currents, taking care of yourself and your partners. Until one day, the sun doesn't come up, and the moon doesn't shine high above. And you're walking in this labyrinth with no apparent escape, wondering how you ever got here.

From that moment on, I was resolved. I wasn't going to make the same mistake as I did with Momma. If my parents needed me, then I would be there for them. I made it a point to show them the love and affection that they deserved. I was grateful for the childhood I had, and so made it a point to provide them as much comfort as I could. And I started with my Dad.

As my father grew older, he had a number of health issues. The many years of smoking finally caught up with him. Even though he had stopped smoking a few years back, it didn't stem the tide of the moon. He was having trouble breathing, and his breath stank which was a bad sign that his internal organs were deteriorating. At times his emphysema was getting so bad, that he had to sleep sitting up so that he could breathe. He went to kidney dialysis four times a week. I could no longer take him out and help him enjoy the things he liked.

For two years I did everything to make my father's life more comfortable. I did a lot of baking during that time, and would bake for him his favorite cakes. Just as soon as it was baked, I would wake him up so that he would have it nice and hot fresh, straight from the oven. I would buy him the most expensive pastries that I could find – no expense was spared. Whatever my father wanted, he got.

Tragically, I was off on a business trip when I got the call that my father was sent to emergency complaining that he couldn't breathe. By the time I got the call, my father was on life support and couldn't be revived. The doctors were going to pull the plug on him. I begged them to wait until I had gotten back home. I needed time to take the next flight out, but they wouldn't listen. I was on the phone with Joel as they pulled the plug. In my imagination I could hear the heart monitor go dead.

I felt cheated and helpless. More than anything, I wanted to be with my father. I wanted him to die in my arms so that in his last moments, his last breaths would carry my love as his spirit went to heaven. It was the second time in my life, where I did not have a chance to say goodbye to someone I loved dearly.

Chapter III.

THE VOW

At the time I didn't have a cellphone, but I did have a pager. The first person I called was Joel, Aunt Elena's son. He was the closest person to me and felt like a brother. We were raised together, and besides me, no one else loved my dad more than him.

My father was a sweet and gentle man. I always saw myself as taking most of my traits from him, and not my mother. He was always very quiet and reserved. Perhaps in my need to be closer to him, I emulated him. Never once did I hear an unkind word and he never spoke out of turn or caused any trouble. He just blended into the background like a sofa chair, never making any noise. He opted to stay at home playing solitaire, while my mom took me out shopping. Growing up I always wondered why he preferred to stay at home and avoided any outings. I wondered if he felt as lonely as me.

I loved my father as much as any son could love anyone. And more than anything, I wanted to spend as much time with him as possible. I could remember all the times he took me out for a bite, and when that wasn't possible, he cooked. He didn't always spend time talking with me because English was his second language, but he communicated with me in other ways. He was an extremely devoted father who worked nights and did overtime whenever he could, to make sure I had the best of everything and everything I wanted.

My mom constantly reminded me how lucky I was to have a father like him. I wasn't sure if this was another extension of the guilt games she played on me, or if it was really true. She told me stories of how strict her father and my grandfather was. In the Philippines discipline was like martial law. You could never speak out of turn, otherwise you got a whipping. Even if you did keep quiet you still got a spanking. It was the way it was back then, but my father was very different. I don't remember him ever raising his voice to me, if anything, he protected me from my mother. Maybe that's why I came to adore my father so much.

One Christmas season I decided to work at the Post Office just to see what it was like. I've never had to stand for over eight hours on concrete. By the time the season was over, the soles on my shoes were full of holes and my back ached. It was a little stressful as there was a lot of chaos while supervisors were continually yelling at the workers over every minor detail. It felt as if I was in an ant colony, but I chose this experience, because I wanted to know what my dad went through.

I remember a time when as a child, I attended my friend's birthday party. My father brought me there, but waited for me until the party was over. He had worked the previous night and tried to take a nap in the car, but it was no good. He wanted to leave early and sleep at home, but I was having such a good time that I didn't want to leave. So he talked to the father of my friend to try to convince me to leave. I was embarrassed in front of all my friends when he openly but gently asked me to leave. All the way home I scowled at him for making me leave, and for a long time I held that against him.

Now here I was, a little older, and working at the same post office as my dad. It was almost a year since my father had passed, and I had nothing but his memories. My dad \worked at the post office for over thirty years, until his retirement. Each day that I worked at the Post Office my feet ached. It was almost a mild form of torture, as I felt and imagined with each step that I took, how my dad felt each day for thirty years. The Christmas season was soon over, and I was glad.

Soon after, I went to visit his grave. I kneeled at his tombstone as if I was at church. I prayed for forgiveness. I prayed for forgiveness for resenting him when he made me leave my friend's birthday party. I didn't understand how hard he worked, how much he sacrificed to make our home comfortable, and what a great father he was to me.

As a child I took things for granted, because I was so used to it. I didn't have anything to compare my childhood to, and so I thought my childhood was like everyone else's. I was sheltered in a private world, unaware that anything else existed outside. I was always with my mom, never really played with friends or cousins, and spent my time at home either watching TV or reading books. It was very routine.

Now, I was on the phone with Joel as he notified me that they were pulling the plug on my Dad. I was in shock. I begged and pleaded with him to stop the doctors from doing so. I needed time to get on the next plane from Denver, but it was to no avail. To this day I don't understand why they couldn't wait one day longer, for my return. I felt powerless as my strength ebbed away, like the life force of my father.

I believe that it was my mom's decision to pull the plug, while I was away. My mom knew me and had I been there, I would have probably gone mad with grief. She knew how much I loved my dad. Perhaps it was for the best. The pain I felt was indescribable. I felt my soul being torn away from my heart. I wasn't ready to let go of my father. I was in hell. Fire and brimstone were burning inside of me. Never in my life have I felt so much emotional pain. It wasn't so much as regret, as it was that I loved my dad too much. And there was no solace – no place to hide. There was no soothing salve to cool my wounds. There was nothing I could do to put out the fire. It just continued to burn and burn.

I didn't know at the time, but that experience would serve me well in later life.

Now I was alone with my mom. In truth, we didn't always get along so well. My dad was our buffer. My mom was a strict disciplinarian, while my dad stayed quiet and uninvolved in the background. I had no privacy with my mom. She entered my room and went through all my journals, monitored all my calls, and even opened my mail so much so that I needed to get my own post office box.

And now, we were going to be alone together, just her and I. I felt like an animal trapped in a zoo. I was a tiger pacing restlessly back and forth in a steel cage. My mother was my handler who cracked the whip at her convenience and whim. She had an explosive temper and her voice was her whip. I never knew when she was going to get out of control. It was the old Filipino way. It was the way her parents had brought her up, and their parents before. My father didn't bring me up this way because his father had passed away early, and he was left to take care of his brothers and sisters. My Dad was a pacifist. And now I had to deal with my mom directly.

Losing my Aunt Elena and then my father, taught me many things. Even though I was always respectful to them, I learned to appreciate the ones you love. And my mom was in very poor health. She had to take an early retirement, because of the condition of her heart. Since that time she had three open-heart surgeries. And her health continued to fail her. I knew she didn't have much time left.

I was struck with a new sense of urgency. Losing my beloved Aunt Elena and my dad, woke me to a new reality. The things you take for granted can so easily be taken away from you. And I've seen how some of my friends had neglected their parents, and how after their funerals suffered deep remorse. Yes, my relationship with my mom wasn't perfect, but she did bring me into this world. She overprotected me, because I was her only child. Her temper tantrums were really the scars of her own childhood. She didn't know how to deal with them or where to go for help, because in those days you never sought treatment. I, on the other hand, read lots of self-help books, so I had a different perspective on things as my mom. It was unusual for a kid of my age to spend his money reading pop-psychology or self-improvement. Instinctively, I think not only was I trying to heal myself, but also my mom. Maybe I was trying to heal generations of my family lineage, but at the time I wasn't aware of this.

I had returned back from Denver taking the earliest flight back home. Strangely, I never felt alone. It was almost as if someone was watching over me even protecting me. It's weird to feel this mild sense of calm, and an unbridled sense that everything was going to be okay. As I boarded the plane, a new sense of mission came over me, but I wasn't sure what it was. I felt strength flow through me. Maybe it was God, but I wasn't certain. I never felt this way before, this sense of total peace. I could have been sitting on the deck of a ship in the middle of a storm and heard the waves crashing violently against the sides, but none of it would matter. Why doesn't it matter, I wondered? Why did it feel like all my worries were swept away?

The next moment I realized I was in front of the pulpit, giving a speech at my Father's funeral. I looked around and saw family members that I haven't seen in years. It's the strangest thing when you grow up and realize your friends and relatives moved farther away. And it's only through loss that you're brought back together again, even if just for one short evening.

I talked about my dad, and how special he was to me. I talked about the fishing trips we went together on that long ago summer. I spoke of his sacrifices and devotion to his family, and how lucky I was to have him. Suddenly a feeling came over me, that I wasn't expecting. I felt as strong as a lion, and stood up straight. I looked directly in my mom's direction. She was sitting there very stoic with a rosary in her hands. And then, out of the blue, I declared that I was going to take care of my mom. At the time I didn't know what that meant. I didn't know if I was to take care of her financially, or just be strong for her. I had no clue.

I didn't know it at the time, but I was going to be her healer. I was going to heal my mom's physical issues and extend her life for as long as I could. If someone had told me that's what I would be doing for the rest of my life, I would have laughed at them. I've heard of people who could heal others, but I never thought of myself as one of those people. Being an intuitive healer or Light worker wasn't on my list of things I wanted to be when I grew up. And I knew no one in the family who chose to be in this profession. So it was a long mystery for me, and especially to my mom, why I would accept such a position.

It was approximately seven years after I made the announcement on the pulpit that I would take care of my mom, when she revealed to me that my Grandfather was a healer. He worked with herbs and instead of taking his kids to the doctor which they couldn't afford, he treated them himself. It was the first revelation I had about where my healing gifts came from.

I never set out to be an intuitive healer.   After the lost of my dad something awoke in me that I never knew existed. It was like a diamond.   It takes the right amount of time and pressure to turn a piece of coal into a diamond. The loss of my Aunt Elena and my dad provided the perfect template. Before that time I wasn't ready, and had pursued it, I wouldn't have lasted. I needed to experience the grievance of profound loss and deep pain so that I could understand other people's pain and suffering. Little did I know that these experiences would relentlessly push me in this direction, because the field is very hard and difficult. Being an intuitive healer is not for everyone. But that was the journey I was about to begin.

Chapter IV.

UNCHARTERED TERRITORY

I had just made the announcement standing on the pulpit at my father's funeral that I was going to take care of my mom. The words just rolled out of my mouth. I had no clue how I was going to take care of her. I was still in shocked that my father had just passed over. But I felt this sudden urge to lay this blanket of protection over my mom. Since my mom and I had a tumultuous relationship, a part of me dreaded being alone with her. My father was the stabilizing post between us. He kept the peace but in a quiet and gentle way. Now without him, we would now be dealing with each other directly and there was no referee. How would we get along? We were like two bulls sizing each other up with my mom being the bigger and stronger bull. Part of me wondered, who would protect me?

But somehow at that moment, I didn't spend too much time thinking about that. My mom had just lost her partner of over thirty-five years. I witnessed my dad's devotion to my mom. He always took care of her. When she was sick ,he stayed by her side until she got better and recovered. He got up early in the morning to bring her to work each day, and waited at the library until she finished, and then brought her home. He did this every day without fail, and so this characteristic was imprinted onto me. Growing up I was taught that family was the most important thing. You sacrificed yourself for your family. In the Philippines you have to work together in order to survive. It's like that in many countries, where the only resource is people. You can't do things by yourself. Everyone needs help. That's why my mom was able to survive when she came to America and knew no one here. She made friends with other Filipinos, and they gave her a place to live while she found work. And it was through these friends that she was introduced to my dad. And throughout time you develop this network where people who are not related by blood are accepted as family. And then your family base expands.

I was born here in America. I feel at times I'm in between both cultures while being an American is my stronger culture. I don't speak Tagalog -our native Filipino language, don't always enjoy eating Filipino food, prefer hamburgers and shakes, and don't enjoy going to Church, while Filipinos are notoriously religious. But I am an obedient son who studied hard in school. I'm very polite, and respectful.

I sometimes wondered who I am, while being born out of two cultures, Filipino and American. Growing up I didn't always understand my parents and how they thought, and even more so with my relatives. I like the freedom of thought and independence most Americans display, but it didn't always agree with my mom who wanted to mold me into what she wanted. She liked the idea that I read a lot of books, but she wished my interests were more educational, rather than pop-psychology, and New Age. I didn't enjoy going to church with her, but I was always very spiritual. She believed in western medicine, and I was just beginning to explore Alternative medicine. In many ways I was an enigma to my mom, while my dad learned to accept me as I was, because basically I was a good kid who didn't get into trouble or had any vices.

In hindsight, I wasn't aware of the forces shaping my life. I had just lost the two most important people in my life – my Aunt Elena, and my Dad. I was crushed emotionally. They were the center of my universe, and now my universe was cracked. Before, everything seemed perfect.

When I was small, they used to take me to the Santa Cruz boardwalk where my favorite ride was the carousel. It was a simple ride where you go around in circles. But riding the wooden horses and zebras while grabbing for those brass rings, that I could throw into the mouth of the giant clown made everything seem magical. And just for a moment I could forget the rest of the world. The organ music played in the background. The animal I was sitting on rose up and down, and when the ride was over, I couldn't wait to get back on. It seemed that life at that moment was going to stay that way forever - cotton candy, sundae cones, and pink popcorn with my family going on rides the whole day. Until the music stops, and the boardwalk closes down. Part of me wanted to believe it would never stop and that life would continue to be fun. I would always have my family with me, and I would never grow up.

As a healer I learned that you can know someone for ten years and still never know them. They can always be nice and friendly to you, never causing any grief or trouble. It's when that person is in crisis that you find what they're really made of. How do they react when they're facing bankruptcy? Divorce? Or a death in a family? During times of trouble your survival beliefs arise. What are they? People change during such times. Do they fold or forge forward?

I can honestly say I didn't know how I was going to react with my father's death. I knew my father was ill, and that he didn't have much time left. But when it happens you're never prepared. Sure you can prepare things in anticipation, but you don't know for certain how you will feel when it does happen. I loved my dad but I wasn't aware how much I did love him. I cried every day at the funeral home. I crumpled to my knees. I thought losing my Aunt Elena was bad enough, but this was worse. I've never experienced so much grief in my life. Even my relatives believed that I would never get over my Father's departure. But I couldn't leave my mom. It wouldn't be fair. My dad took care of her, and he would want me to take care of her as well.

I don't know what it was, but I felt fiercely protective over my mom. Before that time all I thought of was starting a career in the tech field which was booming, getting married, and having a few kids. Suddenly all of that didn't matter. I forgot all of those things, and my main focus became my mom.

Maybe because I felt I didn't spend enough time with my Aunt Elena, and my Dad. Maybe I felt I should have taken care of them better or showed them how much they meant to me. Suddenly all my dreams and ambitions didn't matter anymore. Family became the most important thing to me, and I had made up my mind from then on to take care of my mom. I didn't know how, but I was going to give her the best life I could. The means of which I wasn't sure know. All I knew was that I had made a commitment. And it really came from the most unexpected place. It really wasn't what I or my mom expected. My commitment would challenge everything I knew or thought of myself. Even worst, it challenged everything my mom believed in or expected from her only son. She would never see her son working as a professional in a large corporation. She would never see her son walk down the aisle and get married. And most importantly, she would never play with her grandchildren, or take them to the park and enjoy them. Family is very important to us, and having grandchildren the highlight of a long arduous life. No, my mom would be the only one without grandchildren and a son who is not a professional.

I set out with a commitment to take care of her, and instead I was to be her greatest disappointment. When I took this challenge, I had no idea this was how it was going to go. I didn't know the price I was going to pay. I was going into uncharted territory.

How can I explain it? One day you're walking down the street, and then suddenly a car hits you out of nowhere. You end up in the hospital, and your life changes. Maybe you go through years of rehabilitation. In the mean time you lose all your friends, and maybe even your girlfriend. If you were going to school before, those plans get temporarily or even permanently put aside.

Life is not a straight line. It's curvy. Sometimes you have to make right-turns in a split of a second.

When my father died my old life ended and a new one sprang as a replacement. It was going to be an extremely arduous journey, because I was starting over again. And like it or not, my mom was going to be on the same ride. She had no choice just like I had no choice. An invisible hand seemed to be guiding me. I wasn't sure whether it was God, the spirit of my father, or my destiny...

Chapter V.

THE BIG TEST

For a long time my soul cried out for salvation. The pain of losing my father was at times too much to bear. It's like being stuck in this deep dark pit with no sunlight to give you any comfort or solace. I felt alone with my grief with nowhere to go. First, how was I going to get out of this, and second how was I going to comfort my mom? I didn't know how to answer any of those questions, but if I didn't find a way soon, my despair would overtake me, and then I would truly be lost.

It's the strangest feeling in the world the moment someone dear to you leaves this world. Everybody gathers together and talk about old times. It feels comforting to have so many friends and relatives gather around you and offer their condolences. It has a celebratory flavor. Everyone is shaking your hand and giving you warm hugs, until the music stops and the casket is lowered thirteen feet underneath the ground. Then everything returns to normalcy.

My moments of grief were interrupted by my concern for my mother, and what she was going through. She tried to keep busy by inviting friends over, and cleaning the house several times. On weekends I drove her to the Indian casinos where she would busy herself playing slot machines. It was the only enjoyment she had. Later to atone for the loneliness she felt while sleeping by herself in the master bedroom, she opted to sleep in the downstairs living room. There she invited her sisters and my aunts to stay with her. They were all retirees and widows and it was like a big slumber party, except it was permanent.

One night I had to drive my mom to emergency. She had difficulty breathing, and was experiencing chest pains. Luckily the people downstairs living with us kept a watchful eye on my mom. They alerted me immediately, and I ran downstairs and rushed my mom to the hospital. It was the biggest scare of my life and a wake-up call that I could suddenly lose her just like I lost my dad.

Life, I realize, is held by a thin thread dangling above your head. It only takes the slightest pressure to break. My mom spent about a week in the hospital, while the doctors tried to figure out what's wrong. In the end, they didn't really know what to do or what was wrong. They knew how to stabilize her condition, but it wouldn't be long before she would be back in the hospital and the drama would be repeated all over again. I've seen it happen many times before. It's almost as if people go to the hospital waiting to die. At least it would end their suffering once and for all.

From that moment on I knew that I had to do something. My mom saw her doctor every week, and it seemed each time she was prescribed more medication then the week before. She had so many pills, that once a week they had to be divided for each day. It seemed that she was taking more pills than food, and if she skipped a day, it could have serious consequences. She took pills for her heart condition which caused side effects like raising her blood pressure, so she had to take pills to take care of that. It seem a never-ending cycle and all this time her health continued to deteriorate.

I didn't know what to do. I felt I was in a losing battle to save my mom's life. Like the sands of time I felt my mom slipping through my fingers. I knew that eventually I would lose her, but I wanted to prolong her life. I wanted to give my mom the best possible years. Bringing her to the casino on weekends was good, but it wasn't enough. There were several occasions when my mother had passed out in the bathroom. Luckily the casino manager knew how to act during such times, and the ambulance was immediately called and she was sent to the local hospital.

Visiting the local bookstore has always been my haven when things got sticky. For a cup of coffee I could spend all days studying. Or I could pick up a mystery novel from one of the shelves and engross myself in another world. I feel more comfortable with books than with people. Here was a world that I could escape into. Here was a world where answers were at my fingertips, and tI always remembered he first important lesson I I discovered in a book as a little boy, saying "Knowledge is Power."

It was that day – the first day after my mom returned from the hospital – that I entered the local bookstore with a new sense of purpose unlike before. I was searching for something, but I wasn't sure what it was. Here in this great library must lay the answer of how I was going to help my mom.

I immediately went to the health section. I looked through books on health, diet, and exercise. My mom wasn't going to change her diet as she enjoyed eating Filipino food too much. It was what she grew up on. Exercise seemed a good idea, but the only exercise she did was walking between the aisles to the next slot machine. Plus she suffered low-back pain. And as for her health, she believed in Western medicine too much and the only advice she took was from her doctor.

The final section that I checked out was Alternative Medicine. I never really explored this before, and so it was all new to me. I went through books on herbs, essential oils, and finally energy medicine. Energy medicine was a new term I never heard before, and so I wondered what type of medicine was that. I discovered that the body was composed of an auric field or etheric body. And that diseases or ailments show up in the etheric body before they show up in the physical body. And if this is so, by clearing up the etheric body first, then we could prevent it from manifesting in the physical body as disease. We could also clear disease from the physical body with through the etheric body.

This was somewhat of a new concept for me but the benefits seemed worthwhile. This type of healing required no surgery, use of medication, or even physical touch, as everything is cleared through the etheric body. It could be done from several feet or a long distance away. It seemed impossible, but definitely worth a try.

I found a local teacher, and immediately signed up for classes. I've never done this before, and so this was exciting. I learned about the seven major chakras. I learned all about the auric field, and what it was. But the most exciting thing was when I actually learned to feel the auric field and project energy. I thought this was something done in the movies, but it was real, and I was doing it.

I immediately went outside and started to scan every person I came in contact with. I scanned people at coffee shops, restaurants, and especially at parties. I gave readings to everyone I met, and was amazed at my accuracy. I couldn't stop. I was a kid in a candy store.

And I started to heal whoever allowed me to work on them. And there were lots of people because as I discovered everybody has some sort of pain. I didn't mind, as it was my way of practicing. It was like I had developed an addition to my other five senses. Imagine being blind all your life, and suddenly being able to see. A whole new world had opened up for me.

This didn't go well with my mom. She was extremely religious, went to church every Sunday, and even had an altar in her bedroom full of religious icons and pictures of Jesus. This is typical of Filipinos as they are devout Catholics, and so for her what I was practicing was some sort of Voodoo. Plus she believed in Western Medicine. What made things worse, was that a member of our extended family was a doctor, and she believed what I was doing was hogwash.

My mother didn't accept me. I had studied Alternative medicine with the hope of helping my mom. I wanted to do everything in my power to reduce her visits to the hospital, but it was to no avail. Instead of feeling proud that I was trying to heal her, she was ashamed of me.

Not all members of my family scorned me. A few were open to it as they had exhausted all avenues of care, and were still suffering. The need to prove myself became paramount. If I could provide relief for my relatives, then maybe my mom would believe me.

Conducting healing sessions is fun for me – almost addictive. It helps me accomplish two goals – showing my love for the people I care about, and relieving them of their pain. Getting positive feedback also made me feel good. It gave me a sense of importance and community that I never felt before. I never felt so passionate about anything before. I never finished anything that I had started before, but this was different. Healing became more than a hobby. For the first time I felt that I found my life's calling. Before, I felt as if I was aimlessly wandering through my life. I was a boat with no sail or rudder. I was just drifting along, letting the ocean currents take me wherever they chose.

As reports about my healing sessions surfaced and reached my mother's ears, she became more incensed. Everybody was talking about me, and how they felt better after a healing session. Everybody except my mom. She did not allow me to do any healing on her, but she couldn't stop me from healing my relatives. It was all coming to a head.

My mom liked to be right, and she didn't take kindly to being proven wrong. She ruled me with an iron fist, and what she said was usually the undisputed law. And now, her only son was into something "weird". It went against everything she believed, and she was going to prove me wrong one way or another.

In her most stern voice she called me into her bedroom. I was ready for one of her worst tongue lashings ever. My mom suffered from excruciating back pain. She had gone to her doctor for treatment but nothing helped. She tried numerous massage therapists, but their treatments only further aggravated her pain. At the time my mom was underweight and mostly skin and bones, and was extremely sensitive to the slightest pressure.

Here was the final test that I had been preparing for. I had practiced and studied hard for several months. I was still doing only basic healing, but it had to do. I had one chance to prove myself to her, and if I failed, I would not get another opportunity. And what if I failed, I wondered. How could I take care of my mom then? I had followed my intuition, and this is what I came up with: "Knowledge is Power", I kept repeating to myself. Everything that I had ever lived for had come to this final point.

As I entered my mom's bedroom, I found her sitting on the lazy-boy chair with her arms folded across her chest. "Heal Me!", she barked!

I had a small crystal rod that I had purchased at one of my seminars. Supposedly it amplifies ones healing power several fold. It cost me a couple of hundred dollars. I had spent my last dollar attending these seminars. I had sacrificed everything, and had nowhere to go.

I took a deep breath, and said a small prayer to God. I pointed my crystal at my mom's lower back. Five seconds later her back pain was gone. I wasn't even half-way finished when my mom exclaimed, "Oh Thank you! Thank you! Thank you!" Her back pain was gone. She couldn't believe it, and neither could I.

From that moment on, my mom couldn't stop displaying her pride of me. She couldn't stop talking to me, to her friends or relatives. She became the happiest mother on Earth. And when she saw in the mail numerous checks from my paying clients, it was as if she had won the lotto. Not only was I good enough to heal her, but good enough that people were paying for my services.

It was the first of many hurdles that I had to overcome. I wish I could say that my career flew off in a straight upwards line, but as someone said; a plane never flies to its destination from A to B or in that obvious fashion. 90% of the planes fly in error, but over 99% reach their destiny. The same would also be true for me.

Chapter VI.

THE MASTER APPEARS

I was perusing through the section entitled "Alternative Medicine." I wasn't sure what to look through, but I scanned with my eyes through the entire section. There were books on crystals, fortune telling, and ancient civilizations. I wasn't interested in any of those things. My mom didn't need anything connected to those subjects, much less would be interested in those kind of topics. My quest was to look for books on helping my mom heal and get better.

There was one book that stood out, titled "Miracles through Pranic Healing" by Master Choa Kok Sui. Maybe it was the word "miracles" or the word "healing" that drew me in, but it seemed a nice place to start. The book was simple to read and understand. It described eleven major chakras and how they influence the body. Through cleansing and energizing of these chakras, relief and healing of the human body can be produced. The exercises seemed simple enough, and so I brought home the book.

I finished reading it within a day or two. It was something that I've never been exposed to before. This concept of healing with prana energy was intriguing, but it made sense. I then skipped down to the testimonials of people who have been healed by Pranic Healing. I read each story with interest, and gradually my excitement increased as I felt this was something that could really help my mom. So I searched on the internet where I could find a Pranic Healing teacher. There was one locally – Master Hector Ramos. Master Ramos was one of the original students of Grand Master Choa Kok Sui. It turns out that Pranic Healing originated in the Philippines, and now healing centers were set up in both Berkeley and Los Angeles. Maybe also being Filipino gave me a sense of pride to study this art. Either way, I immediately called Master Ramos and after a small discussion signed up for three courses right away.

Never before in my entire life had I taken an energy-healing course. I've taken NLP, Brain-Gym, and intuition courses, and so on, but nothing on healing. I've had psychic readings done on me, but not one ever mentioned that I was a healer or would take healing courses. Before this experience I felt I was just drifting along the ocean of life, never really going anywhere or feeling passionate about anything. I had long given up finding my life's purpose through self-help books. Nothing worked. And now I was embarking on a new adventure. It was no longer about me, but about my mom. And maybe that made the crucial difference.

The book, "the Miracles of Pranic Healing" served me well and gave me the basic foundation for Level One. And now I was going to experience my first pranic session. I was excited. The first thing I remember was to warm up our hands and get them primed for scanning or feeling the energy of another person. Rubbing our palms together we then directed our palms while facing each other, without touching. We would bring them in and out - closer and then farther appart. I was surprised when I felt energy or warmth. It was like a small bubble that intensified when I brought my hands together and became lighter when I brought my hands apart. At some point I could feel pressure, almost like squeezing a balloon and heat. And then my hands felt lightness and even coolness as my hands came apart. It gelt like playing an accordion.

So this was energy, I thought. And I could even feel it with my eyes closed. My whole body felt alive. I felt the energy move up and down my body as I continued the exercise. I felt peaceful with a sense of joy that I've never experienced before. All I wanted was to be left alone with this feeling. At that point something awoke in me that I can't explain. It felt like I was returning home – an ancient memory, maybe of a past life or something. Suddenly I felt as one with myself and my hands. I wanted to stay in this feeling. Nothing else mattered. The outside world floated away, and I felt at completely at peace.

I could feel energy, I mean really feel energy. It was like another set of eyes opened up. Now I could sense the world in a totally new way. And everything felt different. I could literally scan anything and everything. If there was a plant nearby I would place my hands a few inches from it and sense how it felt. In a restaurant, I would scan my food and feel how much energy it had. But most of all, I would scan people even while walked. I learned where the eleven major chakras were located, and what they meant. Each chakra corresponded to a different body part, and scanning people was like reading a book. There it was: "Knowledge is Power!" I gave a free reading to anyone who wanted one, and each time I learned more and more.

Later in the study, we learned to sweep clean each chakra by using our hands and making a scooping motion while sending the dirty or congested energy into a bowl of salt water. I was surprised that I could actually feel it. Where a person had a diseased organ I felt pin-pricks on my palms. When the energy felt congested, it felt heavy, almost like scooping gravel or sand. And other times when the energy in that area was depleted, you felt almost nothing. It felt like empty air.

You can feel the difference between all three types of energies. Later I learned that not all the students felt energy the way I did. Some felt nothing, and were just going through the motions. Eventually I learned that my palms were extra sensitive. I would describe feeling energy like feeling heat from the oven. You can feel the warm currents of heat inches away from the stove. The pressure is slight like air blowing against you, but with the softness of a feather. In time, I learned to scan a person from a distance, and eventually half-way across the world.

You learn to focus with your mind by targeting each of the eleven major chakras. You start scanning the root chakra located at the tail bone, and slowly scan inches above to the next chakra, until you get to the top of the head. It takes lots of practice, but eventually it becomes like second-nature.

After scanning, the next exercise we learned was clearing each of the chakras while projecting energy through the palms of our hands. We started by sending energy to the root chakra or the tail-bone area. We were to imagine white light coming from the center of our palms and going into the root chakra. My study partner was a young female student. I placed my hands a few inches from her body and started imagining white light. I immediately felt pressure in my palm, and it pushed my hand back a few inches. And then just as suddenly the energy stopped flowing, and I took that to mean, that she had enough.

I was nervous the first time I was energizing another person. And I wondered what if I failed? If I had accidentally energized her around the kidneys or lower back, the mein meng chakra, I could potentially raise her blood pressure. And so I was very careful. My body felt like a huge tuning fork that vibrated simultaneously as I was energizing her. I felt the energy go up my spine and down through my right arm and straight out my palm. It felt like electricity, but very subtle. Almost like a current of water flowing through my body and out the sprout of my palm. At that moment, Master Ramos exclaimed that he saw two angels sitting atop each of my shoulders. It would be the first validation I received, confirming that I was on the right track.

The next day I asked my partner how she felt after I energized her. She told me that she couldn't sleep until five am. I was amazed. I couldn't believe it. None of the other students had the same dramatic effect as I did. Although I was excited to hear such news, my partner wasn't so thrilled. It seemed I had energized her too much, and she didn't get much rest. In time, I learned to refined how much energy I projected, and my hands became more sensitive to blockages in the chakras.

Master Ramos taught me the first three levels of Pranic Healing. I was hooked. I couldn't believe that I could actually feel and project energy. I felt like one of those comic Superheroes. And in order to advance my understanding of Pranic Healing, I had to go to the main healing center in Los Angeles where GrandMaster Choa Kok Sui and Master Co were teaching. For the next four years I saved and scrimped all the money I had, to pay for courses. I couldn't get enough. I went through every advanced course and learned everything I possibly could.

Grand Master Choa was something special. You could literally feel his energy as he walked past you. One could feel his aura from a distance of thirty feet. I used to scan his napkins after he finished his food, and you could feel really strong energy pouring out of them. Sometimes he would be in a meditative pose, projecting unconditional love, and everybody felt themselves pulled forward by his magnetic energy. Even though I tried to resist, I found myself off-balance several times.

Grand Master Choa was my teacher and guru. He taught me many things. I was even lucky enough to get a healing from him. I was suffering from sleep apnea at the time, and he pointed his crystal at my throat and healed me in three seconds. I was surging with energy for two straight days. Never before had I felt so much power in my life.

Sadly, he passed away on March 19, 2007. He's been called one of the greatest masters of energy in our generation. I was extremely lucky to have met him, and that Pranic Healing was the first modality I studied. Even to this day, everything that he taught me has been the basis for every modality and technique I developed. And when I study other healing courses I always check the differences of the chakras before and after, to see how effective these healing modalities are.

Chapter VII.

MY MOTHER'S KEEPER

Hmmm ... okay – so what do I do now!?!

I was standing in front of my mom preparing myself to do the first healing session on her. And I just stood there, frozen. I didn't know what to do. My mind had gone blank. I was nervous. I was scared. I didn't know how to start or where to begin.

For several months I've been going to healing retreats preparing myself for this one event. I went there with a clear purpose of healing my mom. At the retreat you're with a group of like-minded people that are hoping to be called healers at the end of the weekend. It seems kind of short to me that in 48 hours you complete the basic training, get a certificate with no exam, and then go home. It's a lot of information to cram in, and like the others around me, I had no previous experience healing before now.

The lecture was good. We were given several pamphlets with exercises to follow, and then we paired up and exchanged doing healings on each other. Everything went like clockwork. The next moment we were self-congratulating ourselves and each other on what a positive experience it all was, and promised to stay in contact and share our gained knowledge and even do distant healing. We could have sat around a campfire naked singing, "This is land is your land!"

And now the long travel back home. I was tired, home-sick, and the excitement was starting to die down. When I was at the retreat I felt wonderful! I felt like God, not in terms of a vengeful God, but one with such unconditional love and peace. The feeling I felt with Grand master Choa was blissful at times. Now I understood why people continued to review his classes. You can't get the same feeling simply by reading his books or watching his videos. You have to be in the presence of the Man in order to understand it all. And it was the same with my other teachers. In my twenty years I have studied with the best healers and psychics in the world. Each carries a certain charismatic energy that is hard to define, but all are distinctive with their personalities. Some are grumpy. Some are rude. Some swear like a rusty sailor. It redefines what I thought a Spiritual teacher is supposed to be. Yes, they are powerful. And they all have abilities that I can only dream of. But they are also very human.

No matter what, it never seems as if you can learn enough. If I was lucky my teachers had written a book that I can follow or review. Or a small pamphlet that I may be able to follow. Usually they're filled with a few diagrams and instructions for a few exercises, but always lack in content. Most of the time, I had to take hard notes, and I was terrible at taking notes. My mind would often wander off, and by the time I recovered I would find everybody getting paired up and ready to do the exercises. I simply followed everyone else.

The exercises were simple, but I let my partner work on me first, so that I could follow what's going on. It feels good to get a clearing. Waves of energy pass in front of your body like a cascading waterfall. You feel energized. You feel lighter. You feel cleansed as if you just had a shower. And I wanted it to continue. It feels good to have your partner focus on you. It feels like grime being swept off your skin.

The sensation feels like a light tingling. As they passed their hands in front of me, I could feel the movements of their hands. But I wasn't touched, and my eyes weren't following them. Even with my eyes shut, and my back towards them, I could feel the sensations so I knew that something was real. It was hard to define, and part of me didn't believe it, but it was there. And for moments I felt peace – real peace. And I wanted to stay there.

And then it was my partner's turn. I could feel my fingers slowly pull away at something. It was weird, because the pulling sensation was more intense in some, and lighter in others. If I went too fast, I would lose it. And so I went slowly, disposing of the negative energy in a bowl of salt water. We would have to spray our hands and arms with alcohol-mixed water, to dispose of whatever negative energy lingered on our skin.

I asked my partner what she felt, and she told me that she felt refreshed, lighter, and even energized. I felt victorious at that moment, because I wasn't sure I could create such an effect. But it was there. I felt like a magician on stage in front of a large audience. The trick was a simple one. I placed my top hat on the small table set in front of me, and revealed an empty hat with nothing up my sleeve. And as if with a wave of my wand, I pull a rabbit out of the hat, and the crowd cheered. I was Merlin the Magician! My fingers were my wands. I could project energy through them and perform the magical act of healing. This was real magic.

I learned that anyone can learn how to heal. I believe it's in our innate nature to heal, not just ourselves, but also others. God does heal if we pray to him, but he also wants us to heal others by connecting to God. Why? Because anyone can give a gift of money, food, or even time. But healing other people requires something special from the heart. It may be a stranger or a family member. You still need the same compassion to heal either one. And when I lost my father, it triggered in me a sense of compassion for other people's pain and suffering, because nothing can compare to the loss of my father. If I could survive losing my dad and my Aunt Elena, then I could handle anything. And secretly, I was healing both of them. I just imagined whoever I was healing were either my Dad or Aunt Elena. That made it possible to show my love and compassion for this person whomever it was.

And now I stood in front of my mom, ready to do a full healing session on her. This wasn't the same as healing her back. This was different. My mom had several ailments. She had heart disease, diabetes, high-blood pressure, and other conditions that I wasn't aware of. Everything seemed piled one on top of another. Everything in her body ached. And she looked weaker each minute I looked at her.

GrandMaster Choa help me!

Everything seemed so simple when I was at the workshop. Just follow the instructions, and that was it. It seemed fool-proof at the time. If I got in trouble, the teacher was there to assist me. Everybody was cooperative. At lunch we gathered together like one big happy family, sharing our experiences and background. And after class, we continued to gather and talk. It was through my new-found friends that I learned about other healing modalities, and that really fueled my interest in being a healer. I was excited about learning more.

But now I was here alone, and this was real. There was no one to refer to. No one to ask questions or look after my work. If I stumbled, there was no one to catch my fall, and this was my mother that I was working on. Sure we had learned he techniques in class, but nothing compared to real life. Here I were on my own.

A thousand questions plagued my mind, like where do I begin? We had been given a book on Advanced healing, and it had a list of protocols for many diseases. But what if the disease we needed to work on wasn't listed in the book? What if the person has ten diseases or some unknown diseases that science is just discovering? Then what do we do next? What if one protocol interferes with another protocol? Do I start with the first chakra or root chakra and work myself up, or vice versa? What if something happens to my mom? What if she dies?

I was feeling really nervous and scared.

I decided to review all that I had learned in class and then some. I reread my books several times, until I felt I understood the inner principles that ran them. I started with basic cleansing since you can't go wrong with that. I asked my mom what was wrong with her, but all she said was her heart wasn't right. Yet I knew intuitively there was more to it than that. So besides her chakras, I also scanned her organs as well I discovered her pancreas was polluted, and so it became one of the first organs I started to work on.

The pancreas dealt with resentment, especially from her childhood. It seemed my mom had a very unhappy childhood. She had lost her mom early in life, and wasn't given any dolls to play with. Now, as an adult, she decorated her bedroom with lots of dolls. Some she kept in boxes, while others were openly displayed.

In the beginning of learning about Pranic Healing, I started to heal myself. It was easier than healing my mom, because at that moment she wasn't accepting me as being a healer. At that point, my mom and I still continued to have a tumultuous relationship. All of my life she overtook my childhood and even adulthood, and I resented for not being able to live my life independently. It was hard. The funny thing is, that no matter how many times I healed myself, I never really got healed. Something was missing, but I didn't know what.

My mom's blood sugar was going high like a skyrocket. I knew that if I didn't do something quick, she might end up in a coma or worse. She was scared during her first healing session, because she didn't really know what to expect. Yes, I had healed her backache before, but this was still something new. At this point I had nothing to lose. I did basic cleansing, and that provided some relief. And then I focused on her pancreas, cleansing and energizing it repeatedly. From my review of the manuals, I learned there were basic pranic colors used. It took a while to clear her pancreas, but I got it sufficiently cleansed. And then I waited a few days, to observe the the results of healing.

Healing a stranger is a hundred times easier than healing a relative, especially your mother. It's easier to be objective. There's no history that gets in your way of being unconditional. When you're healing a family member a lot of memories and resentment gets stirred up. You can't help it. It just floats from the bottom of the barrel right to the top. It becomes too personal. This was the difference I learned from being in a class or taking it to the real world.

One of the first things I learned even with healing strangers is that there's so much stuff to clear. There is a ton of stuff to clear. All the chakras looked blocked. Some of their organs are really diseased and need so much clearing.

And then there's emotional issues that caused the physical ailments. There's so much to do, and at times seems it'll take forever.

But also I needed healing. I didn't have any health issues, but I had my share of emotional issues to clear. That in itself was a challenge. It's even harder to be objective with yourself – and that's the truth. But I needed to heal that part in myself. I had a lot of resentment brewing with my mom. Being an only child, the way she had overprotected me, meant I had absolutely no privacy. She monitored my calls, opened my mail, and periodically checked my room. My mom constantly advised me what to do, and it wouldn't be so bad if she was mostly right, but she was mostly wrong. And that screwed up my life!

Yes, I had issues. And so I worked really hard to heal myself. But no matter how many times I did sessions on myself, I still couldn't get rid of my resentment towards her. And if I couldn't clear my anger, then how was I going to be able to clear her energy? I mean this was the whole point of taking these classes! I had made a vow at my father's funeral, and now I was stuck. Taking healing classes wasn't what I thought it would be. It brought its own challenges – ones I never expected. Before I thought healing was so cool. It felt magical to be able to relieve people of their pains. It's gratifying to make people feel good. I just didn't expect it to be so complicated.

My mom was getting worse. Her blood sugar was rising, and her diabetes was getting worse. I knew that diabetes causes all sorts of health issues. I was at a dilemma what to do, and so with fingers crossed I started to work on her.

I began with basic cleansing. My mom's aura felt really thick, like molasses. Even though I started from the top of her head, it felt thicker as I worked below her neck and moved down her waistline. My fingers felt heavy with sludge as I flung them at the basin of salt water. After several passes, I could feel her aura become lighter, but there were some areas around her stomach, that needed extra cleansing. I worked her front and her back. And as those areas became cleaner, I concentrated on her pancreas which felt heavy and dull. My mom couldn't stand for more than a few minutes, and so I allowed her to lie down on the couch. Usually we have the client stand in front of us and turn to their back and sides as we clean them, but that was the case only in a class setting. Most people are not going to stand more than a few minutes, and so I had to use my imagination, that I was cleaning their backside even though they were lying on the couch or sitting on the chair. This was my first lesson in doing healing from a distance. You have to imagine the person from all sides even though you haven't met them. We basically have the same standard physique and organs. And so you imagine a 3-d model of the person, in the size of a small doll. It was also helpful to get an anatomy book to know where all the organs were, and after a time I memorized it.

I basically learned there were two basic colors for cleansing which were green and orange prana, alternatively switched between one and the other. These were the two main colors used, except for the heart and brain. With practice, I slowly got to know the rules. If I wasn't sure, then I wouldn't do it. I also learned the root chakra was important in understanding the health of the person. If the root chakra was depleted, then I knew the client was very low in energy, possibly in depression, and was probably in a general state of poor health since it's the root chakra that energizes all the chakras above it. Sometimes the root chakra wasn't easily energized, either because there was blockage in the spine preventing it from being energized or the energy was leaking.

I learned that if the throat, ajna, and forehead chakra were not energized, it showed the person as being low in intelligence or overthinking. But that could change dramatically, if those chakras were energized. If the mental chakras were energized, then the person would think more clearly. As an experiment, I energized one of the students during break. She was complaining that she couldn't feel energy and didn't understand what everyone was talking about. At that time I was skilled enough that I could balance, cleanse, and energize the chakras in two seconds. I was pretty dramatic as I would raise my hand and shout "Cleanse! Energize!" in two waves and it would happen. After the break we returned back to the classroom, and my friend was picked by the teacher to be scanned. The teacher had no idea what I did during the break, and remarked as he scanned her, "Oh – very intelligent!" I had energized her mental chakras to a high level. From that moment on, I could never label people as being dumb, stupid or smart. Because I could improve them by energizing their mental chakras, and their intelligence would improve. Each chakra had both psychological and physical characteristics associated with them. By scanning these chakras and noticing if they were depleted, blocked, or energized, I could tell things about that person very accurately.

One time during a lecture I learned that when a woman is pregnant her second - sex chakra becomes highly energized. The second chakra also transmutes sexual energy to the throat chakra which becomes creativity. Or a large second chakra could also mean a high libido. But anyways I was at a party where I met an attractive girl. Her second chakra was pretty large, and she had a large belly which I took as her being pregnant. I told a friend about it and he went up to her to congratulate her for being pregnant with her first child. Turns out I had misread her. She wasn't pregnant. She was just overweight. Well, that was embarrassing. But I learned to hone on my chakra reading skills.

The next lesson I learned is how healing others had an unexpected benefit. As I started to work on my mom's pancreas, her blood sugar normalized. She also wasn't as irritable as before. I noticed she became calm and relaxed. And surprisingly I felt calm and relax as well. I didn't have the same irritation about my mom as I did before. I almost couldn't believe it. And so I learned that by clearing my mom, I was also clearing myself. It was a big discovery for me, that by healing other people you also heal yourself. And so with newfound vigor I continued to heal my mom, picking up new modalities and trying new protocols. As years went by, it became easier not only to heal my mom, but to love her unconditionally. At the peak of healing her, I learned to love her unconditionally, like the way your dog or cat loves you. I couldn't even get mad at her, even when she was treating me badly.

I was my mom's healer for ten years, until she passed. It was her time. She reported many times of my dad visiting her and even laying by her side of her bed, as she slept. In her dreams she saw my dad calling out for her to join him. Other relatives visited her, and each time she would become sicker, as if they were hastening her death to join them.

My mother didn't want to leave yet. She knew I wasn't ready to let her go. At least two years before she passed, she knew her time was coming soon, and so she prepared me as much as possible by taking care of personal details so I wouldn't have to worry about them. She tried to talk to me several times before she left, but I didn't want to hear it. In my mind I believed she would live forever as long as I kept expanding my knowledge and skill as a healer.

In my time I had performed a few miracles with my mom. Several times she couldn't walk and was confined to a wheelchair. I got her strong enough that she was able to walk on her own. Once she was bedridden, and I worked on her for an entire month before she got up and was never bedridden again. I didn't always know what I was doing, but I prayed to God each time to give me the gift of healing. In the end, my mom was underweight, and was being admitted to the hospital every three weeks. Each time her physician thought she was about to die, and had the priest standing by. Then I would work on her and to their amazement she recovered. It was a constant battle with her doctors, and my mom was tired of going to the hospital and being awaken in the middle of the night by her nurses to take her blood sample. She wanted to live, but not this way.

I believe that a person knows when they're going to die, as does the person closest to them. I sensed it as well, but I can't explain how. Part of me didn't want to accept this reality. And so I took my mom on trips to the casino, and all the childhood places she took me when I was small. If for no other reason, I wanted her last days to be the most pleasant she could have.

The last lesson I had to learn was to love my mom unconditionally. It took ten years to learn that lesson. And when I finally did, my mom decided it was her time to go. She had served her purpose in teaching me how to become a healer. One of my greatest accomplishments was keeping my mom from residing in a resting home, despite her doctor's insistence. My mother would have died of loneliness and despair if she had been left in a nursing home. Instead, she died peaceably at home, surrounded by friends and relatives.

The greatest healing modality is unconditional love, because it's your true intent that makes all modalities work. Because I came with an inspired purpose, I believe that is the reason why I accelerated faster than my colleagues. I had to – if not, my mom would have passed away years ago.

Before my mom's final departure, she told me that my grandfather was also a healer. I never knew this, since my grandfather had passed years before I was born. It seems that I come from a long line of healers. My mom wasn't a healer as it appears the ability skipped over a generation, but she was psychic. Now everything comes full circle. In my family, I am the only one who took up to the healing arts. No one else seems interested. It just didn't make sense why I was so drawn to this field. Losing my Aunt Elena and my Dad triggered a genetic program that had laid dormant before. I wish I had started in my early youth, but I don't think I would have been as interested. You have to be called upon, as the road to being a healer is not an easy one. It takes more than taking a weekend workshop. It takes endless review and infinite practice.

When I finally learned to love unconditionally strangers and friends, then it was time for my mom to leave. She had served her purpose in teaching me. That in itself was the hardest lesson to learn. The power is not so much in the techniques, but in the ability and honesty of the heart. The teachings of Jesus rang true tin the past as they do now.

As I watched my mom slowly dying, little did I know that the next round of lessons were just around the corner.

Chapter VIII.

A TRUE HEALER'S HEART

I still remember the day I got a call from the hospital nurse, telling me that my mom was going into hospice care. I didn't know what the word "hospice" meant, but deep inside I instinctively knew. And it wasn't a good feeling.

My mother had gotten a cold from a visiting aunt, and the next day she was whisked away to the hospital. It was that fast. She still looked healthy at that point, and I thought her recovery would be swift. But there was something that wasn't right. I attempted to heal her several times, but something prevented me from doing so. For the first time I felt ineffective. There was nothing I could do, and I couldn't explain it.

At that point I consulted with every healer and intuitive I knew. All of them except for one, Jane, told me that she was going to live to the ripe old age. And then I asked God, and he told me that my mom was going to die. God's voice was as clear as a bell, that keeps on ringing. I mean, if you ask God a question, he will answer and whether you like his answer or not, you can't deny it. The Truth will hit the core of your soul.

Jane, my intuitive friend, was on the phone with me every night supporting me. One night Jane told me to go downstairs and say goodbye to my mom. She had seen the Angel of Death hovering over my mom. And so I did. My mom had been in a state of coma for several days. Her eyes were open and drying out. After I said my peace, I went upstairs to bed. The next morning my mom was pronounced dead. But what was most strange, was that she was discovered with tears trailing down her face, almost as if saying a final good-bye.

I had gone downstairs to visit her when I was given the news. I practically collapsed on her body. Suddenly I felt my mom's spirit hugging me from behind giving me comfort. I then realize what the Great Spiritual teachers have always said was true – the body is only a shell, but the Soul lives forever.

And I felt at peace.

Nothing prepares you – absolutely nothing – when someone you dearly love departs. You can't say how it will affect you until it happens. I thought I would be spared the pain of losing my mom, but it wasn't so. I didn't suffer from pangs of guilt or regret, because I had spent the last ten years healing her. And I was able to say my last good-byes. No – what followed was unexpected, but just as bad.

I had to deal with myself.

I was in mourning, but that was to be expected. What I didn't expect was that my fears, insecurities, and weaknesses would come to torment me mercilessly. It was as if Pandora's Box was opened and my internal demons demanded flesh and blood. In my most vulnerable moments lay my hardest battles.

Being an only child, my mom was extremely overprotective of me and never wanted to see me hurt. So she took charge over my life. As a child I felt both loved and protected. But as I got older and the people who raised me died off, I discovered this left me feeling incapable of dealing with the outside world. In many ways I still thought as a child and believed my family would always be there to protect and guide me. I didn't learn basic survival skills. I was extremely introverted, and didn't know how to deal with people, much less communicate. The majority of my decisions were made by my mom, and I always had to get her approval.

Now I was left on my own. Suddenly I had a lot of responsibilities, and financial decisions to make. Plus, I was going through a terrible depression. Everything was going really bad really fast, and if I didn't take control, I knew I could lose everything.

For a long time I took a hiatus from healing. I had spent my life healing others, but now it was time for me to heal myself. For a while I thought I did. I healed the rift I had with my mom, but I neglected my own emotional issues. I thought that I would be exempt for all the good work I did, but that wasn't so. It doesn't work that way.

Looking back, I realize that there was some deep karma between my mom and I that needed to be resolved. That's why it was necessary for me to be her healer. I know that my mom and I have known each other for several lifetimes and that in this lifetime we happened to be mother and son. Maybe I was a tyrant to my mom in a past life, and so in this life I had to be in a position where my mom was in control. Either way, we can't escape our debts. One of my Spiritual teachers used to say that the Universe doesn't care what you do. How you live your life is up to you, because we all have free will. We make our own choices in life. The problem is that we don't always see the repercussions of the choices we make. It could be years if not decades later. It can even continue to the next lifetime. In the end, the scales must be balanced.

We pay for every thought, belief, and emotion we've ever had. Think negative thoughts and your life becomes unhappy and negative. Our beliefs limit what we receive or what we accomplish. So if you're not getting what you want in life, then change your beliefs so that they're more harmonious with what you want. You can't suppressed your emotions, thinking they'll go away. Emotions are like snow, building on top of a mountain. Without warning it can avalanche, manifesting as disease or mental illness.

The most powerful thoughts are the ones of peace, gratitude, and neutrality. These three bring a multitude of blessings and good luck. Your mind expands and you find solutions to seemingly impossible tasks. Your stress level goes down and life becomes easier to handle.

Fear is really stress. Fear makes it difficult to think clearly. Everything becomes black or white which leads to depression. Because you only have two options and both lead to dead-ends. Your body becomes full of tension, and your breath shallow. The more fear you have, the more difficult it is to move. In other words, you become stuck. And this can last for years.

Notice I didn't mention love and happiness. Being happy is nice, but being overexcited can make you lose your mind. I've seen too many people go into a blissful state and have a hard time getting back into their body. Love is good, but can be conditional. Loving someone who is hurting you is not good. It's because it's not congruent. It's like attempting to hug someone while they're hitting you. Just walk away and distance yourself. Do no harm, but at the same time allow no harm to come to you. No one has to accept you nor do you have to accept them. Treat them with neutrality, and you'll have a peaceful life.

At first, when I lost my mom, I thought it was the end of the world. It wasn't. It was the beginning of a new world. Now I was free to heal myself. I had built up my healing skills to a high degree, and now I needed to apply the same vigor to taking care of myself. I had paid my karmic debt to my mom, and now I was free.

I was inspired to become a healer because I wanted to heal my mom. Unknowingly, I had built a complete belief system based on keeping my mom alive and healthy. Sounds nice, and it was. I took every healing workshop that I could afford to take. Every waking moment I was thinking how I could become a better healer, and I did. But my identity as a healer worked as long as my mom was alive. And when she died, I didn't know if I wanted to continue healing. I was a runaway car speeding at a 100 mph headed to a broken-down bridge. Disaster was inevitable.

What I didn't know at the time was that I needed to update my belief system from healing my mom to healing myself. My mom passed away within a month after getting that hospice call from the nurse. I didn't know what to do. I was worried about losing my mom, and it was a difficult reality to accept that she wasn't going to be around. What would life be without her?

After my mom passed away I had to update so many beliefs I had about life and responsibility. I was overwhelmed. My life changed, and it would never be the same again. There were a lot of things I didn't know that I had to learn quickly. And everywhere I turned, it felt as if I was bumping into walls. I would be walking casually and a brick wall suddenly appeared out of nowhere, and I slammed my nose against it. After a couple of broken noses I learned this was a sign that I needed to upgrade my belief system - that my old belief system based on old knowledge and experience was no longer working. One way to expand our belief system is by expanding your knowledge through books. I had to learn to challenge what I thought was right, and accept that it may not be right. I had to admit that I may be wrong.

Our beliefs determine what we have in life. Think of beliefs as the clothes we wear. As a child grows up, it needs to get bigger clothes otherwise it will outgrow them. Even as adults we need to change our clothes according to current trends and styles. Otherwise we'll dress dated. Some of us have had traumatic experiences growing up as children. So we build walls to protect and keep us secure. At the time we call these walls castles, but as we outgrow them, they become our prisons. The problem was I felt like I was flowing through life on automatic pilot. As long as things were moving smoothly, I felt there was nothing to worry about. The truth was, things were going wrong, but I wasn't aware of it, because I wasn't aware of what beliefs were controlling my life.

Clearing out my suppressed emotions was the third component that I needed to work on. As a child I had bottled up a lot of emotions, to the point that I was disconnected from what I was really feeling. We didn't always talk about how we feel in our family, and usually I was punished for expressing myself. These emotions don't go away. They stay hidden in your body and mind, until finally they burst as depression and disease.

Suppressed emotions are like subliminal tapes playing 24/7. When I learned to meditate and quiet my mind, I was surprised to hearing my mom's voice like when she was scolding me as a child. Other tapes were of relatives or friends putting me down. And yet other times it was mental videos of my childhood being replayed over and over again. It's not that I was crazy or anything, but this is what's going on at our unconscious level. As an energy healer I began to see blockages not only in my chakras, but also in different parts of my body like my tongue, ears, and eyes.

For example, the ears of people sometimes looked energetically as big as the ears of Dumbo the elephant. That told me these people were very sensitive to sound, like the siren of an ambulance. But also intonation like sarcasm or even a loud voice, can be just as disconcerting. The ears connect directly to the root chakra which when triggered can create a survival response. That's why verbal abuse is more punishing than physical abuse.

Blockages in the eyes tell me a lot. Blockages around the tear ducts tell me the person has gone through a lot of pain and grief. These connect to the lungs. Blockages on the other side of the eye tell me rage and hate. These connect to the stomach or solar plexus. People who have upset stomachs or nausea experience these things. The stomach muscles actually compressed with tension. Blockages in the tongue tell me that this person has so much to say, but that it's all bottled up inside of them. This connects to the throat, throat chakra, and the forehead. That's why these people often feel confused and overthink. It's like there's a traffic jam of thoughts up there.

Blockages in the arms protect the heart and lungs. Blockages in the left arm tells me if they allow other people to get close to them or even get to know them. It usually means they're emotionally very sensitive, and are often afraid to get hurt. Blockages to the right arm connect to the lungs, and that tells me if the person breaths shallowly. And if that's so, then their energy is usually low. It can also mean they feel stuck in their life or find it difficult to reach their goals or even get a job, because when they're under stress their oxygen is depleted.

My skills as an energy healer served me well in determining what issues I needed to work on. In so doing, I was able to unblock myself. It took time. My mind became clear. I could think faster. And my energy improved. I was no longer avoiding people or situations. I started to handle my life better, and things improved.

The way to release your emotions is to allow yourself to feel your emotions. But don't become the emotion. Witness it. Allow it. And then let it go. Meditation helps a lot. Every emotion has a right to be expresses. If not, it will continue to fester and grow. And then you create thicker walls, in order to contain what you feel. Eventually the walls break down, and manifest first as mental illness, and eventually disease.

These three things comprised what I call the "Way of the Spiritual Warrior" – maintaining peaceful thoughts, updating your belief systems, and clearing your emotions. It's not easy. There is no magic bullet that will clear these things forever once and for all. It's a continuous process. As long as you're alive you will always need to upgrade yourself, because life continues to evolve. I work on myself everyday. I have to. It's part of being an energy healer and intuitive reader. If I don't, then I won't be effective healing others. I won't be able to think clearly, and give accurate readings. The problem is that not all healers and readers do enough proper clearings on themselves.

Everything works on a level of vibration. Like attracts like. Opposites repel just like magnets. If I'm healing someone who has the same issue as myself and I haven't resolved it, their negative energy will be absorbed by my body. I know a lot of people who are psychic sponges. Not only do they absorb people's negative energy, but negative people actually seek them out. It doesn't matter that they weren't trained as healers, it's what they do. Healers and psychic sponges who do this type of healing can go crazy, feel depleted, and even stop functioning in life.

It is so important to release this energy into the Earth where it can be neutralized. The reason why it's hard for some people to let go, is that it makes them feel closer to others. For a long time I absorbed a lot of my mom's energy while I was healing her, as well as my clients. I had to learn the hard way to ground myself. I had to learn how not to take it on. Unfortunately, they don't always teach you that most important fact in a lot of the healing workshops I attended.

Most people call themselves healers when they shouldn't. Just because you attended a weekend workshop or know a few techniques doesn't mean you know what you're doing. Some people call themselves "a master" just because they've taken master level training. It takes years of practice and working with thousands of clients to really get the feel. Some people who attend these workshops have never worked on anyone outside of the class. Scanning and clearing negative energy doesn't always feel good. Listening to other people's problems is worse then listening to your wife or girlfriend. Plus you need to be fast and effective. You either love it or you don't.

You need a combination of both healing yourself and others. Some days I do nothing but work on clearing myself. When you are healing others, it teaches you other people's perspectives and how they differ from yours. It really opens the world around you, and I believe is the best psychology course there is. You also learn to become objective and neutral when facing your own issues. You learn from their experiences. It's like peeking through their lives. You actually hear their thoughts and feel their emotions from their perspective, and not only yours. You get an in depth perspective into what makes other people operate. Afterwards, I balance it out by clearing myself.

Always the balance. Sometimes more on myself.

You need to become what I call the "Spiritual Warrior". You can't heal others unless you're willing to either heal yourself or get yourself healed.

Being a healer doesn't make me more special than anyone else. I have problems just like everyone else does. If I don't heal myself then healing others will just add to my problems. I will make myself sick and unhappy. I need to be both clean and clear when healing others.

Each time I heal myself, my psychic immunity gets stronger and stronger. I have fewer psychic attacks and cords attached to me. I become spiritually protected. I can't know everything and so when I'm not able to heal myself, I call upon qualified healers to work on me.   Sometimes we do exchanges.

It took a lot of hard work. It wasn't overnight. It took me years before I felt that balance. Now my mind feels clear. I have a Zen mind.   My energy has skyrocketed. I can read people better than before. I've become super-aware of my energy body and know when it's blocked. I monitor my thoughts constantly, and clear my emotional issues before they become too much of a problem. Life runs smoother.

I'm constantly learning new things, and updating my belief system. Even though I've been doing this for over twenty years, I still have the same enthusiasm and interest just like when I began to study healing.   Each new modality I learn is like starting over, but I learn faster each time. Plus, I can dissect it and add new perspectives from my wealth of knowledge and skill. In the next following chapters I will share some of the things I know.

PART TWO

COMPASS ENERGETICS

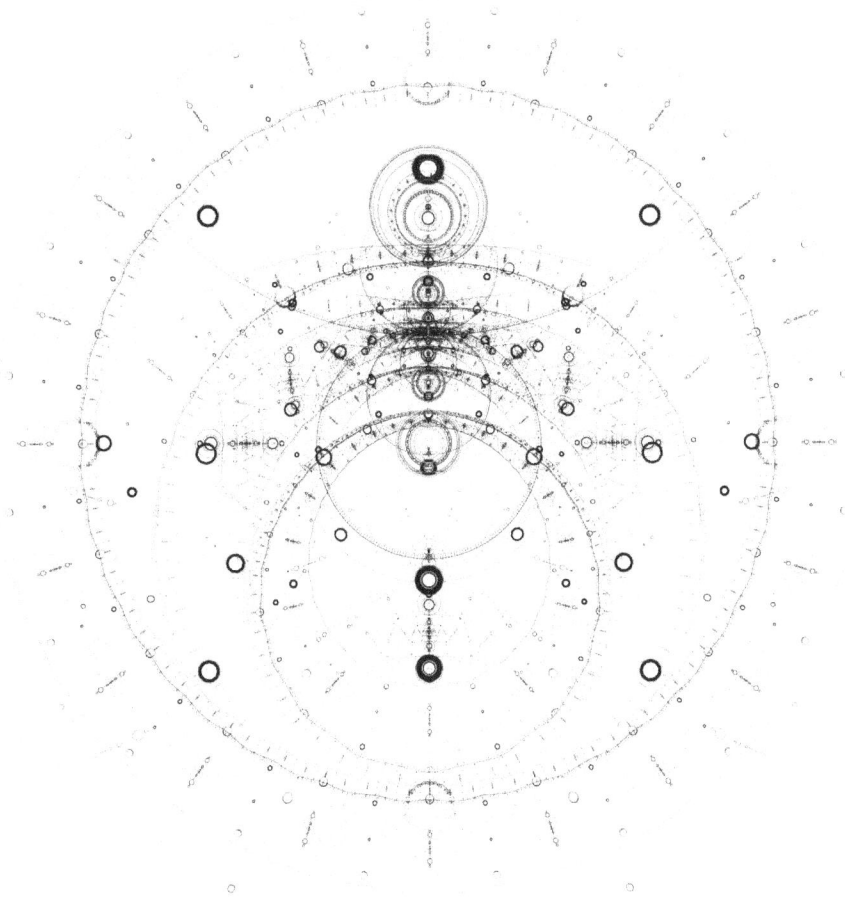

Chapter IX.

THE PRINCIPLES OF COMPASS ENERGETICS

What is Compass Energetics?

Compass Energetics is the culmination of my over 20 years experience as an Energy Healer and Practitioner.
The techniques of this unique method are the tools I use to:
- evaluate and detect energy blockages in a person's aura and energy body
- read and clarify the issues affecting them
- clear and remove blockages that are negatively affecting a person's chi and life-force energy
- replenish individual's chi and restore their physical and mental well-being
- help clarify a person's issues so they have a stronger understanding of themselves and other people involved in their personal life, and finally
- help them make proper choices and decisions for a more fulfilling life.

When a client first reaches out for help, they are usually seeking answers to why their life is not working out for them. They are frustrated, angry, and deeply disappointed that they haven't be able to make the type of gains they set out in life. They seek guidance.

There are four principles that I spell out for my clients right away. If they follow them, it will most often lead them to enjoy great positive results.

1. Until you change the way you think, you won't change your life.
Your beliefs determine the results you get in life. If you are not getting what you want in life, change your beliefs and you'll see changes.

2. All problems of either emotional or physical nature, have their origin in unresolved emotional trauma. Suppressed emotions affect our health, and our mental well-being. If you clear these blockages, then many of your problems will clear as well.

3. When we deplete our Chi, we feel weak, tired, and get easily overwhelmed. Chi is life-force energy. When it is strong, we feel healthier, are able to reach our goals, and find happiness. In this book I share techniques I use to restore and replenish Chi.

4. The main reason why we stay stuck in our problems is that we don't know what are problem is in the first place. It's not that we don't try to resolve our issues - it's that we can't see our issues. We have "blind spots". A good intuitive can see and detect blockages in our aura and energy body, clear them, and then explain what they were. Sometimes all that is needed is a realization of what the problem is. Because once we understand our resistance, it will often disappear on its own, like magic.

Compass Energetics is a technique I created to help me evaluate what state a person was in, what direction they were going, and especially, if I could trust this person. It was created to help me read a person or client directly and fast.

It describes the following four major states:

~ Success and mental clarity

~ Emotional state

~ Failure or feeling stuck

~ Work ethic and action

Each major state is depicted by the four directions of the compass: North, East, South, and West. There are also four sub-directions that are just as important, which are NE, NW, SE, and SW.

NORTH

NORTH is the most powerful direction. When a client or person is pointing North it shows they're successful, moving forward in life, and have good mental clarity. Kinesthetically their body leans forward.They walk with speed and a confidence like they're going somewhere. Their body feels strong and tingles with an air of excitement that can be perceived as charisma. North people lead with their minds, and not with their emotions. Even in the most tense moments, they don't fold and are able to take corrective action or make sound decisions. While everybody else is panicking and freezing up, they continue to forge forward.

EAST

People who depict **EAST** energy tend to be heart-oriented, emotional, and trustworthy. East-energy persons tend to be the nicest people. They're very sensitive and pick up how other people are feeling. They're known as empaths. It doesn't take much to hurt an East person. They can pick up quickly if someone is angry with them and can feel offended even without saying a word. They're so sensitive you don't even need to raise your voice. Just your disapproval is enough to affect them. And that's why East people go out of their way to please the other person or placate them, even when it's not their fault. They don't like to be around a lot of angry energy whether it's with people or being in a stressed environment. Because negative energy affects them so much. It's very difficult for some of them to operate in daily life as they may suffer panic attacks.

SOUTH

People who depict **SOUTH** energy are people who feel stuck in life. They're not moving forward. If you look at them ten years down the road, you'll usually find them in the same place and station. They don't reach their goals much less set goals. They're just existing. It's not like they don't want success or anything. It's just that something seems to keep them anchored in one spot. It can be in any area of their life – business, career, relationships, or others. A person can be successful in their career, but have South energy in their relationships. Usually South energy is caused by some unresolved trauma that has permanently scarred them. There are THREE major locations where this blockage appears in their energy body – the back-heart chakra, the mein meng chakra, and the sternum.

The **BACK-HEART CHAKRA** is located in the mid-upper back. This chakra influences breathing and your lungs. There are FIVE types of distressed breathing like hyperventilation. One or more of these types of distressed breathing patterns shows up as blockages of the back-heart chakra. And the manner of your breath influences the way you think, how your body operates, and if you can function normally. During moments of stress you may hold your breath and not even know it. You won't be in the present moment and may not even be aware that you're not in the present moment. That's because your brain is sensing you are not getting enough oxygen and focuses on the body as it is in a state of survival. During this time you're not aware of your surroundings or even the interactions with people around you. You're not able to think clearly. This is the time when you shouldn't make decisions, and most likely will let other people make decisions for you, as you're not in control. People in South energy feel they're not in control of their lives, because their minds and bodies have shut down.

The **MEIN MENG CHAKRA** is located in the lower back, between the kidneys. It sits above the root chakra and distributes the energy to the rest of the body. When you're overworked or tired, the Mein meng chakra activates the adrenals for quick caffeinated energy. When it is blocked, it can create problems with your blood pressure.

Problems with the Mein meng chakra makes you feel lethargic. You feel as if you don't want to get up from your chair. Instead you feel you want to rest and vegetate on the sofa or be a couch potato. You feel tired all the time. Even if you sleep ten hours a day, you're still not rested. Energetically your root chakra is depleted, and so you depend on your Mein meng for energy. The Mein meng was never meant to be a continuous source of energy. People who have high East energy also tend to have Mein meng congestion which is why they're so emotionally vulnerable and sensitive.

The sternum is located in the front of the chest just below the throat. It's a small bony structure located in the upper center of your chest, covering the heart. This is a major area where trauma is stored, especially when we're children. During distress most children try to hold back their emotions by stifling their breathing. This is when parents tell their children to stop crying and be quiet. It's like telling a volcano to stop erupting. Tremendous pressure is build up in that area, and most children learn to not express their emotions.

Over time this area can be so congested that they literally are not able to move or take action. It doesn't happen all the time, but during times of stress they can be triggered and suddenly they're frozen. Even though they're not deaf and dumb, they'll act as if they were. They may just stare at you in awe and be non-responsive. Many people get annoyed with such behavior thinking they're being ignored, but nothing could be further from the truth. The person is in a state of extreme panic and shock. Their minds have receded in the background, and it's like they're not even there.

WEST

People who depict **WEST** energy are action-oriented people. They're very physical and like to stay busy. They also can be workaholics. The problem with West people is that they don't take the time to take it easy and rest. As such they're also prone to burning out. They don't deal with their emotions or emotional issues very well. If they feel emotionally stressed, they tend to lash out or get angry. Dealing with their emotions is not easy for them. If there is a problem, they try to figure out what they can do either logically and physically. Talking about how they feel is something foreign to them.

North~East

People who depict **NORTH~EAST** energy have high emotional IQs. They're more emotionally balanced and can be described as peaceful and serene. Many of them live to ripe-old age having survived wars, recessions, and family tragedies. Because of their experience they know all things eventually pass, and they don't take life too seriously. Many of them meditate on a regular basis, however that does not necessarily apply to all.

South ~ East

People who depict **SOUTH~EAST** energy are people who have serious emotional issues. You have the South energy of feeling stuck combined with the East energy of emotional distress. Each day is a battle with anxiety and panic attacks. They're usually overthinking. You can find them analyzing and picking apart day's events both past and present. Basically they're stuck either in the past or in the future and seemingly unaware of the present. Their life is one broken record, played over and over again. They need to let go of the past and move past their trauma. Life does get better. No matter what their past is, it's not a life sentence. You can re-create your life so that you're living the life you want.

South ~ West

People who depict **SOUTH~WEST** energy are the ones I watch out for the most. You have the South energy which is feeling stuck, but also the West energy of movement. West energy doesn't like to be contained or stuck so it becomes destructive. South-west energy can go from acting irritable to taking revenge on someone. At its worst, they will try to befriend you in order to get your guard down, and then when you least expect it, they can strike you at your most vulnerable point in order to inflict the greatest damage.

Southwest energy cannot be contained. Depending on how intense the energy is, it must be expressed. In the lighter stages, people become sarcastic. In Medium states they are making threats. Verbal attacks are a prelude to physical attacks or sabotage. South-west people are both liars and manipulators. Some of them are masters of putting up a good front, even so much as to being in good-standing with the community. That way nobody believes them when someone says a negative statement about them. It's also a way to gain people's trust, and to steal from their pocket books.

South-west people tend to attract a lot of bad luck into their lives. Their lives are difficult, full of financial trouble, and health problems. They appear to be charming and even nice, but that's a ruse to gain your trust. You can never tame a snake, and it will bite you when you least expect it. If they borrow money from you, don't expect to get it back.

Anyone at anytime can be in South-West energy. It's not a permanent state of mind. It usually happens during an emotional or financial crisis. You can know someone for twenty years and I can guarantee you don't know them until they're in trouble. How people react to stress is very telling. And when a person is in survival, they're not thinking in their right mind. Misery likes company, and the first person they will make miserable is the one closest to them. It's because they're in a dark space, where they see no place out.

South-West energy can last for years and is a magnet for bad luck. It just attracts all sorts of trouble. Just look at how miserable their lives are. I can detect South-west energy in people, and I just try to stay clear of them as much as possible. Whenever I've violated that rule, I've always regretted it.

North ~ West

People who depict **NORTH~WEST** energy know how to work smartly and efficiently. They have the Midas touch. I would do business or invest with anybody with North-West energy, because success and prosperity always follows them around. They're just extremely smart. They're also the rarest of the 8 compass points.

I developed Compass Energetics by accident. I was studying magnetic healing. Magnets have been successfully used in treating pain and various diseases. Since our bodies are electro-magnetic and this can affect our health, I began to wonder how can this also affect our emotional well-being?

Magnets have only 2 polarities – North and South or negative and positive. As I was observing the demonstration, an image came to my mind. I immediately saw the Yin and Yang symbol.

Yin and Yang are polarized towards each other because they're opposites, and opposites attract. As Yin gains in strength and momentum it becomes Yang, and vice versa. But in the center of Yin, there's a small dot of Yang, and in Yang a small dot of Yin. This represents perfect harmony and flow.

But what if the line between Yin and Yang were wider? What if the space between them was enlarged and the flow disrupted? Then both Yin and Yang would enlarge and they would each get out of control. It would go to over-balance or under-balance. In such a state chaos would ensue. North energy would be arrogance. South energy would be total failure and destruction. East energy would be emotional imbalance. And West energy would be physically destructive.

North and South are the two strongest polarities – you're either moving forward or backwards. East and West create balance and stability. Leaning too much to the left or the right creates imbalance. I used the compass points to help me evaluate where a client is in regards to their issues. Also for direct feedback on how much they've improved after a session or how much more they need to work on. I have brought people into high-North energy and reduced their South or South-east energy. I have also used the compass points in helping me test out my techniques and accomplished that with great effectiveness.

Chapter X.

THREE MOTIVATIONS

There are THREE major motivations that run people. They are power, achievement, and affiliation. If you understand these three motivations and how they operate, then you will have a deep understanding of who you are dealing with. It will give you a profound understanding of where they are coming from, and what to watch out for. You will understand the type of relationship you are dealing with. You will also understand yourself better and how you operate. This may be the single most important tool in reading people as well as yourself.

First, let's define **POWER**. Power is about control, physical domination or feeling you have the upper hand, and emotional and mental manipulation. It's about exerting control over others, and being in control. Power people have a physical presence about them. They tend to look more directly at you, the way a lion looks at a piece of meat. They have swagger and appear confident and strong. They like competition and can be physically active and strong.

They talk with force, and it seems when they make a suggestion there's no other course of action but theirs. They can be persuasive as they have quick responses to counter any rebuttal. It doesn't mean they're right. They may not be even logical and instead use their presence to intimidate. As long as you think clearly and stay calm, you can counter them by rephrasing their illogic to them. Power people at their worst don't think clear or are even aware of what they say.

They are quick to anger and tend to overpower people who have a gentle or nice disposition. Power people look for people who are weaker than them. They are predators who actively seek the ones who don't like confrontations. Power people live by the law of the jungle where only the strong survive, and one only attacks mentally or generally weak-minded people.

Everything is based on how much they can control the other person. Their victims are usually confused, intimidated, and suffer from many anxieties. Sometimes these weaker people actively seek out powerful people, because it fills their own void of feeling powerless. I know women who are attracted to muscular men, because in a bad situation they want to feel they can be protected. Women who seek men with money and power crave security for their future. Sometimes it's influence or merely by association.

ACHIEVEMENT is about results. All relationships of achievement are whether one can help another achieve the results they seek. Their motto is, "you're only as useful to me as you can help me achieve my goals. Afterwards, I'll seek someone else who can further help me." They actively seek people who are in alignment with their goals. And then the next question is whether they have the skills and abilities? Third question is whether they are hard-working or lazy? Achievement people can be ruthless as they don't care about your health, the cost of your relationships, or whether your burn-out and crash. It's all about the numbers. Achievement people are very results oriented, and as a result they measure things. They measure in terms of time, quantity, and quality. They want to be better than last time. They are very competitive and don't like to be placed second to anything. They're constantly seeking information and others to make themselves better or gain the upper hand.

Achievement people are willing to sacrifice. Their motto is the "ends justify the means." They can be extremely single-focuses, and don't like to be hampered by their emotions and especially not by other people's problems. They're not good with relationships, and tend to be loners. They have the ability to do repetitive tasks, because that's sometimes the only way you develop skill. Success is paramount to them. They tend to be very good at one thing to the exclusion of all the rest, but that's where their pride is at.

AFFILIATION people are nice and friendly. They form wonderful relationships and are easy to get along with. They look at people as family, and value close relationships. If you need them, they are there for you. They are reliable, tend to be honest and sincere, and pay attention to how you feel and making you feel good. They're wonderful people.

Affiliation people are sociable. They're easy to talk with, and like to get to know everybody. They are vivacious and exude positive energy. People are attracted to them, because they're easy to get to know and after a while it feels like they're an old friend. They evaluate people whether they're nice or not, and if they have similar interests. They tend to hang out in clicks or groups. They seem to know everybody.

By themselves they can appear listless and depressed. They can't be alone and need company all the time. Sometimes they hang out with someone just to get distracted from their own issues. They can't be by themselves, if they were, they wouldn't know what to do with themselves. Some of them can be party animals and quite talkative, to the point that they dominate the conversation. They just don't like to be alone, but that's sometimes how they feel, even in a crowd of people. That's why it' important to them to form close relationships. They're not competitive and rather seek cooperation than conflict. They like to be surrounded by people they feel care about them. Some affiliation people have entourages with different people who meet and fulfill their various needs.

No one person functions under only one motivation. If that would be so, then it would be easy to classify them. Each person runs through these 3 motivations but in varying amounts. The first and strongest motivation is called the **"major"**. The second strongest is called the **"minor"**. And the third motivation is called the **"mini"**.

It's like dividing a pie. Before you divide the pie, it is whole or 100%. You divide the pie in three slices according to a hierarchy. Even in the animal kingdom where a group of wolves has taken down prey, the first to eat are the alpha males who take the largest chunk. This is to ensure that they stay strong and vibrant. After they finish, usually the females feast. Finally the lowest rank feast. This is the order of nature. If a lower-rank wolf feasts out of order, they are quickly challenged and subdued. They may even be kicked out of the pack where survival is less likely. Doing it this way helps preserve the order of things. It's the same with the three motivations.

The pie must be divided not by equal slices, but by percentages. The major is at least 51% or higher. The minor is 49% or less. And the mini is 5% or less. The major having the largest percentage is the main motivator of a person. It can go from 51% to as high as 95%.This tells you what drives this person. The stronger the percentage, the stronger the motivation whether its power, achievement, or affiliation. It stands out. If it's 51%, then it feels almost equal to the minor motivation. At 51% it can switch from major to minor and vice versa. For example; if the major is power at 51%, and the minor is around 49% affiliation, then the person can switch from being at times dominant and manipulative to friendly and sweet. It can be very confusing to know who you're dealing with. Think of it as if the person were a coin. Depending on the flip of the toss you never know if you'll get heads or tails. And people can switch much less by personalities than by motivations.

The mini at 5% or less is so low a percentage that I wouldn't even bother with it. It's too low. It doesn't have an impact on a person's motivation or agenda. Focus on the major and then the minor. Unfortunately some people focus on the mini which appears sporadically and seldom. For example, a woman is in a relationship with a man who is very domineering. She likes a man who takes charge and is in control because it seems he knows what direction he's going. It doesn't mean that he is always right and at times can be downright wrong. Even if it's hard for her, she looks to those tender moments when he is kind. It doesn't happen often, but that's what makes it more special and can be the lynchpin why she stays in the relationship.

Power and Affiliation is when you feel you have control over another person and also have a close relationship with them – as in parent and child. A parent tells a child what to do and how to behave. Years later when the child grows up and protests how strict the parent was, the parent defends themselves by saying they did it out of love.

Power and Achievement is like a coach telling his players how to train, and validating his expertise by the team's win or loss record. Coaches need to control. They have to control people to keep the team as a cohesive unit. From that level of control, they can dictate their actions and movements.

Achievement and Affiliation is like being the head chef of a restaurant, with a team of cooks behind you. All the dishes need to be executed perfectly and in a speedy manner, especially during rush hour. As long as everyone works together and gets the dishes out in time, the head chef is happy. A well-oiled team is developed over time, and can be as close as a family. But if one cook doesn't keep pace, then the whole operation can be in jeopardy. That's when the head chef will be chopping heads instead of vegetables.

Achievement and Power is getting results with feeling people are subordinate to you. What you say goes, and no one better question you. It doesn't matter if people burn out or complain. Anyone can be replaced. People are just numbers, and the machine needs to keep running.

Affiliation and Power is having a group of people that you treat as family, but you get to tell them what to do or they seek your advice in all matters. The head of a household is a prime example. It could be a small family or a family composed of lots of relatives. The thing is there's one person who acts as the king or queen of the kingdom and everyone defers judgement to them. They're highly respected and usually hold an esteem position. They could also be someone who has lots of money and can change the fortunes of others.

Affiliation and Achievement are people who know how to motivate and influence people. They know how to communicate and their understanding of people is unparalleled. They're very smart. They're able to emphasize with other people, and this gives them a unique insight of what makes other people tick.

In order for people to dominate or control you - POWER, you need to allow them to control or dominate you - POWERLESS. In order for people to lead you ACHIEVEMENT, you have to feel they know better than you or you don't know what to do LACK OF ACHIEVEMENT. If you haven't been successful in the past or are entering unfamiliar territory, getting a trainer or coach is helpful. People who seek affiliation are people who don't like to be alone. They need support and people they can talk with. The trick is to pick the right people who have similar or like interests as yourself.

People who seek too much power are people who feel out of control with their lives. They have very low self-esteem. They need to control and influence other people. They like telling people what to do. It makes them feel good even important. They even wonder why people don't thank them for all their advice and help.

People who are high achievers sooner or later burn out. Their tenacity and dogged determination strangely comes out of anger. Maybe they have something to prove. Maybe they were poor and never want to be poor again, and so they pursue business ventures. It usually stems out of some form of insecurity, or a need to feel good at something. What brings achievement people down is their inability to deal with their emotions. They're really out of touch with their feelings, and don't know how to deal with them. Sooner or later their emotional issues catch up with them, and they literally shut down.

People who put affiliation above everything else, tend to live the longest and happiest of lives. They have communal meals and like to stay clustered in small towns where everybody knows each other. They're never alone. They don't achieve much in terms of success, because they're more focused on everyone else. Their personal ambitions are not as strong as much as making others feel welcome. The only disadvantage is as they grow older and watch several of their friends pass away until they're the only ones left behind. Memories are important to them.

Incongruity happens when your motivations don't match the other person's motivations, or when you misperceive their motivations as being your own, which they are not. If a person craves power, they will seek people who are subordinate to them. If a person is trying to achieve something, they need to feel you have skills and abilities to help them achieve their goals and are willing to follow their lead. If someone seeks affiliation with another, one should be nice and have similar interests.

Control and domination ~ POWER~ means you're subordinate to them. Achievement means you're following their lead. Affiliation means you're a good friend. It only works if you allow it. Otherwise you'll be looked on as a traitor who betrayed them. They will despise you and treat you as a traitor. They will turn on you, even though you don't feel the same way. It's because you changed, and the relationship only worked as long as things stayed status quo.

People only look at things from their perspective, and naturally assume the other person thinks the same way. And this is where people get fooled and taken advantage of. This is where people get conned. These are your blind spots.

A friend of mine was a lonely widow. For a long time, she craved being in a relationship with someone. She didn't have much money, but was a healer. She knew and taught Reiki. Reiki teachers pass along Reiki attunements to their students. Depending on who you go to, a session of Reiki attunement can be quite costly.

She met a gentleman who wanted to learn Reiki and get these attunements. The problem was he didn't have any money. He was a bit of a player and knew how to swoon my friend. His main motivations were Achievement (because he wanted to get the attunements for free), and Power (manipulate her to give him the attunements). Power and achievement don't always appear evil, because if something appears evil you would run away. And that would defeat the purpose.

Power and achievement means doing whatever is necessary to achieve domination and results. If you have to be nice, then you become gracious. You say the things the other person wants to hear, and are careful not to offend them. So how can you know if the person is sincere? Time – no one can keep up with appearances for very long. Eventually, the cracks in the mirror become more evident.

My lonely friend who was a widow sought affiliation with the opposite sex. It's been a long time since anyone paid attention to her. She assumed the other man was also seeking a long-term relationship, because that's how he appeared to her. Once she passed the Reiki attunements to him, he left. It's because he had achieved his goal. There was nothing else he wanted.

As a healer I also read clients on the basis of their motivations. I read what is their major and what is their minor motivation. I read their percentages, with the higher percentages dictating their intention and agenda. I know their major and minor motivations can change or switch in an instant. I'm especially watchful when a person is going through a crisis, because it tells me what they need or are looking for.

It's not always easy, and I'll admit I've been fooled. We all have our needs and desires and they play a stronger role in us than we suspect. Our motivations are dictated by our beliefs and emotions. No one is perfect, and that's why we need to continually update our beliefs and clear our suppressed emotions. That way, we can achieve what we want in life without manipulation or dependence.

Chapter XI.

SEVEN DIVINE INTELLIGENCES

There are what I call the SEVEN DIVINE intelligences of the brain. Understanding them has helped me profile my clients. Everyone thinks differently, and no two people think alike. So in order to get along and avoid misunderstandings ,we have to understand and respect how other people think differently from us. But it's more than that. This is how we process information, make errors in our judgement, as well as make the best possible decisions.

This is the way your brain thinks, and how it thinks is different from everyone else. Get familiar with your pattern. Order them from your strongest to your weakest intelligence. If you can do so, then it's like using the right key to open the lock in your brain. If not, then it's like using the wrong key. Use the right key and you will open your brain's optimal potential. If not, then you'll be mired in confusion, frustration, and erroneous thinking.

Each person learns things through their strongest intelligence. It's the first step that helps them understand how things work. If you try to understand things through your weakest or even second strongest intelligence, your learning will slow down. You won't pick up things very fast. You will end being frustrated and confused because it seems no information is properly absorbed by your brain.

The secret is to identify your strongest intelligence first. Then retranslate the information so that it fits that intelligence. Re-organize the information that makes sense to you. You don't have to follow exactly what the author is saying in the beginning.

Also understanding the SEVEN DIVINE intelligences can help you to better understand other people. It can help you understand their problems, and why they are the way they are. This can help clear out a number of misunderstandings.

INFORMATION GATHERERS

The first group are the information gatherers. Information gatherers, as the name implies, like spending their time with books. They love reading books, and are always ordering new books to fill their library. For them knowledge is power, because it opens a whole new world where all doors are open for them while closed to the ignorant. The more information they gather, the more fascinating the world becomes. Because they learn how to do things. Knowledge opens them up to new experiences. The more you know the more options you have and that makes you feel unlimited. The less you know, the fewer options you have. It's expansion versus contraction. When you feel limited, you have less energy. Your world looks dark and bleak. In contrast with expansion of knowledge, where an inner world of knowledge and endless concepts flourish in your imagination. And each time you add more information to that world, more colorful it becomes.

The best way to describe the Information Gatherers is that they prefer books over people. Each one that I've met has their own private library. They love reading or more like hoarding information. For them, information is power and some of them are experts in their field. They can be described as introverts, or people who like to spend a lot of time alone. Their world is that of information. Their genius lies in that their knowledge is so wide-based that they can connect things together from ten different sources that may either be related or unrelated. It doesn't matter. Their creativity lies in ability to combine pieces of information together and connect them in new and innovative ways. And that's why they need a lot of alone time – they're always thinking or imagining.

Information gatherers have very active imagination. They turn information into pictures in their minds. Every concept they learn, has to be turned into a picture where they can see it, feel it, and hear it. They live in their imagination reviewing concepts in their mind like watching a movie over and over again, until they understand it. Their genius is that they can associate other concepts, even from different and unrelated sources, and connect them in new and innovative ways. This is what makes them brilliant. This is how they come up with new and novel solutions. It helps them learn faster.

They also tend to spend a lot of time alone especially as children. Parents label them "the good child" because they don't cause trouble and tend to keep to themselves. They may look quiet but deep inside they are brooding. They can be highly sensitive and a single word can traumatize them. That's because they keep rehashing the event over and over in their minds until it's blown out of proportion and becomes a trauma. The mind can be our worst enemy and information gatherers spend most of their time in their heads.

Some are very in touch with how they feel and their emotions. Because they spend so much time thinking they tend to overthink. They overthink everything. They overanalyze. They go over their interactions with people and review everything in their heads. They analyze what was said, why they said it, and how it affected them. This can be really bad, and can create a type of neurosis.

As children they're often seen playing by themselves. They're very quiet and don't cause any trouble. If they get scolded by a parent, they become even more quiet and still. They may be seen sitting in the backseat of the car not moving or saying anything. But inside them brews a cauldron of emotions. They're very sensitive children who get easily hurt. They keep it inside where the hurt continues to grow. Eventually this hurt morphs into a trauma that they'll spend the rest of their adulthood trying to undo.

Energetically I see huge energy bubbles circling their heads like the rings of Saturn. This is where their knowledge exists. This is where they keep all their concepts in place. Imagine having several computer screens each with their own information that you can access but feeding into the mainframe or your brain. That's exactly how it is.

SOCIAL NETWORK PEOPLE

Social network people are the friendliest people around. They're very comfortable meeting new people. They have no problem coming up to you and saying hi. They wonder why that disposition could ever present a problem for someone.

You can drop them into any group and by the end of the day they'll know everyone and not only be on a first-name basis, but will know most of the people's contact information or have given their own. They're hugely popular and well-liked.

They love social media. They seem to be very open about themselves, and don't mind sharing personal information. I sometimes think this was one of the reasons why Facebook and other social platforms were created. Interestingly, Social Network people can easily share personal details about their lives even with complete strangers. What some people consider personal is not so personal to them as they like to share everything. But that's the caveat – some people believe that when someone shares personal information with them, that they are suddenly close or friends. But for Social network people it doesn't mean that just because they talk about themselves they feel it's personal or that they trust you. For them, it's just sharing information and learning from each other.

Their friendliness can be misconstrued as flirting, but it couldn't be further from the truth. Just because they talk with you doesn't mean they want to get together with you. Sometimes it doesn't go beyond just talk. Yes, they know how to dress nice and greet you with a happy smile. But it's just practiced social skills that anyone can acquire, but not everyone does. This gives them an edge in diplomacy. They often take helm as leaders, because it's the skill of listening and talking. They're like information gatherers, but instead of reading books they get their information from others. They'll ask the same question 10 different people, listen intently to their answers, and pick the best solution. Then, they will present the solution as their own and be looked up as brilliant. An example was Thomas Edison. Edison was a great inventor, but he didn't come up with all his patents. Instead, he employed many engineers and inventors. Whatever they came up with or invented would be under the intellectual domain of Edison, which he would later patent and cash in on.

Social network people are smart. They know that the more people they know, the more help they can get when they have a problem. If they need their house repainted, they'll reach out to their friends who may know someone who can paint or someone who needs money and will do it for free. They can be manipulative as they know how to persuade people to help them get things done. If a teacher in a classroom asked a Social Network person a question, and they wouldn't know the answer, they would talk to everyone possible in the class and ask what they think the answer is. Selecting the best answer they'll covertly claim it as their own and take all the credit.

But leave them alone in a room and they wouldn't know what to do with themselves. They need to interact with people. In some cases, interacting with people distracts them from their own issues and that's the problem. They know how to flow with people, but they lack the skill to deal with their own emotions. In some cases they don't know how they feel. Dealing with them intimately can be superficial. They know how to smile and make you feel good, but it's not always genuine. They usually have a lot of friends, but very few close ones. That's why they can be very free and friendly with you. Because it's not personal. They don't understand why it's difficult for other people to socialize, when it's not a problem with them. People who have a hard time making friends gravitate towards them, because they may be one of the few people that talk to them.

Social networking people great psychic ability is that they can read people. They pick up how people think, their quirks, and their needs. They operate mostly from their heart chakra. Clairvoyantly I can see their heart energy enveloping and overwhelming the other person, or even a large group. You feel and bathe in this heart energy where it fills all the lonely, empty cracks of your soul. Sometimes I see the energy coming from their second - sex chakra. They have huge sex chakras, and you can see this energy going up towards their throats and out their mouth and eyes. You'll see it as a twinkle in their eyes like they're happy to see you. Their voices are musical tones, happy and uplifting. Sometimes it's fast and rapid. Love and lust are two very powerful energies that they emanate. These energies project like a beam from their heart and sex chakras. But there's a difference between love and joy, lust and passion. People get a big mix-up about that. Just because someone says "hi" doesn't mean they want to be your friend. Just because they slept with you once, doesn't mean they want to see you again or that it meant anything to them.

Social networking people can be manipulative. Clairvoyantly I see light rays emanating from their body. It's like the legs of an octopus. It's like a shooting rays of light hitting your hands so you can't see, your Third eye - sixth Ajna chakra so you can't think, your heart so that they have your trust, and so on. I stay friends with them because basically they're nice people. But I don't get too close to them. Why? Because they look at me as they do everyone else – a resource. They're always looking for ways to save themselves, and the best resource for that are other people.

WORDSMITH PEOPLE

As the name implies, Wordsmith people are good with words. They love to journal. They also like to talk as a way of clearing themselves out. They put things in the most eloquent manner or are good with metaphors. They're also people of great intellect, because they write everything they think and observe. Through their notes they give themselves feedback. They're the great scientists and historians of our ages.

Wordsmith people need to talk and write it out. It's their way of clearing their minds. When I work with a Wordsmith client I allow them to do precisely that. If I don't, then they usually don't feel valued. Also, at the same time, listening to them tell their story helps me pick up impressions and intuitive signals. They're wonderful people who instinctively know writing things on paper clears their mind and helps them to think more clearly. Often you can see them at local cafes journaling or writing blogs. They love to write and express themselves. If they're not writing, then they're talking. They're talking constantly and are the first to dominate a conversation. They need to, because communication is the way they clear themselves. That's why if they can't write, then they'll talk which is why when they have a problem they will call up several of their friends and use them as therapists.

There's nothing wrong with needing to express yourself. Many people do this, especially women. I often see a pair having lunch with each other, where one girlfriend is recounting her life to her other girlfriend. I think it's positive and men don't do it enough. It's not so much about complaining, as it is about clearing the air objectively. The problem is that some people repeat the same thing over and over with no end in sight. This is a sign that the person is in survival, and the reptilian brain is very active.

The REPTILIAN BRAIN is the oldest portion of our brain. The brain can be divided into 3 stages of evolutionary development – the reptilian, the limbic, and the cerebral cortex. This is a very simplistic model, but it works for us right now. The reptilian brain basically deals with fight or flight. The limbic brain deals with our emotions and can activate our reptilian brain when we're in fear or stressed. The cerebral cortex is our newest layer of brain matter and it deals with higher thinking.

When our reptilian brain is active we need to calm it down. The easiest way to do this is repeating the same action, whether it's saying the same thing over and over again or doing a physical action like chopping wood. It's like repeating a mantra over and over to yourself. This gives the reptilian brain something to focus on and over time it calms down. It doesn't matter if the action repeated solves anything. It's just something to keep the mind occupied.

Wordsmith people either think out loud or they journal to observe their thoughts. They need people as sounding boards. And so they look to friends who are good listeners. It's not so good for their friends, because it doesn't feel good to be an emotional sponge, but that's how wordsmith people clear themselves.

They need to see and hear it. This is the way they get things. Interacting with large groups of people can work with them, but they would rather talk with one person who they feel comfortable with. That's because it's not so much as getting other people's feedback, as it is to get their own feedback of what they think and feel.

Wordsmith people take in information through lectures, listening to tapes and by reading. They actively think as they're doing both. And then they need to express what they learned. And the cycle begins again. If they're repeating the same thing with no end in sight, then it's like a computer that's malfunctioning. This is a sure-fire sign that they're stuck. Usually it's a repressed emotion that needs to be cleared. Energy healing is the most effective method I know, and properly done it can be successfully executed in minutes.

EGGHEADS

Eggheads are smart and knowledgeable. They can be a walking encyclopedia of knowledge. They're run by logic, and if it doesn't make sense to them logically, then it doesn't make sense at all. They're not very emotional or in touch with how they feel. They despise people who are not as smart as they are. They can be control freaks as they like to be in control. Mostly, they like to be affirmed or told that they're right or how smart they are. But if you can't follow their logic or thinking, then they dismiss you.

They like to be told that they're right and be admired for their intelligence. They're the thinkers and planners. If they have a viewpoint, it's often fruitless to argue with them, as they've thought ahead of all the angles and feel they have the strongest point.

Eggheads need to make sense of the information they are reading before they can accept it. It has to make sense or it doesn't make sense at all. They use their reasoning power so in case of a debate, they can argue successfully. They need to develop a viewpoint first and foremost with a strong foundation. If not, they become unsure of themselves which makes them uncomfortable, because they like to be both right and affirmed by the other party. When talking with people in a group, they've already formed their own opinion. They're just there to prove their point is the best.

Eggheads like to make all the decisions and solve problems. Some people like them, because eggheads take control and they can just follow. But logical people are far removed from their emotions and feelings. It's like communicating with Spock from Star Trek. If you're a highly sensitive person, you may not get the nurturing you're looking for when with them.

Eggheads think their actions through. They weigh things in terms of the benefits, or why something is the right choice. Let's say your partner is an egghead, and you're both going to the electronics store to buy a TV. You may be thinking that you are going to check out the different brands before making a purchase. An egghead has already made the choice for you. They will have done their research beforehand, comparing brands and options and already know the best brand at the right price. You're just tagging along for the ride.

For Eggheads, there can be a protocol for everything. They may want their dishes set in a certain way or their clothes hanging sequentially in the closet. It's because when things are in order, it helps them think clearly. They know where everything is. When things are out of order, then there's chaos. Some Eggheads bring a lot of rules into a relationship. As long as people follow the rules, there's no conflict.

Eggheads are smart and efficient. They get things done and don't let their emotions rule them. Success is paramount to them, and they are usually high earners and achievers. We need them, because they create order out of chaos.

Working with Eggheads can be difficult at times. Some try to be spiritual or follow a spiritual path, but usually it feels like they're following guidelines. Spirituality is facing your own inner demons, which is difficult for them to do, because one's issues cannot always be solved through logic. It's what you feel. You can't solve your problems like a Rubik's cube. Sooner or later we all have to face our inner demons. You can run for a while, but eventually you'll run out of road. Trauma shows up in the body as aches and pains and eventually disease manifests. These energy blockages can be cleared quite easily. There are many effective modalities for this. But what most healers fail to do, is to re-energize the body and mind through chi. In the later chapters I will discuss more about this important topic.

MUSICAL PEOPLE

Musical people know when someone is lying. They can detect a lie from a mile away. You'll hear them saying: "That doesn't sound right." As such, they also tend to be more honest and sincere. If they don't believe something is right, it's very hard for them to perform. That's why I always try to look for musical people – because you can trust them.

Musical people focus more on the tones and inflection in people's voices, rather than what is being said. When something sounds out-of-tune, then they question what is said to them. They wonder if this person is being deceptive, manipulative, or that they just don't know what they're saying. Musical people are practiced lie-detectors. They ask questions like: Do they sound confident? Do they sound like they know what they're talking about? Or are they making it up along the way.

You can't lie to them. They can read the intent of what you're saying. If you're a liar, then they don't want to be in your company. It also makes it difficult for them to lie. They can be direct and blunt, but don't take it personally. They're just letting you know where they stand. If you're in a relationship with them and there's a problem, they will bring it up. They can't hide what they're feeling or just ignore things.

If a Musical person does begin to lie, then they are going against their nature. This is a sign of great inner-conflict and insecurity. A musical person cannot do something they know or think isn't right. You could say that Musical people have integrity. But if they are stressed they'll not only lie to other people, but also to themselves. In such a case it is guaranteed that they will make wrong decisions, because they're going against their own truth. If you're a musical person and you're going through a major crisis in your life, then my best advice to you is: do not make any major decisions until you talk to the right people and think thoroughly.

As you can guess, Musical people connect with their ears. The ears connect directly to both the root and heart chakra. The root chakra deals with security, survival, and safety. The heart chakra deals with relationships, feelings, emotions, sincerity and care.

The reason why Musical people can detect insincerity is because it triggers the root chakra. Something about what you say threatens their survival or safety. And that creates an immediate, strong reaction.

Imagine yourself in a forest and you spot a deer. The deer may look up from its feeding and stare at you for a while, but if you stand still and don't move, it may think you're a tree or something harmless. At this point you don't pose a threat. Motion travels faster than sound, but motion and sound will trigger the survival response in the deer. Without hesitation, the deer will scamper off. It's because nature has built into the deer, that a single sound is a cause for alarm. And if it doesn't heed the warning, then it may not be able to escape. Musical people are like deer. They scamper off. But if they don't scamper off, then they're ignoring the signals from their root chakra. The law of self-preservation is being ignored or the alarm is not sounding off.

Musical people also operate from their heart chakra. That's why melodic tones or words melt them. They're empaths and feel what people are feeling. Sounds nice, but if they're with someone who is angry or full of grief, then they really feel the intensity of those emotions. This may make them ignore the signals of their root chakra. At first the alarm of their root chakra is as loud as a fire truck, but the longer they stay with this person, the alarm starts dimming and they get used to it.

It's not easy to balance between your heart and root chakra. It's not always easy to make the right decision or take the right course of action. The battle for self-preservation and empathy for others, is a war that needs to be constantly negotiated.

Musical people like to tell the truth, because they're afraid you'll find out the truth. They live in truth and therefore live in integrity. That's why if something is not in their truth, it's very hard for them to take action.

When working with them, I try to keep the tone of my voice low and soothing. I try not to speak in loud or startling tones. Saying "hello" is different from saying, "HI!!!". This would startle them. I also tell Musical people to have their friends keep their voice calm, especially when they're angry. It doesn't take much to hurt a Musical person. One harsh word can break them in half, and they won't be able to hear what you're saying.

When I'm conducting a session with them, I try not to talk so much. Silence is golden for some. Or I change the topic to pleasant things while at the same time clearing them out energetically. They often ask me for a reading, but I have to be careful as they can be sensitive. They do want to hear the truth, but I need to tone it down and be nice as to not trigger the root chakra. When you talk to them you have to make sense, otherwise they don't believe you. At this point it's not about insincerity, it is about whether you know what you're talking about.

SPORT HEROES

Sport Heroes like action and movement. They're very attune with their bodies and like to get things done. They're extremely disciplined and follow agendas, schedules, and programs very well. They're very good at keeping records, because they want to know if they're improving. They measure everything. They weigh everything in precise amounts. That's what makes them great athletes. Because they follow the science.

They pay more attention to their bodies, sometimes to the exclusion of everything else. They may not know how to express things very well. Some have to train themselves to not feel, so they can focus on both their opponent and their training session. By the same token, they don't have the time to listen to other people's problems either.

I know this one bodybuilder who explained how he got into shape. Each day he eats at least six portions measured out by protein and calories. He keeps records of his workouts which he follows religiously. But he told me his real secret was being able to stay focused and committed despite doing the same boring routine everyday. He doesn't let anything get in the way. And that also means not wasting time listening to other people's problems.

Everything is in precise amounts. That's what makes them great athletes. **Kinesthetic** people like to move. They like to stay busy. They have a lot of natural energy to burn. They easily pick up anything physical. They can hardly sit still for very long. Sitting in class and not moving is very hard for them. They quickly become bored and listless. Sport Heroes don't know how to express things. They're not comfortable saying how they feel or what they need. Hurt quickly turns into anger and even rage. Often you see them angry or quick-tempered. They see what needs to be done, and when it doesn't get done, they get upset. Sometimes they need to walk away.

Because motion is movement they have a psychic sense of how things are flowing. Are they moving up or down?   They can sense when the momentum of things or even locations change. For example, I have one client who invests heavily in real estate. She can sense when a neighborhood is going up in value about two years in advance. And when the neighborhood feels as if it's going to sink, she knows it's the perfect time to sell. You can also do it with stocks and commodities. Many Sports heroes flip houses as well. They can walk into a house and just feel what's not right. They know, that by taking a wall down it opens the living space and makes the house seem larger.

Sport Heroes who do Feng Shui easily pick up its principles and do well. I met a woman who later became a close friends. She was a Sports Heroe type. She was a dynamo. She could work 14 hours a day for weeks at a time. She taught me a lot. She taught me that you needed to have open windows to let natural sunlight in. How a mirror could make a room seem larger or putting in the dining room adds warmth and comfort.

VISUALS

Visual people learn best through pictures, diagrams, and maps. They're extremely observant and notice everything. They're affected by motion, therefore anything that moves catches their attention.   A lot of them are natural speed readers. They go through a book as if they're watching a movie. They're literally able to turn words into pictures.

One of the things I've noticed with Visual people is that they pay attention to people's facial expressions. They read their body language. They're masters at it. They do pay attention to how they look and dress. Some are vain while others are not. Many don't like watching violent movies or fight sports. They're too sensitive for that.

It can be difficult to communicate with them if they don't see the picture of what you're trying to say or do. They model example so it's best to demonstrate it in front of them. Other than that, they are the fastest learners I know.

When I work with a Visuals they prefer to see me in person. It doesn't work for them when I'm using the phone. If it's a long distance client, then Skype will do best. Seeing me gives them comfort to know I'm present. I usually get a feeling that they're reading me as much as I'm reading them.

They can be difficult to treat, since you're changing a false picture of how they see the world or themselves. It's these negative images that keep them stuck. They see the world through their inner pictures and when things don't go according to their perspective, they can be most unhappy. But it's these pictures that hold strong emotions.

Visuals see things their way. They are strongly opinionated. For example, let's say they don't like another person. Not only will they talk badly of them, but they'll go out of their way to sabotage them. What doesn't correspond with their opinion of how the world should be, gets deleted. Their visual pictures is what limits them. That also needs to be changed.

Clairvoyantly I look at their eyes. If there are blockages in their left eye, then I know they see people with their heart and easily forgive them. The corner of their left eye shows blockages of grief. The other side shows rage. And when they look at you directly with their left eye, it's like you violated them and they're seeing images of betrayal.

Clairvoyantly the right eye is about seeing opportunities. I call it the searching eye, because it can look through the ground and detect gold from fool's good. Or it could be blocked energetically, and they wouldn't know if opportunity was knocking right at their door. Blockages on the tear ducts show anger or a curse. But when they see prey or opportunity, they look with the right eye, and it's a direct look.

Visuals build up a rolodex of images in their mind. They love looking at magazines. They often talk about how their ideal wedding is going to be. Many have a good picture of what their future would look like.

SEVEN Divine Perspectives

This is the way I read people. All of us use all SEVEN Perspectives interchangeably. This helps me understand how people think, and how they form their thoughts. When I tell or sort the order of these divine perspectives, they begin to understand themselves. It's like shining a flashlight on someone's trauma. Clearing their trauma is as simple as reorganizing their blocks. Their trauma was created when they used their weaker perspective, and not their strongest.

I used to believe that people used a preset pattern of perspectives, and that this pattern never changed. But after working with my clients, I see that our strongest perspective is different depending on the situation. It's like using the right tool for the job. But most people use the same tool for everything. Sometimes you use a wrench, and sometimes you use a screwdriver.

Chapter XII.

SUBTLE ENERGY AND THE BRAIN

As well as learning the latest in energy medicine, I continue to study the latest in neuroscience and psychology as well. I think it balances my approach to healing when I combine both Eastern and Western medicine. Western science is backed up with thousands of case studies and reproducible lab experiments. It takes the guess work out of it and is backed up by empirical data. This gives me the sound foundation I need to advance my energy work.

But Western science is slow. It can take years before it trickles down to the mainstream. And it takes millions of dollars to fund this research with teams of the best scientific minds working together. It's great because all I have to do is read the reports, and then I do my energy experiments and make my own findings.

I study all the research, and the discoveries they've made. Then clairvoyantly I see what's happening in the mind and body. What blockages appear in the aura and chakras? How does the kundalini energy flow? What happens when you remove the blockages, and how does it appear in the energy body?

I then run different experiments moving the variables around like a scientist. I can track a person back in time. I can compare it with different stages in a person's life, which is something difficult for psychologists to do, unless they have been tracking someone for ten years. Then I can see how they differ from the results. Many times I'm able to advance the theories various psychologist and neuroscientists made. Eventually, they can make the same discoveries as I do, but it takes much time and money.

Studying their research really gives me a peek into how the mind operates, and it is scientific. I simply confirm what I see clairvoyantly, analyze it, and further my understanding. There are things you can simply do clairvoyantly that are faster, easier, more profound and can't be done scientifically. Science hasn't developed instruments sensitive enough to detect these subtle energies, but I can. By marrying both Western and Eastern approaches I have a more balanced view while testing one against the other.

Bottom line is the feedback I get with my clients. I learn so much from them. I use the findings of neuroscience and psychology to help me read my clients better. After the readings, my clients tell me if I'm accurate or not. They know immediately if I'm off the mark. This helps me hone in on their energy blockages, and when I remove or clear them, they give me feedback about the difference it makes for them.

Positive energy feels lighter and more expansive. Sometimes you feel the energy flowing in your body. Some clients have described it as feeling "ticklish" in their arms and legs. Negative energy feels tense, muscles contracting, and overall tightness or becoming smaller. Positive energy feels good. You can think clearly. You feel calm and less emotional. You no longer feel depressed. Your energy soars, and you want to take action.

What follows are some of the discoveries I've made testing various modalities. All of them work, and have provided effective treatment to all of my clients.

BRAIN SPOTS

Brain spots was a term I coined while I studied modalities like EMDR (Eye Movement Desensitization and Reprocessing), and others. With rapid eye movements you're able to access parts of the brain that were previously unaccessible. By directing a client's eye movements using a pointer for them to focus on, you can alleviate negative trauma. Brain spots was my take on this.

In Brain spots, I didn't use any rapid eye movements. I noticed that when a client was relieving an unpleasant memory, I could feel these energy bumps on their forehead. Curious about them, I poked my finger towards their forehead where I felt these bumps, and was surprised that the client felt relief.

So feeling a modicum of success, I asked the client to bring up this painful memory even more strongly. I also told my client that they didn't need to tell me any details, and could keep it privately to themselves. All I asked is for them to think of the negative event affecting them.

I then did the same thing as before, which was to press with my finger pads the energy bumps on their forehead, but this time with rapid succession of all four fingers of my right hand. I'm so used to scanning people that my hands work automatically. Some energy bumps are bigger or taller, and so I would press on them longer, but never more than a few seconds. The whole process takes about a minute or so.

When asked to bring up the painful memory, the client would respond that it was difficult to bring up. It's almost as if I've erased the memory. But even though the client feels cleared of the experience, I can still feel there are more energy bumps. And so the client would think of the memory again, and I would clear it out again with my fingers. Overall I would repeat the procedure three times, to make sure it's really erased.

Scientifically I know the frontal lobe deals with mental clarity. Neuroscientists have discovered that negative emotions like disgust, fear, and anger are registered in the right frontal lobe. The left frontal lobe deals with planning a sequence of actions, happiness and high self-esteem. Low activity in the left frontal lobe is associated with depression or feeling unhappy.

When I look back clairvoyantly, I see energy bumps on the right side of the forehead. The bumps resemble buildings to me, and the bigger the skyscraper, the more intense the negative emotions are, such as fear and anger. Energetically the right forehead seems larger. If I were to scan the right forehead, I could feel like an energetic bubble several feet in front of the person. All I'm doing is popping these energetic bumps, and that's why the client feels immediate emotional relief. Once done, then I energize the left frontal forehead so that they can think more clearly. Problem solved.

The energetic bumps of the right forehead feel really strong. It's like they control what a person focuses on. At its worst, it keeps repeating itself like a broken record, and can make a person go crazy. Popping these energetic bumps can help a person with obsessive thinking.

If a client keeps on going over past events, then these energetic bumps can resurface again. It's like planting weeds. As long as you water them, they'll multiply. The next thing, you'll find yourself controlled by your emotions. You won't be able to think straight.

This technique is fast and effective. I usually do it during demonstrations where I only have a few minutes to demonstrate. It takes five minutes, and the results are dramatic.

GENIUS POINTS

I've always been curious about child prodigies. I've often wondered how is it possible that little kids are able to obtain skills and abilities that would generally take a lifetime to achieve. Researchers discovered that these children have acute senses, higher than normal. They see things visually in 3-D. Hearing and touch is also advanced. Basically they pick up more information, and this information is fed to their brain.

In the New Age world, it's usually explained that child prodigies were very accomplished in their past lives, and brought that skill set into this lifetime. So accessing these abilities is a matter of downloading. If you were an accomplished painter in the previous lifetime, then you can still access those skills in this lifetime. If you weren't a great painter, then you can't access what you didn't have. It's as simple as that.

Some of these children are able to remember who they were in their past life. They can recall details of who they were, where they were from, and even the circumstances of how they died. Usually this lasts until the age of five, and then they start forgetting. Past life regression does help bringing these abilities alive. I know so, because in my first past-life regression, I was able to access skills from when I was a healer in previous lifetimes.

And so energetically I wanted to find out what makes child prodigies different from all of us. Let's take the root chakra. All the chakras except one, are dependent on the root chakra for energy. That's why it's called the root chakra, because like the roots of a plant the energy flows upward from its base, along the spine, to the top of the head. Therefore essentially if the energy of the root chakra measures 100, then the forehead chakra will also measure at 100. If the root chakra is measured at zero or depletion, then all the chakras above will be starving for energy.

But what's intriguing, is that when I measured the root chakras of these prodigies, their upper chakras measured differently. Let's say the root chakra measures at 100. The forehead chakra, for example, should measure at 100 as well, but it doesn't. It measures at 500. Why the discrepancy? Something must be supplying the forehead chakra with extra energy, because it doesn't appear in all the chakras.

Clairvoyantly what I saw, were these nodules around the outside periphery of the chakra it was covering. I don't know what they are, and I've never heard of them described by any of my teachers. They average about three to seven nodules, and they seem to energize the chakra directly, increasing their strength and enhancing the characteristic of that particular chakra.

I wondered whether this theory was correct or not and so I scanned very successful people from all walks of life. I was intrigued with the story of this burglar who was caught and jailed for several years. When he got out of prison, he started a business developing security products that thwart burglars like himself. His products were innovative and revolutionary in design. Soon he was making more money than when he was burglarizing. When I scanned him, I observed seven nodules in his root chakra. This was also the case with millionaires. The root chakra deals with survival, security, and trust. Making innovative products and coming up with creative ideas does increase your ability to not only survive, but to thrive as well.

Bruce Lee had several nodules in his solar plexus. The solar plexus chakra deals with taking action, movement, and your basic emotional needs and desires. One of my teachers who has a 5th degree in Okinawan karate, also had these nodules in her solar plexus, as did her son.

As I later learned, these genius points can appear in any part of the body and not just in chakras alone. They can be also in your hands, as a result you would have gifted dexterity and finger control.

And so I wondered if they could be artificially created. The first group of volunteers, I placed several subtle energy nodules in their forehead chakra, just to see what would happen. All reported not only greater levels of mental clarity, but a profound sense of joy and happiness. I was surprised, but it makes sense that our emotions are processed through our brain. If our brains are energized through the forehead chakra, then it enhances our sense of well-being or feeling good. Still, I was a bit astonished.

One of my volunteers, a young woman, wanted me to place genius points on her sex chakra. Marilyn Monroe had several nodules in her sex chakra and they clairvoyantly shone brightly. And so I placed the same number on this young woman, to see what would happen. She told me later that she went to a party with her girlfriend. Her girlfriend was beautiful, and had recently broken up with her boyfriend and young men were usually swooning over her.

But strangely this didn't happen. Instead, all the young men at the party were surrounding my client. They were magnetically drawn to her and left her girlfriend alone. Experiments with other females brought similar results.

Everywhere they went they were patronized, in the supermarket or the hair dresser, and even friends they've known for many years suddenly began flirting with them. In the end, the experiment was stopped because they didn't like getting so much attention. Some were married, and others felt uncomfortable and didn't know how to handle the attention. They felt flattered in the beginning, and then it became annoying.

Either way the genius points stayed only temporarily, maybe a few days. I also made a discovery of something that I call the "Einstein" point. I call it that, because I noticed it when I saw a poster of Einstein. Instead of being on the outside periphery of the chakra, the "Einstein" point is located in the center. Only a few people have the "Einstein" point.

HEMISPHERES

The brain is composed of two hemisphere – the right and left hemisphere. Science tells us that the left hemisphere deals with logic, structure, words and so on. The right brain, on the other hand, is more our creative muse, connected to our intuition, and emotions. That's putting it very simply.

From what I observed, the left brain is more like a movie director. The director may cut or delete scenes. He can change the plot of the whole movie, and give it a different outcome. That's why some directors may direct the same movie with three different versions, and then select the best one to their or audience's liking.

I watch a lot of court TV. I'm frequently amazed how defendants will change the story of what actually happen to make them appear innocent. Just like a director they'll delete or change whole events and tell you a different story than what actually happened. Sometimes they'll look you in the eye and say they can't recall what was said or what happened. It doesn't matter even if there was video, a police report, and ten witnesses... they'll still deny they were at the crime scene. You'll see it in their faces, because they're either looking away or downward or looking you straight in the face with defiant eyes.

Clairvoyantly, it's like their left hemisphere has spread across the brain and is smothering the right brain. The right brain is like the DVD copy of the movie. There's only one version of the movie. The left brain seems connected to the Ego, and so if it doesn't like the movie, it will conveniently delete those scenes.

From what I've observed energetically, the left brain hides the truth or suppresses the truth. That's why I see it covering up the right hemisphere. People who have this energetic configuration are liars, because they'll come up with ten versions of the same story. And in each version they're always the victim. They're always innocent. It's always the world that conspires against them. It's never their fault.

In one therapy that I read about, the client is told to recall the event descriptively. If the incident happened in a room, they have to describe the room. They have to describe who was there, as if objectively describing a scene of a movie. And then they're asked to repeat it per verbatim and describe the scene in an even greater detail. You see, the left brain is trying to delete certain details. Most people just try to block it out, but by doing so, they're only suppressing very strong negative emotions. And these emotions can't stay bottled up forever, before they re-surface as some type of psychosis.

One characteristic of people who are very left-brain dominant is that they're also highly opinionated. They believe they are right and everyone else who doesn't agree with them is wrong. They have their own reality of how things work in the world. And sometimes their views are not very realistic, but they impose their habit of thinking onto other people. They have rules and expectations. And whether spoken or unspoken, it's like they expect everyone to read their minds and just follow along.

And when people don't follow their rule of reality, then they enforce it. Sometimes they'll manipulate people. Sometimes they'll commit sabotage. They'll do smear campaigns. They really do believe they are right. They can be pushy, even aggressive in their views.

"This is the way things are, and this is how things are supposed to be". They believe in it so much, that you don't know in some cases how far they'll go. I remember watching this case where a man set up his own brother for a murder he was going to commit. He set up his brother to be the fall guy, ingeniously. Planning a murder for two years and manipulating his own brother is beyond cold-hearted. He was very meticulous. He was very smart.

I've seen left-brain domination with all types of people in all walks of life. They're easy to spot. They're usually very sensitive or reactive and tend to over-rationalize things. They can't take blame. But in all cases they're always a victim, usually stemming from childhood abuse. They repeat their childhood story both to themselves and to anyone listening. And each time that they do this, they're re-traumatizing themselves and keeping themselves stuck in the hole, forever.

The subconscious mind can really be our worst enemy. It doesn't like unresolved emotional conflicts, and will frequently bring them up to a person's consciousness. The subconscious mind will even set up the person, so that they recreate the same destructive environmental conditions, in an attempt that the person would finally deal with it.

I remember I was at a coffee shop where a couple sat close by. They're weren't in a relationship, but just friends. The female was telling her male friend how a lot of her girlfriends treated their new boyfriends as if they were the old boyfriend, that they broke up with. In such a case, even though it's not the same guy, old issues from their previous relationship creep up and become the problem in their next relationship.

With the left hemisphere constantly changing outlines of what actually happened, it suppresses these negative emotions more deeply, until you don't know what is real. The saying, "The Truth will set you free" is so true. Deep down you know the truth. Getting yourself to acknowledge it, is very cathartic. You can stop running away from your demons.

If the left hemisphere is the director, then the right brain is the CGI or computer-generated images. The images can vary from beautiful-fantasy to impending doom.

I saw a court case where a man fell in love with a married woman. They carried on with the affair for about a year. Later, the woman would recount how her husband was physically abusing her, and how she wanted to run away with her lover. The lover went crazy with envy and killed her husband, but was soon caught. The woman, now a widow, became rich due to a life insurance policy. She was charged, but not convicted because her lover declined to testify against her.

Peeking through his brain clairvoyantly, I saw an image of his former mistress. The image of her was like that of the Virgin Mary – beautiful, and majestic, with rays of light streaming around her body. The woman looked nothing like the image in this man's brain, but that's how he saw her. He was willing to die in prison for her, while keeping that image of her in his mind.

It's not all negative. Sometimes it's a romantic tale with happy endings. Many of my friends recount that their boyfriends or husbands waited for them for as long as eight years, before they were single. The boyfriends recount the first time they saw them and were instantly hooked. It could be as simple as walking past them in the hallway or seeing them for the first time at a party. There may have been eye contact, but usually the guy's eyes were averted to avoid direct contact. Either way, the women don't recall the first moment they met. And if they did, they recount it as uneventful. Nothing special happened. They didn't hear the trumpets roar or the angels sing. It was just an ordinary day, like any other.

But the men remember it like it was yesterday. It's like they took a photograph of that day and they have been looking at it everyday, until they reunited with the woman they fell in love with. And their love and devotion lasts through the years. Even with decades going by, in their husband's eyes, their wife still looks as beautiful as the day they met.

It's because the right hemisphere is blocking information from the left hemisphere. Clairvoyantly, the right hemisphere is smothering and suppressing the left hemisphere. It's like there's a fence between the two hemisphere and one hemisphere decides to push down the fence and take over that side of the property.

Sometimes the images are that of impending doom. Conspiracy theory abound and the end of the world is coming soon. These images can be frightening, of course, but they feel so real. You believe it is real, and that it is happening right now. And so you act out. Paranoia sets in.

In some of my clients, this can become so challenging, that they shut down. Some stop working, while others have never worked a day in their lives. They could be successful professionals, and all of a sudden they're no longer able to function. It's like a complete mental breakdown.

Energetically I see blockages in both the back heart and the Mein meng chakra. The back heart chakra is located in the center of the upper back. This chakra affects the lungs, and so when blocked, the person has a hard time breathing or stops breathing momentarily. The Meng mein chakra is located between the kidneys and adrenals. When the Meng main chakra is blocked, the person feels overwhelmed, easily fatigued or has no energy. They may also feel extreme anxiety, feel overeager, overly attached, or even obsessing about things. Many hoarders have piles of junk that they're attached to and even affectionate with.

The predominant thought pattern with the right hemisphere is that there isn't enough time in the world. Some people feel rushed or that things are passing them by so fast, that they can't compete everything. Even when given all the time in the world, they can't get started because everything is too much for them. Sometimes it's an internal clock that's pressuring them, and they suffer bouts of anxiety.

Space is the second predominant thought pattern with the right hemisphere. How do I define space? The space to move around in your environment. When you have a lot of space you feel limitless. If you live in a closet, you become claustrophobic. You don't feel there's room enough to move or grow.

Space is interesting. It could be outside of yourself, like you feel people are blocking you or are in your way. Sometimes you feel that people don't want you to succeed or move forward. It's a very real feeling. Or space can be an invasion of your inner space. This feels like you don't have room to breathe.

Many children who grew up without any siblings talk about this. Because they were the only child, usually the mother overprotects them. I've heard tales where one parent or both, monitor and listen in on their child's phone calls. They enter the room and go through all their stuff. This is an invasion of the child's privacy. They may grow up feeling their parent's presence even years after the parents have passed away.

When I work with clients, I find it necessary to energetically clear both hemispheres. I see the connecting lines to the chakras, and disconnect them. I've studied numerous modalities and psychological approaches, and this seems to be the most effective approach.

FLIP YOUR BRAIN

The concept of "Flip your Brain" came from these TV shows where they took a dilapidated house, bought it at a discount, later renovated it and sold it for a healthy profit. I was reading a book where an author talked about how he could change his mind from a negative to a positive state in mere seconds.

I was intrigued.

Basically he focused on positive values, realizing when he did so, his brain operated optimally, and he was able to come away with solutions to his problems. Being in a negative state, he found it difficult to concentrate and it just kept him thinking about his problems. And so for two months, he focused on bringing on a positive state, until it had become a habit and he could clear his mind in seconds.

Being a clairvoyant, I decided to peek into his brain to see how this was done energetically. I saw that when he was in a negative state, there appeared to be sparkles of blue, black, and red colors. And when he was in a positive state – the moment he flipped his brain – his brain seemed to light up with bright glowing lights.

I started to experiment to see if I can do the same thing with my clients. Whenever they thought of something negative, I noticed the same thing with the lights inside their brain – black, blue, and red lights. One by one I transformed them into bright lights, until the whole brain looked like someone turned on the light in a dark room.

Strange as it may seem, it kept preventing negative thoughts from reoccurring. Combined with "brain spots", these were the two most powerful techniques for neutralizing trauma, and even PTSD. Why? Because it neutralized the brain and emotions, so that it wouldn't occur again. The process can be repeated as many times as necessary. Even when it seems completely neutral for the client, I can still detect some blockages, and so continue to clear them energetically.

BRAIN PLAQUE AND THE HIPPOCAMPUS

The Hippocampus is the part of the brain that's connected to emotions. Each time a client brings up an issue to clear, I've noticed the hippocampus is energetically blocked. That means the negative emotions associated with the trauma can still be regenerated. The same way I clear out the chakras, I put my intent on the hippocampus and clear it. This further neutralizes the issue.

Brain plaque is like the plaque that develops on the surface of your teeth. This plaque exist between the neurons, and slows down communication and connectivity. I first became aware of this when I was shown slides of people's brains. The ones who were very negative had few dendrite connections between the neutrons of the brain. Their neurons appear to look like dead trees. While the brain slides of more positive and intellectual people looked like healthy trees with bushy branches.

An experiment was done whether I could energetically clear the brain plaque of not just my clients, but also myself. After less than a week, greater energy and even a reversal of mental decline was visibly observed. My theory is that brain plaque is caused by stress and trauma. It makes sense that the brain produces more cortisol during periods of great stress, so why not brain plaque? Removing brain plaque is difficult if not impossible, but what if it could be done energetically? Then it would be a new revolution.

REPROGRAMMING THE BRAIN

Reprogramming the brain is just the reversal of clearing. Now since the brain has been cleared of emotional residue, we then imagine the positive image or outcome. If we could change history and turn-around a tragic event, what would it be? What would we ideally like to have happened, so that we could lead a peaceful, happy, and successful life? What conditions would we create or provide for ourselves, now that we have the wisdom and experience?

Some of you may say that isn't realistic as it didn't happen that way, and that we're just fooling ourselves. I disagree, as the mind remembers events both imaginary and real, but how we remember them will determine if we stay handicapped or empowered. It's the reason why they put erasers on top of pencils. We all make mistakes. But an eraser shows us that mistakes are not permanent, and that we can change our answers and learn from them.

First, you re-create history by thinking of the most ideal outcome for your issue. Then you see the energy around your head expand brighter and larger, so that it will send a beacon to the universe of what you wish to attract.

THREE Guiding Principles

When creating your ideal image, you need to follow three guiding principles that are basic motivations for everyone. The more you follow and use these guiding posts, the easier time you will have manifesting.

1.   We are all basically animals, and as such like to hang out in groups or packs. We all have our community or tribe that we feel we belong to. As such, the biggest punishment we could receive is banishment or expulsion. It's as old as history. Acceptance into our group is most welcoming. That's why when you think of your goal, it's important to connect it to the good for humanity, rather than a small group or gathering. That way you're less subjected to the rules and authority of the a few select individuals.

2.   Pain and pleasure – we gravitate towards pleasure and avoid pain. Well, not always. Some people accept a lot of pain in order to gain a little pleasure. And still others view pain as pleasure. If so, then that needs to be reversed and cleared before making your goals. Make pleasure your guiding post as long as it doesn't harm anyone including yourself.

3.   It's difficult to learn anything unless it's very interesting or very important to you. Find your reason.

Finally, you measure your desire against each chakra, to gauge the acceptance of your desire. For example, you imagine your desire and then scan your root chakra. Are you feeling secure? Do you feel safe pursuing your dream? There could be resistance, and if there is, then you would do a body scan to discover where you are blocked. If you are blocked in your ears, then there is something you still don't want to hear, that's threatening your sense of safety and security. Those things need to be cleared, otherwise you won't be able to move forward, because the root chakra controls the movement of your legs and feet.

The more thorough you can background-check each of your chakras, the faster you'll be able to manifest your goals. Periodic checks will maintain your progress and growth.

Root chakra – You feel strong and secure moving forward. You feel there are people you can trust to help guide and support you. But if you come across people who are less than trustworthy, you feel confident you are able to handle and discern who they are.

Sex chakra – You sense a strong interest and excitement going after your goal.

Solar plexus chakra – you take action.

Heart chakra – lion-heart or the courage to face overwhelming odds and obstacles.

Throat chakra – the ability to openly express your truth. Expression is very powerful as it exposes your insecurities and weaknesses. Remember, darkness fears the light of exposure. It's as simple as turning on a light switch. Once you do, you realize all those things you were bumping into in the dark were just ordinary objects, that really posed no danger.

Forehead chakra – thinking clearly and logically.

Crown chakra – spiritual health.

Navel chakra – energizes all chakras. If your chakras are not energized, it's like driving your car without gas.

Spleen chakra – initiative or doing things on your own, without someone else having to tell you to do things.

Mein meng chakra – distributes energy of the root chakra through entire body. If blocked, then you are using adrenaline like coffee and caffeine. It's sustainable when you're young, but when you get older, you'll pay a heavy price.

Backheart chakra – the way you breathe controls everything. If you are feeling in any way stuck, have less energy, or are unable to concentrate, the improper breathing is the cause.

PART THREE

THE HEALING PROCESS

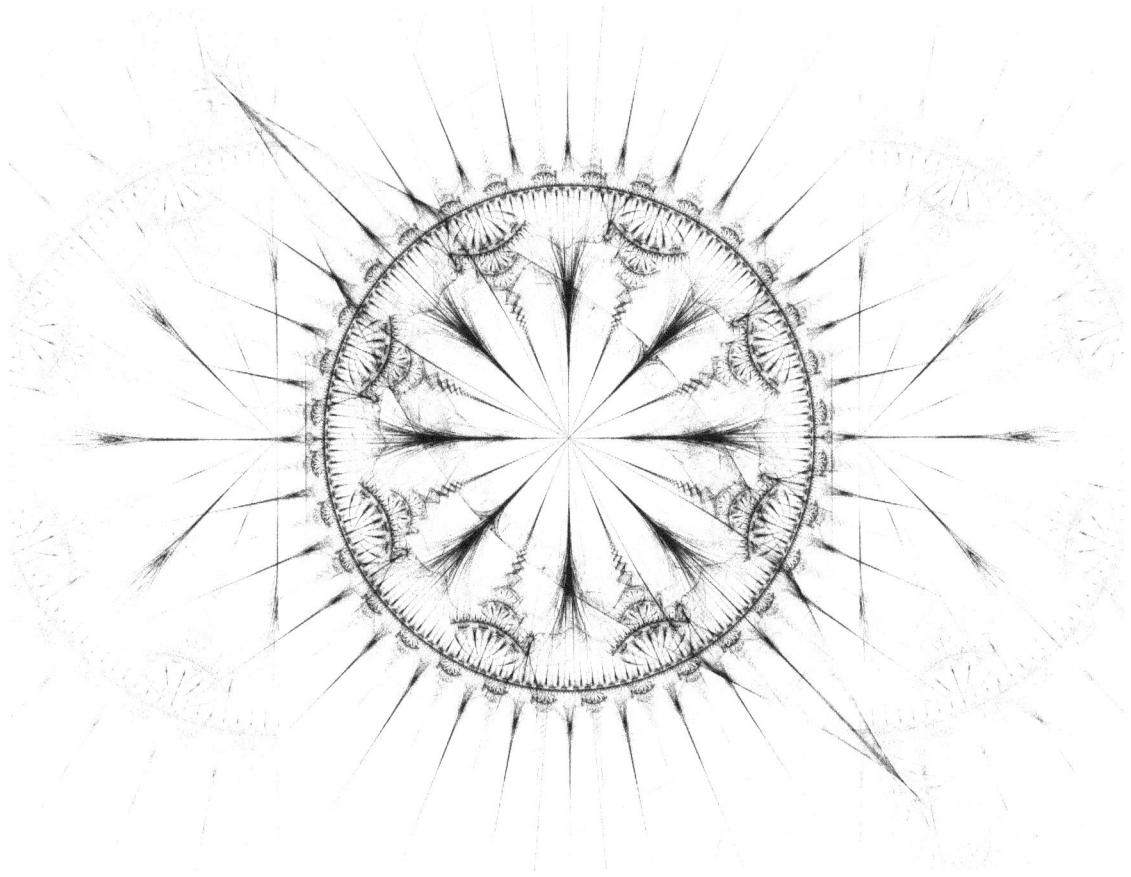

Chapter XIII.

CLEARING EMOTIONAL TRAUMA

Everyone goes through bad times in their lives. And sometimes it's really serious. We all have traumatic moments. And often it goes well beyond that, and turns into a PTSD or post-traumatic stress disorder. In this chapter I will talk about the various methods I've encountered to deal with trauma, and the solutions that I've found to deal with these difficult issues.

A lot of people like to talk about their problems either with a therapist or a good friend. It feels good to unburden yourself to someone. It makes sense. But is it effective? It may be for the moment, but energetically, you're polluting the other person who has to listen to you. It affects the listener, and most people don't know how to clear themselves afterwards, unless they are a healer.

What about the person who's doing the talking? Does it work for them? I'm an energy healer who specializes in emotional clearing. I know that people feel the need to express themselves, because they're going through so much anxiety. And I've listened to people – sometimes for hours both as a healer and as a friend. And in my opinion, it may relieve them temporarily, but it doesn't solve anything.

People talk about whatever they think about. And people think about whatever they talk about. And when people think and talk about their issues constantly and repeatedly, they make themselves miserable. Because by the Law of Attraction, you manifest what you think and talk about constantly. I understand that these traumas are really affecting you, and there seems no end in sight, but unless you have a lot of friends or a good therapist to unburden yourself, it's not effective in the long run. Because each time you rehash your issues, you're essentially re-triggering yourself. You're reliving the memories and analyzing the details of what happened to you.

SELF-HELP BOOKS

I personally like self-help books. I have whole libraries in all the rooms of my house. They're interesting and thought provoking. And I'm constantly collecting more of them each day.

I do learn from them. They help me understand myself and others. But I've never come across any book that reflected my life or the lives of my clients perfectly. That's because there isn't any book that does that. Sure there are books that seems to help you understand yourself better, and maybe others as well. But we're all uniquely different, like our fingerprints. There are general patterns that we all can be categorized into, but we all have our own specific themes. Two people can experience the same event at the same time, but each will have their own perspective of what they witnessed and felt.

When I work with my clients, I sense and feel the various emotions that comprise their emotional experience. It's hard to describe. Before I did healing work, I thought that grief was grief, and anger was anger. But for me, it's no longer so. I have felt grief in my clients in various shades of color. Grief, for example, comes in different intensities and in their own themes or beliefs. Grief can come in when a person feels invisible. Grief about the loss of your favorite pet. The intense grief of a breakup, and so on. Each feels different to me, when I'm reading a client. My mind gets flooded with pictures and scenes of a client's life. Sometimes I hear words or get messages about how the person is feeling. And other times I feel it physically.

I'll never forget the first time I had a booth at a psychic fair. A young lady sat down at my table, and wanted me to read her father who abandoned her when she was born. At first I was angry that someone would abandon their responsibility, but that was me being judgmental. She reunited with her father later in life, and wanted me to read him.

Suddenly I felt a crushing blow to my chest. It was like a baseball bat slammed into my chest, and I couldn't breathe. It wasn't so much physical pain, but overwhelming guilt and grief. I didn't expect that and I gasped in horror.

She saw my expression and clearly saw I was distressed. She then told me that her and her father had reunited amicably and everything was okay. I was upset with her for the moment, and told her "Why didn't you warn me?!?" She was puzzled by my reaction. I had a preconceived thought that her father uncaring and callous. Instead, I saw a man who was scared, and the guilt of abandoning his daughter really haunted him all those years. And I felt all of that crashing down on me in just a few seconds. I wasn't prepared to feel this avalanche of emotions and it took some time to compose myself. I told her that her father was really a good guy, and that he really did love her and was sorry. She confirmed everything I said was true. But it was difficult to handle, at the time.

But such situations give me clues to better understand where they're coming from, and how to help them. My clients feel I understand them, because I understand their issues from their perspective. I don't casually say, "We all go through bad times" or "You'll get over it."   They feel understood. Most importantly, I know how to clear these energies and how to clear myself afterwards, so that I don't continue to carry around any negative energy.

BELIEF SYSTEMS

I've met the best psychic readers in the world. It's fun. I've been read by them, and I've studied with them. They can be uncannily accurate. One of the problems with getting a reading is that the more answers you get, the more questions you have. It's a never-ending cycle. Because you want more detail or explanation and before you can ask your question, they've moved on to another subject.

When I do psychic readings I let the person talk or explain what they want. Just listening to what they say helps me connect with them. My mind gets flooded with pictures or I hear messages. It's like a carnival of sensations.

I worked with this one teacher whose modality was changing belief systems. Our belief systems influence and dictate every aspect of our lives. So it makes sense that if we change our belief system, our lives change as well.

Because of my expertise with reading chakras, I can read a person in seconds. This comes in handy, especially when I'm evaluating different modalities. I attend workshops all over the country and during a demo where the teacher is calling a volunteer for a demonstration, I read the volunteer's chakras before and after the demo, to evaluate the effectiveness of the technique.

One of my teachers was extremely psychic and detailed in class the beliefs of this volunteer. My teacher was spot-on, and brought the volunteer to tears. It can be very traumatizing to hear your beliefs, especially in front of class. It can break you down even after being changed, because there's a string of emotions that are attached with each belief.

The chakras of that volunteer looked blown-up afterwards. It taught me a lot – to be careful about what you say to a client. Reading beliefs is like peeking into a person's darkest secrets. Telling them what you read, can be like stepping on a landmine. Over the years I've learned to be tactful and careful in my wording. It is necessary to have the person understand their beliefs, because without it they won't be able to understand their issues. Clearly I had to find a balance between both.

ENERGETIC CLEARINGS

I've watched my share of masters doing both physical and emotional clearings. A volunteer is called up for the demo, and us students observe. After each clearing a client needs time to process as their body and mind heals. That's to be expected. Sometimes the client feels lethargic after a session and needs time to rest. Sometimes the conditions become worse before they become better. That's natural as another layer of their issues comes up to the surface. Our issues take years to develop and manifest on the surface. So it's unlikely everything can be cleared in one session. Usually it takes several or even on-going sessions to clear these problems. Things do improve and you do feel better.

Sometimes these clearings can be difficult and even traumatizing for the client. I'll never forget when my teacher was clearing this young woman of emotional trauma. He was clearing her solar plexus, and also the seat of the solar plexus chakra. The solar plexus chakra deals with our base emotions like anger, envy, and anxiety. Many of our suppressed emotions are stored there.

Witnessing her clearing was like watching a horror movie. My teacher was using a crystal wand which is a common energetic tool used in healing. Quartz crystal amplifies our healing power several fold. Clairvoyantly I saw thought forms in her solar plexus resembling snakes, spiders, and scorpions coming out. And she could feel them. It was a good clearing, and it did help her release a lot of stuff that she had been holding onto. But she was hysterical and screaming during the process. She never returned to the class.

I knew then, that if my clients had to go through that, I would lose half of them immediately. Some clients like that feeling, because it lets them feel, that they're getting a good clearing. I call it the "bitter medicine" syndrome. If the medicine isn't bitter to the taste, then it's not strong enough.

CORDS, ENVIRONMENT AND CHAKRAS

Whether it is trauma or physical illness, everything leaves on us an energetic fingerprint. Doing energy work is like being a detective, solving a mystery. It's the most interesting aspect of being an energy healer. It becomes even more fascinating, when you know where to look and you learn to always find the right answers.

Cords are energy strands linking you to another person, place or even objects. They are emotional attachments that are constantly feeding into us as well as us feeding them. For example, if someone is thinking about you a lot, then you may dream about them next night. If they're angry and sending you angry thoughts, you may have a cord from them to your head area. This may result in you having headaches. I've cleared many headaches simply by pulling the cords from my clients head. Immediately they feel a 50% reduction. The other 50% is clearing the residue left in their head, and then it is all gone. If the cord is attached to their kidneys or lower back, then my client may experience low-back pain and also lack of energy.

My teachers used to quote that "Environment is stronger than your will." And it's true. People go to study at the library, because it helps them study better. Similarly, the moment you enter a casino and start gambling, you start to lose your ability to control your money. The environment including the friends you hang with, influence you the same way a chameleon changes colors to match its surroundings. Feng shui is very effective, because it's the study of improving your house in order to change your well-being, including prosperity. If your office is messy then it creates a disorganized mind. That's why the offices of executives are very neat and orderly.

Chakras are very effective for reading yourself and others. There are 7 major chakras in the body. In Pranic healing, we have 11 chakras. I highly recommend anyone to study Pranic healing, because it taught me how to scan, read, and clear the chakras. In my opinion, it's the most important skill. It has served me well, no matter what modality I've studied. The chakras are consistently accurate and reliable. Each chakra has specific characteristics for both mental, emotional, and physical aspects. When the chakras are blocked or not functioning, well it helps you pinpoint the cause.

One time I was having a very difficult time in my life. I felt stuck, and couldn't move forward, no matter how hard I tried. I did a lot of clearings on myself, but still it wasn't enough. I checked and rechecked all 7 major chakras and they all looked clear. But I knew there was still something wrong, and I couldn't find it.

But it had to be there. It had to be! Everything leaves an energetic fingerprint in the chakras otherwise it wouldn't exist. It was only when I reviewed all t 11, not just 7 chakras of Pranic healing, that I found the source. It was in my back heart chakra which controls breathing, and my Meng mein chakra which deals with adrenaline. During times of stress, I felt like I couldn't breathe and that would stop me in my tracks. Because suddenly I had no energy, because I had slowed my breathing my adrenal glands were overworked.

I couldn't find it earlier, because I had limited my search to the 7 major chakras. According to Pranic Healing, we have 11 major chakras, and not 7. It took a lot of work to clear those two chakras, but I finally did and felt better. Interestingly, I discovered that these two chakras were blocked in some of my clients who never had a job. It's not as if they didn't want to work. It's just that something shut down in themselves that prevented them from looking for a job. Even successful people who seem to have everything, can suddenly have a mid-life crisis where they lose it all. At the time it seems unexplainable that very smart and successful people suddenly stop functioning. It's like somebody pulled the plug on them.

These two chakras – the backheart and the Meng mein are the main culprits. I studied them extensively to help me understand them, and how they function. I wondered if they were the roots of all our problems. This led to my biggest discovery, and the most effective emotional clearing technique I know.

BREATHING PATTERNS

In my previous chapter I talked about brain hemispheres. It makes sense, since it's our brain that controls how we think and feel. I wrote about the characteristics of each hemisphere, and how they function. Clearing our hemispheres can clear more than 50% of our emotional issues, without even having to go into detail of our trauma.

When I work with a client, I ask them to give me a 5-minute synopsis of their issue. If they don't want to talk about it because they want to keep it private, then I ask them to think about it – that's all. It takes me a second or two to scan the energetic blockages in their hemispheres and I just go about energetically clearing them out. During that time my clients can stay and talk with me on phone, cook, dance, or even exercise. It doesn't matter, because I've locked in on the energetic fingerprint in their hemisphere and that's all I need. I'm just used to it. I always tell them that I need only 10% cooperation from them, while I provide 90% of the work.

I also discovered accidentally that your breathing pattern is connected to your trauma. Breathing is the most underrated technique for improving our health and well-being. Breathing controls everything from how we think, to our energy levels, and even how we digest our foods. Breathe incorrectly and our energy goes down. We may experience panic attacks or high anxiety. When the brain does not get enough oxygen, we experience brain fog and it literally stops us dead in our tracks.

There are 5 types of distressed breathing patterns – reverse breathing, breath holding, hyperventilation, Pause-haling, and Code 911.

Reverse breathing is when we exhale when we should inhale and vice versa. Because of that, we don't get the proper amount of oxygen. It's not natural and goes against the way we normally breathe.

Breath holding is when we're holding our breath. This usually happens when we're hyper-focused on a particular task. The funny thing is that we don't really notice when it's happening, as it is unconscious. The usual signs are when we're yawning or sighing a lot.

If you've ever gambled at a casino, and place a large bet on the table, chances are you held your breath. You become so focused on your bet and the dealer's hand, because you could lose or win a lot of money in seconds. It's like the fate of your life is determined by turn of a few cards. You forget that you are hungry or thirsty.

At times when in certain situations, I've tried to notice when I'm holding my breath. It's funny. I know I'm holding my breath, but I can't force myself to breathe. It's like I'm locked in, and can't move.

Hyperventilation is when you're breathing very rapidly. This causes an imbalance between carbon dioxide and oxygen. When you're hyperventilating, you are either inhaling too strong and exhaling weakly or exhaling too strong and inhaling weakly. Either way, you're rapidly depleting oxygen levels and soon feel faint.

Sometimes hyperventilation is subtle or you may not be breathing so rapidly. It doesn't matter, as it sets off a chain reaction. You'll notice your anxiety levels go through the roof. Hyperventilation breathing is the most common breathing pattern associated with trauma and especially PTSD.

Pause-haling is when you inhale half-way and ex-hale half-way. It's like you stay in the middle, and don't know which way to turn. It's like you take snippets of air in and out.

This type of breathing controls your thinking process. People who take long breaths tend to write longer sentences. People who take shorter breaths, write shorter sentences. That's because how you breathing is connected to how you think. Every time you have to take a breath, it disrupts your thought process and you have to start over. Imagine giving a speech and inhaling every 2 or 3 words. It's disruptive not only for yourself, but for the person listening to you. That's because breathing controls attention spans.

Code 911 breathing is connected to PTSD. It usually starts out during childhood where you're not sure when or where you're going to be attacked or punished. The body is so used to being attacked, that it tenses and contracts intermittently. It could be a physical or a verbal attack, and some psychologist equate a verbal attack more lethal than a physical one.

In the military, they train new recruits for the battlefield by having their drill sergeants scream and yell at them repeatedly. It's to train them for when they go off into the battlefield. They figure if you can get used to the screaming and yelling, then you it won't be so bad when you have bullets and bombs going off around you. Unfortunately, nothing duplicates the extreme conditions such as when you're in a war. And physical and verbal abuse at home, is just as bad as being in a war.

Energetically, I can sense which breathing pattern is associated with my client's trauma. There are usually two or more breathing patterns. I then scan how intense each breathing pattern is, and then clear it until I sense nothing. The client is usually unaware of how they breathe. To my surprise, clearing their breaths also clears energy cords and reduces the influence of their environment. It makes sense, because how you breathe controls your response, and response controls perception.

These two techniques are extremely fast and effective. The client does not have to re-live their trauma and therefore doesn't get re-triggered. The clearing process is so fast and streamlined, that they don't even feel the negative emotions being cleared.

Imagine a giant chalkboard. Written on it are all the experiences, beliefs, and traumas of your life. You can do a life review. You can take one experience and dissect it to its tiniest details. But if you do, you'll create a stronger connection as the memory becomes stronger and thus becomes an even more powerful trauma.

When I clear your brain hemispheres and your breathing patterns, it's like I take a giant eraser and wipe it off. That's it. Trauma gone. You can't even go back to the chalk board and find it, because it's erased. The memory and trauma is gone. If you try to revisit it. you'll find it hard to recall or the trauma will be more neutral.

I can't erase your whole chalk board, because it's too big. The bigger your trauma, the more writing on the chalk board needs to be erased. If I was painting a room in a house I could only paint one side of the room at a time. I can only paint one room at a time. Depending on how many rooms are in the house will determine how long it takes for me to paint the house.

It's the same thing with life. Sometimes it takes several days to paint one room. If I sit back and read the graffiti on the wall, I may not get the job done in time. I may just sit there and just read the wall. Just paint the wall, and it'll look brand new!

Chapter XIV.

SCANNING ~ INTENTION ~ IMAGINATION

People have asked me how I would describe the aura. I would say that it's like a chicken egg. You have the yolk which represents the body or the person. The egg white is the chi or life force. The egg white is what feeds the yolk and gives it the nourishment it needs to grow and become a chick. The egg shell is the aura that contains both the yolk and the egg white. The egg shell is very strong. If you were to squeeze an egg in your hand, the egg shell compacts and become stronger preventing it from cracking.

But if you were to take a stick and poke at the egg shell, it will crack. Dirt and germs are able to enter the egg easily thereby contaminating the egg white, which in turn contaminates the egg yolk. The egg white starts leaking out of the chicken egg, thereby depriving the yolk of much needed nourishment and arresting development of the chick inside.

Whenever you get angry, it's like poking another hole in your aura. Every time you lose your temper, it takes a lot of energy from you. You feel tired and fatigued afterwards. And it takes a while to recover.

Each time you lose your temper, it creates another crack or fissure in your auric field. This allows entities to embed themselves in your aura, and these entities feed off the angry energy you project. Soon they multiply and so the thirst for more anger energy increases. The next thing you know is that you lose your temper at a whim, and soon need to attend anger management classes.

It's the same thing with drugs or alcohol. The moment you start taking drugs or alcohol, your emotional maturity stops growing. No matter how old you get, your maturity level stops at the moment you develop a drug or alcohol problem. But the entities remain.

I remember watching on the news about a drug addict who massacred his family. Even though unfortunately this isn't an unusual occurrence, a reporter interviewed a close neighbor to get her opinion of this tragedy. The reporter wanted to know if there was anything in this suspect's character to make him a murderer. The neighbor said no, and believed it was the drugs he took that influenced the murder spree.

I remember scratching my head as a kid in disbelief. I'm not saying the suspect wasn't responsible for the deaths of his family, but I do believe the entities inhabiting his aura played a crucial part.

The solution is repairing and re-sealing the aura, removal of entities, and increasing the chi or life force energy. All of these things are way beyond this book. These are all separate specialties that require a lot of experience. Even if you learned the techniques, each person is unique and different. There is a difference between studying surgery from a book, and doing surgery on the operating table.

HOW I PERFORM MY CLEARINGS AND HEALING

Over the years I've had to develop numerous tools to help both myself and my clients. I use techniques that I've learned in my workshops, but I've also had to innovate techniques myself. At this time I've been studying Energy Medicine for over twenty years. I also study neuroscience, psychology, nutrition and more, to give me a broader scope of how the mind and body work. Then I translate this information with my knowledge of energy medicine, to perform what seems like miracles.

From my early training in Pranic Healing, I learned to use my hands and fingers to scan the chakras. It was the first thing that I learned. I can't describe the magical feeling I felt, when I realized I had this ability. At first I couldn't believe what I was doing and that it was real. Not only could I scan the chakras, but I could also read them.

Scanning was magical for me, and from that moment on I started to scan anyone and everyone who gave me permission to scan them. I couldn't get enough of it. Every time I had to scan a client I learned something new. I discovered things outside of the chakra system that I didn't know before. It was a new world that I was discovering, and I couldn't get enough of it.

Everything has an energy signature. In the beginning, like learning how to spell, you need to learn the alphabet. But once you learn the alphabet, then you learn how you can rearrange the letters to form words. And from words, you learn to structure them into sentences. And through sentences, you learn to convey your thoughts and ideas. And this is exactly how I perform my clearings.

From Pranic healing I learned how to scan the chakras. I learned their positions in the body and where they are located. Next, I learned to detect blockages in each of them, and what they mean. Then it was the process of clearing them out and energizing them. And this was the basis of my subtle energy alphabet.

As I said before, everything has an energy signature. Everything flows in distinct lines and circles. If a person is angry with you, can you not feel them sending hostile energy towards you? If someone is looking at the back of your head, doesn't it make you turn and look at who it is? Can you not feel love from someone who cares? Or how a place can either feel cold and dead, or warm and inviting. These are all energy signatures, and like all things they have a distinct flavor.

Some people don't feel these things, and it's because they're not attuned. It takes practice. In the beginning, I was illiterate about energy, just like some people can't read a book. But like everything, you just have to be taught how to read energy. Then reading people or situations becomes like reading a new book. A whole world of adventure opens up to you. The more you read, the more you want to know. Later you learn to specialize in one area. And so reading people becomes like reading a book.

What surprises most people at first, is when they learn I can read people by their first name. I have them repeat the name three times in order for me to get an energy read. Let's say their name is John. There's 10 million people with the first name John, but the John I'm reading is the person you know, or the one in 10 million.

I did make one mistake in twenty years. And that was with this hotel clerk who was nice enough to share her sandwich with me, late at night when the hotel restaurant was closed. As an exchange, I offered to read someone for her. She told me the name Michael who was the father of her child. And so I proceeded to do my reading. Afterwards, she told me I was accurate, but it wasn't the right Michael. And so I asked her: then who is this Michael that I read for her? She told me this Michael is the father of her other child.

The next most powerful thing I learned, was how to manifest my intentions into real-time results. By real-time results I mean if they have pain in their shoulder, it goes away usually by the end of the session. If they're depressed, I relieved them and they feel neutral and more grounded.

In energy healing you learn to set your intention. You discover that your thoughts and even your words are very powerful, and they do manifest in the real world. It doesn't matter what healing modality you use, it's your intention made with unconditional love, and that's what creates results.

In the beginning, I didn't think this was possible, but when my mom got sick, you do whatever you have to do. I mean, there's no time to think or question. You just do. And when she got better or experienced pain-relief I wondered, "Did this actually happen?" I couldn't believe that I was able to help my mom, when the doctors couldn't. And that's what encouraged me to become a healer.

Intention is like a muscle. In the beginning, when you go to the gym, your muscles are very weak and flaccid. Later you get stronger. It's the same with intention. You learn to direct your mind, and focus on the healing intention of your client and even yourself. If your client is in pain, you ask where they are feeling the pain. You then focus on that area, and in minutes they experience pain relief. It's that simple.

The third tool that I use in healing is my imagination. I imagine my client in the most ideal healing environment. In this environment I may imagine crystal bowls of different tones generating sound waves at different body parts or chakras, a gemstone cavern where they are sitting in the center being healed by the stones, or being surrounded by angel's singing choir. There are no limits to my imagination.

I just don't imagine these things in my head, I also monitor the healing as it goes on. I'm watching the healing energies as they flow into my client's body, and clear and remove any blockages that I see. I focus with intent on what type of healing the client is coming for, so that we know what end result we're looking for. Sometimes I get messages that I convey to the client.

And then I witness. I witness the process as it goes on. I check and recheck the chakras to see how they're humming. I scan numerous body parts to see how they're developing. Of course I ask feedback from my client and depending on what they tell me, I readjust the healing according to other parts that need to be healed. It's a multi-sensory experience for me, but I enjoy it.

The client could be sitting, standing, or walking around. It doesn't matter. It has no effect. Sometimes I do the healing at night while the client is sleeping. Sometimes the client either doesn't have the time or likes to talk about his personal experience. The point is I get permission to do the work and am told what to work on.

The next day or two, I consult with the client on how they're doing. I allow them to process during the intervening day, and then I get feedback on how they're feeling. Usually I find out right after the session. If it's pain then I inquire if it is gone or what percentage is still remaining. If it's an emotional issue, then I ask if they feel neutral and clear. At the end of each issue, I energize them with chi energy so they feel good, and have great mental clarity.

Following are a few techniques that I use with my clients.

HONEY BEE

Honey Bee was something that I read about in the book, Medical Medium, by Anthony William. In his book he made mention that the buzzing that honey bees make in a hive is very healing. I was curious about that. I didn't know what type of healing, but I wanted to try. Since I didn't have access to any bee hives, and I don't like to get stung, I experimented by imagining my clients in the middle of a bee hive.

One time I was at the airport waiting for my plane. I had two classmates who were also waiting, but for another plane. Since we had time to kill, I asked if they would partake in an energy experiment. They both agreed.

We were sitting across from each other and I just imagined them in the middle of a bee hive. The experiment lasted about 20 minutes. During that time we were talking. Every now and then I would scan them with my fingers and make adjustments to their energy body or redirect the buzzing of the bees. At the time I didn't know what was going to happen as this was my first experiment.

The next time we met they told me they've never felt so relaxed in their entire lives. It seems while they were in my imaginary bee hive, they were releasing copious amounts of stress and tension. They felt they were in a Zen monastery meditating, and this feeling lasted up to four days.

WASABI

I think I was having sushi when I thought of this technique. Sometimes I try to come up with names that are easy to remember or are common. When I think of Wasabi, I think of raw fish. When I think of raw fish, I think of how it is to swim in the ocean.

I remember reading this book by a scientist who mentioned that he believed we descended from the ocean before we came on land. And that's why we like to go to the beach, because it reminds us of our ancestral home. He cited numerous compelling evidence facts, that this may be true. And so some of us need to be near the ocean or the coastline. A lot of people find being near water very relaxing.

And so I decided to create a technique using water. At first I experimented putting my clients in a hypnotic trance where they would imagine themselves on a deserted island, walking along the shoreline. There they would swim with the dolphins while having fun. But some people objected to being hypnotized, and so I had to scrap that idea.

I know from my energy training, that water holds energy and that salt breaks down negative energy. Swimming in the ocean is very cleansing especially if you have cancer. If you're not near the beach, then filling your bath tub with salt water is the next best thing.

Then I heard of Watsu that was invented in Harbin Springs. You're placed in a warm pool of water with a nose guard. In the pool you're pulled while in water by a Watsu practitioner, who pulls you by your arm and leg across the pool. He slowly descends you under the pool, and then slowly brings you up where you take a breath of air. Some people call it water ballet. I've never had Watsu performed on me, but I got the idea how it works.

Wasabi is where I imagine my client in the middle of the ocean. We can be over the phone or in person – it doesn't matter. As I'm imaging them in the water, my arms are moving their body across the ocean. After a while, I imagine moving the currents around their body parts.

For example, if they have a headache or tension around their neck and shoulders, I imagine the water gently massaging those areas. I imagine their body buoyant so that there's no muscle tension anywhere, and their muscles beginning to unwind. It's like they're getting a massage.

I usually do this at night for three consecutive days. I invented this for men or people who have a hard time expressing their emotions. After three days they feel renewed, refreshed, and invigorated. Somehow it releases whatever emotional tensions they were repressing, even though they haven't told me what their issues are.

All I'm doing is taking principles and energetically putting them, in order for it to work. I take the idea that the water is our ancestral place of origin, and so we feel at home in our original birth place. By imagining my clients as a dolphin, I imagine them having fun and being happy as dolphins. The salt water breaks down negative energy so they feel renewed. As this is all happening, I scan them with my hands and redirect the water energies where I sense blockages. It's that simple.

DRAGON'S BREATH

This technique has nothing to do with breathing, and it has nothing to do with a dragon. Being Asian I just thought it was a cool Eastern term. That's all.

There are 5 places where chi or life force energy enters our bodies. They are the palms of our hands, the soles of our feet, and right below our tail bone. I also read that in the past, the earth's magnetic field was way stronger then it is now, and that Qigong masters used to practice standing on lodestones or magnetic rocks while practicing. You can get very powerful gauss magnets on the internet. And so I combined all three together.

In my imagination my clients are laying in the Giant Redwoods. I imagine them in a part of the forest where no man has ever set foot. Right there, the earth, air, and water are the purest and brimming with energy. My client is laying on the ground, totally comfortable and relaxed. Their hands and feet are touching the ground below them. Buried in the ground are 10,000 gauss magnets that are strategically placed below their palms, feet, and tailbone. This is to help magnify the energy of the earth many fold.

My client is there relaxing and breathing in the fresh air. I'm also standing there beside them, monitoring the flow of energy through their bodies. It's not like I can stand there as if I'm watching a movie. It doesn't move as smoothly as that.

The feet or the hands can have blockages that are keeping the energy from entering. Sometimes even after opening those portals up it doesn't reach pass a few inches upwards. It is required to watch that the energy flows up the spine, while circulating throughout the body.

All during this time, the client is relaxing. I encourage them to breathe deeply in and out through their nose. This way, the air they inhale and enters their body is warmed by their nostrils. Exhaling through their nose releases the air more slowly, while increasing carbon dioxide in their bloodstream which helps oxygenate their body even more.

Qigong is the art of moving chi throughout the body, using slow movement. If that is so, then I figure why not maximize the amount of chi going in the body using the earth and magnets. Finally I clear the blockages by scanning them energetically, and thereby increasing the flow.

My analogy of Qigong and other internal exercises is that chi is water flowing through our body. Our bodies are made up of pipes or meridians, that the water-chi flows through. In the beginning the chi doesn't flow well, because our pipes may be filled with lots of gunk. But over time of practicing Qigong, the sediments in our pipes are slowly removed and cleared. Later, the pressure of chi flow builds up the pressure even more and over time enlarges our pipes.

It's obviously easier to practice Qigong than to do Dragon's breath energetically. It requires a lot of concentration, and I don't do it too often on myself or with clients, as it is quite taxing. But in time I'll get better and the technique will get easier. Clients tell me they feel very energized and gain a lot of mental clarity.

HARVEST MOON

Harvest Moon is a ritual one of my teachers learned in Africa. It is performed once a year on September 15. This is when the energies of both the Moon and the Sun coalesced. It is done at night. You say a few incantations whereby you release a substantial amount of negative energies into the flame of a candle. Afterwards you express gratitude. It is said that you age regressed by two years.

I've met people who have used this technique and they do appear younger. They have less wrinkles and less gray hair. But there is a downside to the ritual. Each time you perform the ceremony, you will re-experience whatever emotional issues you had during the past two years. It's the same for physical issues. If you had to have braces to straighten your teeth, imagine your teeth getting crooked again.

Not everyone wants to experience those things. And a few people that I spoke with, to my surprise, didn't mind getting old. They actually treasure getting old with their friends, and look upon it as a mark of passage. Plus you can only do this technique once a year. I didn't learn the technique, but I did meet with someone who did. She explain how the ritual went, and as she did I started scanning what was going on energetically. Remember everything has an energetic signature.

The first thing that I noticed was what looked like a film around the auric surface. It looked like a dirty smudge that was embedded around the energetic body and was coming up to the surface. It created a hazy cloud of dispersed dust circling around the person. There I sensed strong emotions of anger, hurt, and grief.

Some of this energetic dust did go into the flame of the candle, but most of all was still lingering around. My first thought was that I needed to get rid of this dust cloud as much as possible. Otherwise the longer it lingered, the more the client would be suffering.

I was having a lively discussion with a fellow healing practitioner. He told me that rituals are like training wheels on a bicycle. Training wheels were never designed to be used forever. With a ritual it's useful to follow the exact steps, because you don't know what you're doing. Later, after you familiarize yourself and get attuned with the energies, you can perform it better without the ritual, because you'll have known how it goes.

An example was when I attended a pranic healing workshop. A young student was cleaning my solar plexus chakra with green and orange prana. She would switch between green and then orange prana ten times in total. She must have done a thorough job, because afterwards I ran to the bathroom having the worst case of both vomiting and diarrhea.

But it taught me a lesson. Never have an amateur healer work on you. In retrospect, she didn't do anything wrong. She was just following protocol. She did exactly what the teacher instructed her. Later as you become more experienced with healing, you learn that you don't have to clear the solar plexus with ten green and ten orange pranas. Sometimes you only do six green and three orange pranaa. It depends on the client. You have to intuitively feel how much the person needs and can tolerate. Through focused intention you can control the intensity of the prana you're sending. But in the beginning, you need to follow protocol or a ritual, until you understand what you're doing.

When I started experimenting with the Harvest Moon technique, I would notice a lingering layer of old emotional energy. I surmise this is what makes us look and feel old. It's emotional baggage. Even people who perform this ritual have health problems.

So I had to figure out a way to get rid of this energy. I imagined a toilet overflowing with waste, and myself taking a giant plunger to help it flush down the pipes. And so I would lift both my hands gathering as much of the dust cloud as I could, and pushed it down into my imaginary candle flame as an offering to the moon.

It still wasn't enough. And so to emphasize plunging down the cloud of dust, I would yell, "BOOM!" as I brought my arms down. It did help. But there was still more. And so I would yell, "BOOM" several times, as I brought my arms down. And that really worked.

I didn't wait until September 15 of each year to do the Harvest Moon ritual. Remember, with imagination you can create the right environmental conditions anytime and anywhere. As long as you can sense the energy signatures, you can re-create almost anything.

I've done the Harvest Moon ritual as much as three or four times a week. My clients report to me that they are feel really great! They feel younger. They move with greater agility. They have more energy, and so on.

I think that it's just the release of emotional stress that burdens us both mentally and physically. We all know of people who have been through a lot and they look as if they've aged ten years. The Harvest Moon helps.

Overall I practice these three skills – scanning, intention, and imagination on a daily basis. As I continue to learn, I put these three skills to work. They help me come up with new innovations and techniques. I don't try to take anything away from my teachers, but instead I honor them. I'm constantly learning new techniques, and I don't know everything. These tools that I use make my field adventurous and fun. There's always more to explore.

Chapter XV.

HEALING MODALITIES

During my twenty years of practicing Energy healing, I've been exposed to all types of healing styles. These are the main ones.

CLEANSING

Many modalities just cleanse. They remove negative energy and dispose of it. This allows the chi to flow and helps clear blockages that are preventing the person from healing. It is simple, universal, and it works.

Clairvoyantly it looks like a traffic jam of congested energies in one central location in the body. The theory is that the body sends an emergency flow of healing energies to one part of the body. It could be the chest or a leg that is injured. You can feel it as you pass your hand in that area, and it feels like a cloud hanging above that part. All you have to do, is sweep the energy away and dispose of it in a basin of salt water.

As you do, you'll notice the area feeling lighter and lighter until the cloud is no longer detectable. The energy starts to flow into that part of the body and the patient feels relieved. It can be used for pain or just about anything. It is very effective.

ENERGIZING

A few modalities only do energizing or sending healing energy to that part of the body. It is simple and easy to do ,as you're just sending energy to the body. The premise is that the healing energy is intelligent and so it knows where to go. You don't have to do anything. It's the reason why this form of healing is very popular, as it doesn't require scanning unlike cleansing.

It is effective. The idea is that in the client's energetic body are areas that are depleted of energy. Imagine a land parched by drought. Water revives and brings life to the land.

It's not my favorite technique for healing, as it doesn't clear away the negative energy or the congestion. Also when you energize the client's body, it forces negative energy to come out of the energetic body. This is why some practitioners get contaminated with the client's energy. I've known many practitioners who abstain from healing, because of this effect.

CLEANSING BEFORE ENERGIZING

For many years this has been my main rule of thumb when healing. I always use the analogy, that you never use a dirty plate before putting fresh food on it. You always have your plate clean or use a new plate. In that way, when you put fresh food on your plate, it doesn't get contaminated. And it seems to combine the best of both worlds.

ENERGIZING AND THEN CLEANSING

This is sort of reverse healing. As far as I know, I'm the only one who uses this type of method. As I mentioned before, when you energize the etheric body, negative energy flashes out because it's a direct reaction to the positive energy sent to the energetic body. Positive and negative energy repel each other.

The problem is that the negative energy usually splatters over the healer. The solution is simple. I create an energetic wall between myself and the client, that acts as a barrier. So as the negative energy is coming towards me from the client, the energetic wall transforms the energy from negative to positive returning it back to the client. This insures that the client doesn't have a loss of energy, and needs less energizing.

Energy is energy. It cannot be destroyed. But it can be transformed like steam into water and into ice. It's all the same element.

HOW CAN I MAKE YOU HAPPY?

This is the newest concept that I've come across. All ailments whether emotional, mental, or physical are a form of unresolved or unattended conflict. It could be resentment from many years ago that you still haven't let go of. It could be incorrect beliefs that continue to bring you misery and failure. Curses, ancestral lineage, genetic beliefs – I've heard it all. It could also be lack of nutrition, exercise and movement, or just not getting enough rest.

There are two main ways of doing this method – having an internal dialogue with your disease, and sending rapid pictures of whatever it needs. Both take time to master, and you have to allow your intuition to provide the answers. But when done properly, it's the most effective healing method I know.

LET NATURE TAKE ITS COURSE

When people think of energy healing, they believe they'll get instant results like Jesus from the Bible. Healing is not always miraculous. It does happen. For example, relief from pain is immediate, but even an amateur healer can do that. But physical disease is something else.

It can take weeks or even months to heal from physical disease. The difference is, that what would otherwise take months can with energy healing take weeks or even days. In other words, it's accelerated healing.

If you allow nature to take its course, it can heal everything. The problem is that this does not mean your condition improves immediately. It may get worse before it gets better. If you were feeling pain before, it can become even worse. Your grief can transform into depression. But gradually it gets better and improves. And when it's healed, it doesn't come back.

ALWAYS ASK PERMISSION FIRST

Before you heal someone, always ask permission if it's okay to heal them. I know this sounds like an oxymoron question to ask, but a few people have declined my offer.

I remember when I was first starring to heal, I wanted to heal the world. I wanted to heal everybody. In the beginning I didn't ask – I just did. I figured it was good karma for me. Through the years I've asked my teachers this same question, "Can I send healing without asking permission?" I've gotten so many responses. Some said yes, and some said no. Some said if the person doesn't want it, then it'll just bounce back from them, and so no harm. Others said it interferes with the person's karma or their destiny to learn their lessons.

The best explanation I've heard is from one of my teacher who's healed thousands of people of cancer, and other serious diseases. He told me even when a person gives you permission, it doesn't mean they want to be healed. Because some people identify with their disease so much, that it's becomes a part of their identity. In other words, they wouldn't know how to live without their disease.

Now that sounds strange to me. Why would a person want to suffer? Some people may get attention for the first time, from people they love. Some people get benefits from the government or that blue handicapped placard. And some people know that their disease is being fed by hate or resentment, and they're not willing to let it go.

When my teacher has healed or started to heal someone from their disease, he's gotten one of three negative reactions – resentment, anger, or revenge. And I concur. I had to learn to allow people to be, and to do so without judgement.

BALLOONS

Balloons are energetic thought forms. I discovered them by accident while doing a healing session on myself. They appear to be round and of different sizes. Some are small and some are large. They can also be elongated and wrap around your body like a boa constrictor. Some are outside your body, and some are inside your body. And some are lined up like a set of dominos. This usually signifies the past connecting to early childhood.

They're like water balloons containing your negative thoughts and emotions. And when you pop them, they release a lot of negative energy. Left untouched, they re-contaminate your chakras and your energetic body. That's why no matter how many times you clear your chakras, they seem to re-contaminate.

For example, bubbles around my solar plexus contain a lot of anger and resentment. Sometimes it's so much, that it spreads out of my solar plexus and forms a belt around my waist. I can feel the tension in my stomach or that queasiness of anxiety.

Bubbles around my right hemisphere are filled with the harshest criticism. Bubbles around the left hemisphere are a traffic jam of thoughts, all wanting to be expressed. That's why when you talk with some people, they come up with a thousand reasons why they're innocent and you're wrong. It looks like they think fast, but they don't know what they're really saying. They're just blurting out ideas.

Bubbles around the ears are repeated dialogue with people from the past, that you keep repeating to yourself. It's like having imaginary arguments with yourself and your past friends. And each time you do, it brings you back to that same emotional state. You get angry.

Bubbles around the eyes deal with grief and sadness. This is the so-called, "rose-colored glasses" that people wear. For some people it's all they see – sadness.

And so when you pop these bubbles, it releases a lot of stored emotional energy and thoughts. It's almost like magic. For example, I would demonstrate by asking a person to think of something that really bothers them, but not telling me what it is. I then take my finger tips of either hand and imagine I'm popping bubbles in their forehead. The bubbles in their forehead are their thought bubbles, and I just pop them like soap bubbles.

I ask them then how does it feel when they think of their incident, and most of them say it's more neutral. And then I ask them to think of their issue again, I pop even more bubbles. After three or four popping actions, they say it's so neutral that they can't bring it up. If they say it's not neutral or it's still there, then they didn't focus on one issue but interchange issues.

VORTEX HEALING

One day I noticed that I can see tiny vortexes on a person's body. They just appeared out of nowhere. They look like miniature hurricanes. Some are large and some are small.

So, for example, when someone has a cold, I would notice tiny vortexes around their chest, throat, and nose. I would then spread my fingers, and imagine my fingertips were touching the outside perimeter of each vortex, and then bring my fingers together to the center and close them. And then the symptoms of their cold would go away.

Simple. After two or three sessions, their cold would be gone.

I've used this for back aches, sinuses, and headaches. People ask me in what direction was I moving – clockwise or counter clockwise? And I tell them I don't pay attention to those things. I just close them.

Some vortexes are large while others are small. You can feel them with the palm of your hand. But to feel them properly, you have to position your palm to the correct angle of the vortex. For example, sometimes they're pointing at a 45 degrees or 30 degrees.

Most of them I close, but a few I open because they seem to open special abilities. These are my favorite vortexes.

THE HEART VORTEX

Sometimes a client will call me during an emotional meltdown. I don't have to be in front of the person to see that their heart vortex is overactive. I can just feel it. It can be as big as a movie screen.

All I do, is I imagine my fingertips touching the outside perimeter of the vortex and bring my fingertips to the center. Sometimes the vortex is resisting and tries to open up, whereby I just close it up again. Within a few minutes my client calms down and becomes rational.

SLEEP POINT VORTEX

This is a vortex located at the back of the neck. I simply open it, and it seems to help the client have a good night sleep. It also seem to release a lot of bodily tension.

ROOT CHAKRA VORTEX

The root chakra vortex is located at the bottom of the tailbone. From the tailbone it drops to the floor like a skirt. I open this vortex mainly to help the person feel more grounded, but it adds an unexpected benefit.

I discovered by accident that it seems to keep a person sober. I didn't believe it at first and so the next time I decided to get drunk along with my friends. Even though we drank more wine than usual, we didn't seem to get inebriated. We didn't get drunk. Our speech wasn't slurry to the least. I couldn't believe it, especially since I'm a lightweight when drinking.

Not only that, but after the 3rd or 4th time even friends who are alcoholics suddenly developed a distaste for drinking. This even extended to smoking. It just seems that the root chakra vortex releases tensions and anxieties, and so we become less addicted.

MAGNETIC VORTEX

I used to gamble in my early years but I've stopped. I still gamble occasionally, but mostly to scan myself as I gamble or watch clairvoyantly other gamblers to observe how they energetic bodies operate.

There is a vortex located in the lower chakras that operates when you're gambling. It's amazing as it drains energy from the upper chakras and you feel as if you have no will. Actually, it's difficult to think as it seems you are led by your emotions or vices.

It's a magnetic pull, that even when you know it's time to leave, you just can't. Perhaps it's the danger or excitement you feel when gambling, but I noticed it's the same vortex when people are uncontrollably attracted to swindlers or hustlers. You want to leave, but you can't. It's like you feel this irresistible urge to come back, and the more you resist, the less willpower and mental clarity you have.

One time I was passing a casino on my way home, and suddenly I feel this irresistible urge to gamble. I remember the magnetic vortex and proceeded to close it down.

It was like snapping out of a trance. It was weird. Suddenly I became aware of where I was and that I was driving my car. It's like waking up from a dream or snapping out of someone's hypnotic control. But it worked and so far I haven't gambled since.

THE HEALER'S VORTEX

I've met some of the best healers on the planet. One healer, I know, has healed more people of cancer successfully and consistently. I had a chance to watch him work and knowing what I know about vortexes, I wanted to see if there was a vortex for healing.

There was. I observed a vortex coming from his forehead cascading down like a waterfall down to his feet. At first I was confused as I thought it would be a vortex from his crown, and so wanted to test my hypothesis.

I was having dinner with a friend at a wonderful Mexican restaurant. I proceeded to tell her about the workshop and what I've seen. I demonstrated the vortex by energizing her glass of water. She noticed that the water tasted much sweeter and could feel the energy emanating from it.

I then transferred the vortex to her and instructed her to charge the paper napkin. She was amazed that she could do it. The napkin was so energized you could feel it several feet from the table. She then tried to energize a 2nd napkin, but it wasn't as energized as the first.

The vortex that I had downloaded on her was diminishing. It seems that it lasted only for a few minutes, but it demonstrated that just by opening the vortex, a person can become a healer, even without any prior training.

BODY INTUITION

Take both your hands and have your palms face each other a few inches apart. Slowly pull them apart, and then bring them close together. As you bring your palms close together, you'll start to notice an energy bubble between them, and when you bring them apart the energy bubble feels lighter. This Is an old technique for sensitizing your hands.

I wanted to develop a technique that would make me more sensitive to the intuitive signals of my body. All the other clairvoyant abilities like clairvoyance or clairaudience come later, but feeling your body signals is the easiest one to develop.

YES ~NO

Yes~No is your basic questioning. Most people use a pendulum as it's the easiest tool to train your intuition with. But I wanted to figure out a way to read signals from my body.

So if you do the palm exercise as stated above, I want you to feel your forehead. Close your eyes and repeated the word "YES" out loud. Then bring the palm of one of your hands to your forehead without touching it. Now feel your forehead as you say "YES".

The majority of people will feel a slight pressure as they bring their palm to their forehead. That's because when you say YES, you're usually thinking clear and there is energy in the forehead chakra.

Now do the same with the word "NO". The majority of people will feel no pressure on the forehead. It will feel void. But the pressure does appear on the lower back and you may feel your lower back stiffen. That's because when you say "NO", you're making a declaration and you have to stand strong to opposition.

Now I said that these signals for YES and NO show up in the majority of people that I've tested, but not all. Sometimes there is no energy in the forehead when people say YES. That's because they may not be sure or feel confident of their "YES". Sometimes their "YES" is really a "MAYBE".

The same thing with the word, "NO". With some people, when they say "No!" I would scan that their heart chakra is overactive, which means that they are sensing the other person's reaction, rejection, and even anger of being refused. They may say "NO" but it's a weak "NO" that can easily be overcome.

Some people have their "YES" and "NO" in reverse. Probably due to early childhood trauma. I noticed that people who were molested as children have their "YES" and "NO" in reverse, probably because their boundaries have been crossed over so many times.

It's really important to have your "YES" and "NO" in proper order. Otherwise, how can you make wise decisions? How can you know what's best for you?

SAFE AND UNSAFE

Safe and unsafe are the next two important words along with "YES" and "NO". Are you in a safe environment or in danger? Your life may depend on it.

When I tested the word, "SAFE" I notice my body feels comfortable, as if it's ready to sit down and relax. My lungs feel expanded, and my mind feels clear and serene. My upper body feels relaxed and light.

With "UNSAFE", I notice my stomach contracts and everything feels tight around my mid-section. There's a sense of anxiety that grows, and depending on the sense of "UNSAFE", I feel like I want to leave.

Many people get SAFE and UNSAFE confused, especially with UNSAFE. It's because you're flirting with danger, and with danger comes excitement. Sometimes you feel a buzz of sexual excitement like the magnetic vortex acting on you.

The signal of SAFE and UNSAFE are very clear. The problem is that we misinterpret the signals. For some people SAFE is boring and monotonous. UNSAFE is exciting like playing with fire. The problem with that is that sooner or later you're going to get burned.

PART FOUR

MAPPING

Chapter XVI.

BRAIN MAPPING

Brain Mapping took me several years to develop – mainly because I needed my scanning skills to advance. The basic premise of brain mapping at the time was, that there was only one brain map – the way a person was wired to learn new things. And so it was presumed that this was the dominant way a person's brain was wired.

But through countless observations and feedback from my clients it didn't make sense. A child growing up will go through countless brain maps as their personalities change. How you solve your problems may consist of two to three brain maps. A brain map consist of the sequence of your SEVEN INTELLIGENCES of your brain. Which intelligences you use determines how the information you are gathering is being processed and developed.

There are basically two types of brain maps for every segment of your life – the success brain map, and the failure brain map. The success brain map when followed, leads to greater success and decision-making. You have more energy, and have greater problem-solving skills to get you out of whatever jam you're in. You also have greater luck in your life, and things seem to flow more smoothly.

The failure brain map is the wrong sequence of using your Seven Intelligences of your brain. This happens when under stress you use one of your weaker intelligences to solve your problems. It's like water – it seeks the easiest path. The failure brain map is formed when under stress, trauma, or fear. And when you repeatedly follow this type of brain map, it becomes a habit and eventually takes over your personality. Overtime, this will make you more reactive, increase your anxieties, and decline your mental clarity. You'll make more mistakes. You'll experience more failure. And your life will generally become unhappy. It will seem as if your life is plagued by the same recurring problems.

So how does it work?

Each brain map is sequenced from 1-7, but you only need to know the sequence from 1-3. That's because sequences 4-7 follow directly in line and are influenced by the first 3. The success brain map always starts out with your strongest intelligence, followed by your second strongest, and then the third strongest. The rest, from 4-7 intelligences automatically become aligned, so you don't have to worry about it.

The failure brain map is any intelligence, except your strongest. It could be your 2nd strongest – it doesn't matter. You always start out with your right foot forward – anything else will get you off-balance.

Each of your 7 intelligences has both a strong and a weak side.

INTRAPERSONAL

PRO – creativity, contemplation, and innovation.

Intrapersonal is connected with free-association. For example, let's say you're studying the color blue. How many things can you associate with the color blue? The night or daytime sky, crayons and markers, your clothing, and so on. Now take all those associations and connect them in new and novel ways that you never did before. For example: the night reminds me of Van Gogh's "Starry nights" painting. The painting reminds me of when I was a kid, hiding underneath the blanket, or the sparkly lights I see in the dark. One association leads to another which leads to new ideas.

CON – extremely quiet and still, non-communicative, reviewing things over and over in your mind.

The best example are children sitting quietly by themselves, especially after being scolded by their parents. They're usually hunch down, not moving a muscle. Parents usually label them as "good kids" because they don't cause any trouble or fuss. They're easy to handle. And it seems they just want to be left alone. But inside the child's mind is a flurry of I bottled up thoughts, emotions, and feelings. It's like a tornado of negative energy, swirling inside them and they're holding themselves very still and tense to contain the explosive angry or sadness inside. Their minds are out-of-control. They are picturing all sorts of negative scenarios, and in each one of them they're victimized.

INTERPERSONAL

PRO – leadership, gathers advisement and opinion from others, great social skills.

Interpersonal persons know how to get along with people and make them feel comfortable. They're great communicators. They know how to listen and ask questions. Because of that ability, they have a deep understanding of how the outside world works. They get informed of the latest news, and so are able to capitalize on new opportunities before anyone else.

CON – manipulators, con-artists, and good talkers. They know how to talk, but it's basically all they know.

They may have many friends, but few personal ones. They can be superficial. They tend to use people as resources or "what can I get from you?". They're not easy to get to know. They know how to make you feel good, but it has no meaning.

LINGUISTIC

PRO – expressive, articulate, and well-read.

Linguistic people are good in all forms of oral and written expression. Some speak well, and some write well. They also tend to read a lot and are very educated. You'll find them journaling where they express their thoughts and feelings. This makes them more aware of themselves and their surroundings. They're very observant. Also writing and talking out-loud helps them release their inner tensions and clear their minds.

CON – can be annoying to listen to constantly.

They talk incessantly. You can't shut them up. They're like a ball of string that continues to roll until completely unraveled. They go over the same details or repeat the same things over and over again. They recount past events. They complain a lot. They ask a lot of annoying questions and expect you to explain it logically and complete to their satisfaction, otherwise they'll pester you with more questions.

LOGICAL

PRO – problem solver, mental clarity,
and goes about focus on the solution rather than the problem.

They tend to not let their emotions get in the way of their perceptions. They find shortest path. They're good at making decisions. They tend to be task-oriented, because they know that action brings results.

CON – know-it-all attitude, bad logic leads to wrong conclusions,
highly opinionated and closed-minded.

People who are too logical are usually closed off to their emotions. They pride themselves on their intellect, even to the point where they like to be reminded of how smart they are. They like debates as long as they're right. They like to make all the decisions. But they're not always right. Sometimes their thinking is not always so logical or clear, but illogical. And that's where they get into trouble. They're constantly coming up with the wrong conclusions or ideas about things. At the same time they won't admit they're wrong.

MUSICAL

PRO – honesty, integrity, right action.

People with strong musical intelligence tend to tell the truth. I look for them when I'm buying something at a store. They also tend to be more ethical, and can't carry out actions that they think are wrong. So everything they do has to feel right, otherwise they won't do it. They can also detect deceit or lying. It just doesn't sound right to them. And so they know who to trust, or not trust.

CON – gullible, easy to manipulate, wrong action.

They're just the opposite of the description above. They tend to believe the lie and dismiss the truth. Even though they know what the truth is, it's difficult for them to accept, and so they go along with the lie. They go against their very nature and take the wrong step. They trust the wrong people, and scurry away from the ones who really care about them and try to realign them back onto the right path. This is the most destructive intelligence, because it takes a long time for them to learn. They will literally block out people helping them, because they won't listen.

KINESTHETIC

PRO – full of energy, sense of timing, results oriented.

Kinesthetic people are always moving, and can't be enclosed in small places. They measure everything in inches, numbers, and especially in regards to deadlines. This is how they measure results and are therefore usually highly successful. They get things done and figure out ways to shorten their cycles of actions, to become even more efficient. They can also sense if things are moving in the right or wrong directions, and can make corrective actions. They're excellent in feng shui. They're very good at flipping houses, because they instinctively know how to make a place feel inviting and comfortable.

**CON – prone to anger and outbursts, feels stuck,
and unable to take action.**

When your kinesthetic intelligence is working against you, you're usually going through a lot of anxiety. The anxiety can be extremely debilitating. Your body may feel tense or awkward to move. Mornings can be greeted with aches and pains. Taking action to move forward can be very difficult, sudden, or even remain permanent. I've seen people move from being highly successful to homeless failures. Look for stuck breathing patterns as it contributes to their low energy.

VISUAL

**PRO – ability to create concepts into well-defined mental maps,
fastest learning intelligence, clairvoyance, observant.**

Visual people are the fastest learners. They have the ability to turn everything they see, hear, or read into a mental movie which they can replay over and over in their minds. And like with a movie, they can slow, stop, or reverse and review things in their mind. They learn from observing. They can also be image conscious, and dress fashionably. If they're reading a book, they see pictures and not words, which makes them excellent speed readers.

**CON – body issues, imagining worst case scenarios
leading to unparalleled anxiety and worry,
can't stand to watch violent movies and sports.**

Some of the most beautiful people have body issues. Perhaps because they're judged on their looks so much, they want everything to look perfect. In other words, they see imperfections. Watching violent movies and sports is disturbing to them to the point of shut down. Their imaginations can go wild and out-of-control, leading to worry and anxiety.

A success brain map always begins with your strongest intelligence first, and then your second and third. In this way, you'll use the pro of each intelligence.

If you start out with even your second strongest intelligence or other, you will demonstrate the con side of your intelligence.

Every issue like relationships, business, money, or work, has both a success brain map and a failure brain map. If you're in crisis, then you're definitely using the failure brain map. Stay relaxed and calm and soon you'll change into your success brain map.

The problem is that we're all unique, and no two people think alike. Figuring out your brain map either for success or failure takes time and practice. You can't follow someone else's formula for success, because the way they think will be different from your way of thinking. That's why you can read books on success, but it may not work for you, because it's geared to that person's brain map and not yours. You need to translate what they say and write about into your success brain map.

Now to make things more complicated, each intelligence is governed by either the right or left hemisphere or both. So for example: your logical intelligence can be either right or left hemisphere predominantly or balanced. And this goes for all 7 intelligences.

LEFT HEMISPHERE

PRO – logical, sequential, writing, steps.

You need the left hemisphere to put things into words or actions. For example, Beethoven may hear the music in his head, but without the left hemisphere, he wouldn't know how to translate those notes into his compositions. It takes the ability to make a reality, something that you imagine in your mind.

CON – don't get anything done, revises reality to divert blame or responsibility.

Some people continue to think and think, but they never take action. They don't see the steps or complete the steps to make things a reality. For example, some writers can work on a book for years without ever getting it published. It doesn't mean that the book is very good – they just never get around finishing it.

The left brain can be akin to a movie director. A movie director may take a historical account of a story, but in making a movie he will delete, revise, and even change the outcome of the movie in order to create more drama, missing plots, and add high-selling elements. I see it often in court cases, where the defendant denies responsibility or even participation, despite the police reports and eye witnesses to the contrary. The left hemisphere will protect the ego and will delete details from the person's memory, so that the person always sees themselves as an innocent victim, despite the crime they committed.

RIGHT HEMISPHERE

PRO – creativity, imagination, beauty.

The right hemisphere deals with emotion, creativity, and imagination. Through it, we are able to access unlimited knowledge and information that is outside our limited consciousness. In other words, we step out of our limited boundaries, and see things outside the box.

CON – impending doom

Impending doom is exactly what it says it is. We may foresee disaster where none exist, but we believe it. It affects us, because in our mind it's very real and true. It's so real that it's going to happen, and that becomes our basis for reality.

The left hemisphere controls the right side of the body. The right side of the body is considered the masculine aspect or action, business, money matters and material wealth. The right hemisphere controls the left side of the body. Emotions or emotional blockages are stored on the left side of the body. The left side is considered the feminine side of us.

When I read people, I tell them what their success and failure brain map is for any subject in their life. It could be for any life issues, or where they're feeling stuck and want to improve. That's why it's taken me years to develop – I had to perfect my scanning skills.

The brain maps are pin-point accurate. Because your brain determines how you think and feel. The hemispheres determine how you perceive things and create even greater refinement. The left and right sides of the body bring it into full refinement.

We learn through our five senses, but our five senses get their information from the body – our whole body. Our ears deal with sound and our eyes deal with sight, that's obvious. But other body parts feed other information to other parts of the brain that is necessary for the way we make decisions, how we feel, and what we know. For example, our legs tell us where to go, retreat, or if we feel stuck. Our arms tells us what to do, how to protect ourselves, and how to fight or defend. It's the layering of more refine maps that explain our consciousness.

Chapter XVII.

BODY MAPPING

The brain is fed through our FIVE senses – sight, hearing, taste, touch, and smell. And the five senses get their information from our entire body. The body feeds the brain with information both conscious and unconscious-intuitive. The brain then processes this information and sends it back to the body about the decisions it made. If the brain is properly connected to the body, the body will receive these commands and you will achieve your goals. Most people think that the main information they feed the brain, is through what they read or listen to, but this is not the case.

The brain communicates through the body via the central nervous system. And the body provides feedback to the brain, so that the brain can make adjustments to its goals and intentions. For example, if you wanted to pick up that glass of water with your right hand, your brain would send a signal to your right arm to extend the hand closer to that glass of water. You would measure the distance to that glass with your eyes, coordinating your arm reach, and finally your hand and fingers would grip the glass of water. The pressure of your grip would signal to the brain how tight or loose to hold it, in order to pick up and bring the glass of water to your mouth. Before it reaches your lips, the scent of the water would tell you if the water is fresh or stagnant. Your tongue and lips determine temperature, taste, and texture of the water. And so on.

So naturally, we take all that for granted. But what if instead of a glass of water, our aim was setting goals, like starting a business, a new relationship, or learning a new skill? The same mental and physical processes would apply. You see someone you like at a party. Your eyes pick that person out of a group of several other people, and focuses on that one person. Your ears pick up that person's voice and the intonation, which tells you if they're friendly, negative, or just plain moody. Your legs bring you closer to that person in order to meet them. Once you are physically close to them, you take in their scent which can tell you if they are friend or foe. Your tongue articulates the words and intonation to gesture with them. Your eyes and ears tell you that person's receptivity and reactions to your presence. The brain takes all this information and formulates whether you like this person or not, and whether they like you or not. From then on, you can decide either to pursue this person or not. But at least you initiated the steps that bring you one step closer to finding someone you may want to be in a relationship with.

In a similar scenario, but with a different result, another person spots someone at a party that they like. You take in that person's full dimensions and size up if it's to your measure or not. But let's say you approve. You then imagine how it would be with that person in the future and excitement builds.

But even though you can feel your heart beating rapidly, excitement building, and your eyes locked into place, you don't make a move. Your mind tells your legs to walk towards that person's direction, but there's resistance. Your legs wobble. You make your first steps in that direction, but your head turns away at the last moment.

Nothing is accomplished.

Maybe that person was interested in you, but because you couldn't execute the moves to make your presence known or make a simple introduction, you'll never know. It may be one of several attempts you've made in the past, that never came to fruition. Half-attempts do not count as they never reach the finish line. Now this scenario could easily be repeated in your disposition to career, business, diet, fitness or personal goals.

You have a goal in mind, but in order to accomplish that goal you have to take certain steps to accomplish that goal. And you accomplish your goals by feeding your brain via your five senses which get their information from your body. Every part of the body is like an antennae picking up information, both conscious and unconscious or outside of your physical realm. The brain is like a computer that needs data to analyze and sort through. It then sends commands to your body in order to execute the actions that will bring your goal to fruition.

But ...

What if your body parts are sending incomplete, blocked,

or incorrect information to your brain?

What if your brain couldn't send the proper signals

to your body parts to execute moves?

When we think of our FIVE senses,

we think of them purely on a physical level,

like we listen to sounds with our ears.

But what if they're more than that?

What if they also represent our beliefs, traumas, and inner conflicts?

Then no matter how much we want to accomplish our goals, we feel resistance.

We may even sabotage ourselves.

This can determine why we are successful in one area, but not in others.

You have ears but cannot hear. You have eyes but cannot see.

When I do readings for people, they ask me why they are stuck in their life. They want to know why they can't reach their goals or start a new relationship. They've tried everything. They've read books, gone to workshops, and even went to psychics. They've spent thousands of dollars on consultants who promised them success, but still to no avail.

I don't need tarot cards, crystal balls, or charts. It's not necessary to go into trance and describe your past lives. I just read their body energetically, and the body tells me most everything. The body does not lie. The body tells the truth. The body tells me the heart of the problem that my clients have been searching for.

First of all, we need to divide the body in separate segments. There are the neck and face, chest, arms and legs. Each have different functions. When I'm reading the body, I'm not reading body language, otherwise I would have to see them in person. It doesn't matter if they're in front of me or not, because I'm reading their bodies energetically. And what I am looking for are energy blockages. Energy blockages tell me if that part of the body is providing the right information to the brain, or if the brain is able to communicate with that part of the body.

Right side of the body represents taking action to reach our goals, make money, and create results. If the blockage is on the right side of the body, then we don't feel safe, secure, or confident in ourselves. It may also mean we're not receiving the information needed to create the steps to reach our goals.

Left side of the body represents our emotional well-being. How do we feel? Do we like or dislike that person, place, or thing? Do we feel comfortable or uncomfortable? Are we scared? Do we hate that person, place, or thing? How do we feel? We can try to suppress or hide how we feel, but everything shows up in the left side of the body energetically, and that will influence how we walk in the world.

THE FACE AND NECK

The face and neck represent how we express ourselves to the world. It also represents how we take-in the information from the world. This is the major area of the body that gives our brain the most amount of information.

EYES - block out what we don't want to see or what we can't handle.

For example, blockages in the left eye keep us from seeing the other person as they really are. Let's say it's a partner who's abusing us. If we're not comfortable confronting that person, we simply block out the abuse. If we're not able to leave that person, then we try to see only the good parts of them in order to rationalize staying with them. Even if it happens in front of our eyes, if we can't handle it emotionally, we'll block it out. Our friends can see it, but if we can't see it in our mind's eyes, then it doesn't exist.

We block out what we can't handle emotionally. Or sometimes I see like a large movie screen in front of the left eye. It's a fantasy image generated from the right hemisphere of an ideal future. Maybe they see themselves marrying this person and living happily ever after. This vision is what they see 24/7 and it blocks all other information contrary to it.

The right eye forms mental maps of concepts you've studied. It shows everything in order, like a working clock with all its gears moving. Imagine the alphabet strung out in wooden blocks from A-Z. You can pick any letter in the alphabet and can tell the letter before and after it. The right eye controlled by the left hemisphere gives you logic and order, and helps you plan the steps necessary to reach your goals.

Blockages in the right eye keeps you seeing the information even though it's right in front of you to read. For example, you can read a book and mouth out the words and still not know what the books is about. That's because you haven't turned the words into pictures and without pictures you have no meaning. You just see words, but your brain hasn't translated it into ideas or concepts. That's why some people who have really strong visual intelligences can read a book like watching a movie.

I sometimes see a lot of rage, anger, and grief in both eyes. Grief shows up in the tear ducts. Focus and determination shows up in the center of the eyes. Rage and revenge show up in the outside corners of the eyes.

Clairvoyance shows up as vortices around the tear ducts and also in the center of the forehead or 3rd eye. A simple experiment is to close your eyes and imagine something in your mind. Slowly bring your finger to touch your head where you see the image. You will be pointing at the 3rd eye.

There are two types of images I see in a person's eyes – internal and external. It's like a giant movie screen that's either indoors or outdoors. The external picture keeps them from seeing what's happening in reality like blindfolds. The internal image is what they see in their mind's eye. Either one is different from reality or what's actually happening.

EARS - blockages in the ears represent only: hear what you want to hear, and what you don't want to hear. They can cause the person to be extremely sensitive to loud sounds, such as people's voices or sirens. Blockages in the ears can shut a person down both mentally and emotionally. And when they are shut down, they can't respond to what you say or tell them to do. They just stand there, frozen.

People who have blockages in the left ear can't stand people who are sarcastic. They like people to talk softly to them. It doesn't matter if you greet them with a happy "Hello" or most especially with an angry tone. They enjoy quiet.

People who have blockages with the right ear talk loud. They like to hear themselves speak. They'll ask the person to re-explain things a thousand times, but they still don't get it even though they say they're trying to hear you correctly.

Blockages in both ears also represent internal and external dialogue. For example, internal dialogue is repeating an old dialogue you had with people in the past. It could be put-downs, self-criticism, or old arguments from family or friends. They're just old audio tapes running 24/7. If you feel limited, then these are old tapes about putting yourself down or why you can't do something.

External dialogue is interesting. Mostly it represents clairaudient abilities or the ability to hear other people's thoughts. The problem is that unless you understand that you have clairaudient abilities, you can't differentiate your thoughts from the other person's. Most people's thoughts are very negative and condemning and so if you can hear what other people are thinking about you, it can be very insulting. If you think that's bad, then you ought to hear what babies say to their parents. But once these blockages are cleared, these people make excellent readers. Some people have the gift of gab which is really telling people what they want to hear by reading their thoughts.

NOSE – represents the olfactory sense which is the oldest and earliest of the five senses to be developed. It creates the strongest memory connections. Anything you want to remember permanently, you connect to smell. Blockages in the nose represent odor associated with trauma. For example, fear puts out a sweet smell.

The left nostril smells if this person is someone you can trust or not. Before the early Hawaiians were united, they would visit the other islands. The chieftains would greet each other by bringing their nostrils so close, that they could inhale the other's exhale through their nose. That way they inhaled the other person's essence. Blockages in the left nostril means you can't tell who you're dealing with, and get wrong impression about people. That's why people wear perfume.

The right nostril helps you determine if this business deal will bring you fortune or bankruptcy. "There's something about this that doesn't smell right" or "the sweet smell of success." "Follow your nose! It always knows!"

Blockages in the right nostril may keep you from finding the right opportunities. And some people tend to pick the wrong opportunities, simply because they're attracted to the wrong smells and don't know it.

TONGUE – deals with articulating sounds, thoughts, and ideas. It clarifies our mind by letting us express what we think, and releases build-up of thoughts or overthinking.

When I see blockages in the tongue, I see the tongue energetically wagging back and forth like a dog's tail. It doesn't mean the person's tongue is literally wagging, but it feels tense and folded inside the person's mouth. It means they're holding back from saying what they what to say, or their tongue is generating lies.

A wagging tongue generates words or thoughts even though no sound comes out of the mouth. Because these thoughts or words are unexpressed, they crowd the mind and create traffic jams to your mental clarity. This means you can't take in information, because your mind is crowded with too many thoughts or simply thinking too much.

I know a lot of people who are accused of talking too much or interrupting when people are talking. They're trying to clear their heads of congested thoughts. Sometimes you just have to let their mouths roll like toilet paper dropping downwards. They won't stop until the whole of toilet paper is finished, and then they can listen to you.

NECK - expression, creativity, and goals. The color of the throat chakra is blue and it's connected to both your arms, because creativity is expressed through your hands. Now imagine this blue light sending beams from your fingertips. Clairvoyantly, if the blue light extends 5 ft. from your finger tips and crisscross, then it means you can reach your long term goals. If it extends 1-2 ft and crisscross, then it means you reach your short term goals. If the blue beams don't crisscross either short or long, then it means you work hard but you never finish anything.

Blockages in the neck are when you're beams never crisscross or the blue beams are at different lengths from either the left or right arm. In many cases I've seen the blue beams never go past the fingertips. They may go halfway up the arm, which means the person doesn't have any goals or direction in their life.

UPPER CHEST – represents heart and lungs and serves for breathing and circulation. Heart represents flow with life, with the people in our lives or our connection to people. Lungs deal with grief and pain. The chest represents your identity in this world.

People who have blockages around the heart area, keep people away. They either push people away because they don't want to get hurt again or are afraid to risk getting hurt. It's like a force field around these people, and you'll find them difficult to get to know. Energetically it can feel threatening to other people, even though the person appears to be friendly and nice.

Lung blockages show up in the upper back, but also in the front of the chest. People with lung blockages suddenly can't breathe or have breathing issues. It can either be sudden or constant. It will literally stop you in your tracks. Nothing gets the attention of the brain when you suddenly can't breathe. You can't focus. You can't think. Whatever you're doing, you'll immediately stop. This is the most detrimental blockage in the body, because you will not be able to function. You will immediately go into shutdown. I have seen people who were extremely successful lose their business and career overnight.

When you have a blockage with your breathing, which is usually triggered by emotional issues connected to your heart or relationships, your energy will dwindle and you will need to rest more. You'll feel more fatigue which leads to mental fog. Some people are not even able to hold a job or pursue their goals, because they don't have the energy or the ability to think and learn. It can be so bad that life itself is too stressful, so you spend most of your time at home vegetating.

Also look at suppressed anger and resentment. The upper back will appear to be tense. Tight shoulders represent massive burdens and responsibilities placed on that person. Droopy shoulders or sensing the person is folding inside themselves, represent protecting the heart from being hurt again. Shoulders pulled back with chest protruding feels like the person is ready to fight, and you can sense energetically their hands balled into fists.

ARMS – protection, defending, and vulnerability. The arms protect the chest and face from attack. The arms can also be used to attack or fight. Vulnerability is when the arms are raised or hang uselessly at your sides.

When the arms are used for protection, you can energetically almost feel a wall between you and that person, or a push-back sensation if you get too close. If the wall is not too strong and you push hard enough, the aura feels squishy like jello which means extreme vulnerability. In other words, they may put up a strong front, but it is only paper and not brick. If the wall is strong, then you really sense their presence in the room and it feels intimidating.

Blockages on the outside of the arms mean they are trying to protect themselves from the environment or people. They are hard to get to know or get close to. Blockages on the inside of their arms represent two aspects: with their left arm a lot of self-criticism, or their right arm that tells them they can't perform tasks or learn new things.

HANDS AND FINGERS – fingers are tactile, and palms are what we hold or get attached to. Energetically we feel and check out things with our fingers, to see if we like it or not. Palms are used for holding things and sometimes not letting them go.

Energetically we use fingers to grab what we want or are attracted to. People who are obsessed with things or other people, I see their fingers reaching out. It's the tactile sensations they feel that make their goals tangible. When you're trying to learn something, imagine feeling it with your fingers and sense how it feels. If you can't touch it energetically, then somehow it doesn't feel real, or it makes it harder to understand what you're trying to learn. If I feel it energetically in a person's palm, then it like the person is saying "This is mine and I'm not letting it go". This also shows up when a person is not able to let go of another person or relationship. It's because they're holding on to it. When the fingers and palm open up, there's a sudden sense of release.

LOWER MID-SECTION, BOTH FRONT AND BACK– the front mid section is usually where you feel anxiety, anger, or lack of power. The lower back is adrenaline, always on the defensive or on the go and can't rest.

Left front mid-section is emotionally anxiety. Right front mid-section is anxiety dealing with money, job, or security. Also self-doubt. You can feel the auric energy extending from either the left or right sides. Lower back blockages mean they can't relax and are always working. You'll also see a depletion of energy in the root chakra.

PELVIS OR GENITALIA – It can pull like a sponge all the energy of the body including the brain to the pelvis. This means you will be influenced by your desires i.e. sexual, drug, and hobbies, and so on. You will not be able to think clearly or have any willpower to resist. The craving will be overwhelming and will increase until fulfilled. You will be influenced by your desires and what you think are your needs. It looks like a huge funnel and acts like a black hole that sucks in everything in its wake. This is an external blockage.

The opposite is the internal blockage. Usually as we age our life force energy diminishes drastically. If the external blockage was attraction, then the internal blockage is repulsion. Desire then become emptiness. Enjoyment of even the simplest things such as a walk through the park becomes minimal. There is no joy or even excitement. Clarity diminishes also and thinking becomes more rigid.

HIPS AND LEGS – how we move in life. Do we move forward? Do we retreat back? Or are we stuck in the middle? Energetically I can see if a person's legs are walking forward, walking away, side-stepping or avoiding, or stuck like their legs are in cement. Sometimes I see one leg moving forward while the other is moving in the opposite direction. Sometimes you want to move forward with your right leg, but your left leg is saying, "I don't feel comfortable or ready."

Blockages on the outside of the knees tell me how comfortable they in their environment. If it's the left knee, then they'll avoid areas where there's a lot of emotional tension with the group working there. If it's the right knee then it's not the right environment for work.

Blockages on the inside of the knees signify how comfortable they are with themselves in a workplace or home. Some people have to move from place to place, no matter where they go. They say they feel bored with a place or people, but it's really with themselves, and they can't stand to be in the same place for very long.

The front of the right knee blockage is tremendous ego. This shows up in hustlers or scammers. You need a tremendous ego to scam your friends and associates or even people you invite to your house or home. Scammers don't think about the people they're hurting. They may even display great confidence and charisma. This is all due to the fact that their ego is telling them how great and wonderful they are.

The front of the left knee blockage is that of psychopaths. They are blocked from their feelings and emotions, and can become anyone that they want. They can appear normal and even ordinary which makes them very difficult to detect. They can raise families, and hold down jobs like everyone else.

The front of the knees represents power or move forward despite obstacles. You need strong knees to support your body, and where you walk is where you find opportunity. No matter how hard you're willing to work, if you don't walk or run where opportunity is, you won't get your chances.

FEET AND TOES – balance, stability, and energy.

Toes are funny. They remind of bloodhounds when they're searching for a scent. But in this case, they're looking for the right direction to go. The toes definitely lead the way. Energetically I see them sniffing different directions, trying to figure out the best way to go. And when they find the place, I see them scrunch up like they're grabbing the earth. Sometimes they let go and release that piece of earth, which tells me that they're flexible in changing and adapting to new plans or goals. Few people have the ability to let go of long-laid plans for better plans, as circumstances dictate.

Some people's toes are not even moving, which tells me they don't know where they want to go. And others are bent like they are scared of life. Sometimes I see the toes raised like they're afraid to touch the ground.

Energetically the ball of the foot tells me if they're excited about moving forward with their goals. Sometimes if they're too enthusiastic, I see them leaning too much forward and they'll lose their balance and fall over. This tells me that they're too impulsive and need to watch their actions.

The middle sole tells me if they're balanced and grounded. If the middle sole is not touching the ground, then it's like they can't stay in one place for too long or need to keep moving. The imbalance shows on the outside and inside ridges of their feet.

Blockages in the heels tell me either they're stuck to the ground and can't move, or they can handle whatever challenges come their way. It gives extra stability to their grounding. If the heels don't touch the ground, it tells me they don't feel safe or are ready to pivot into different direction. It all depends upon the circumstances and what feels right.

INNOVATIVE REMEDYING

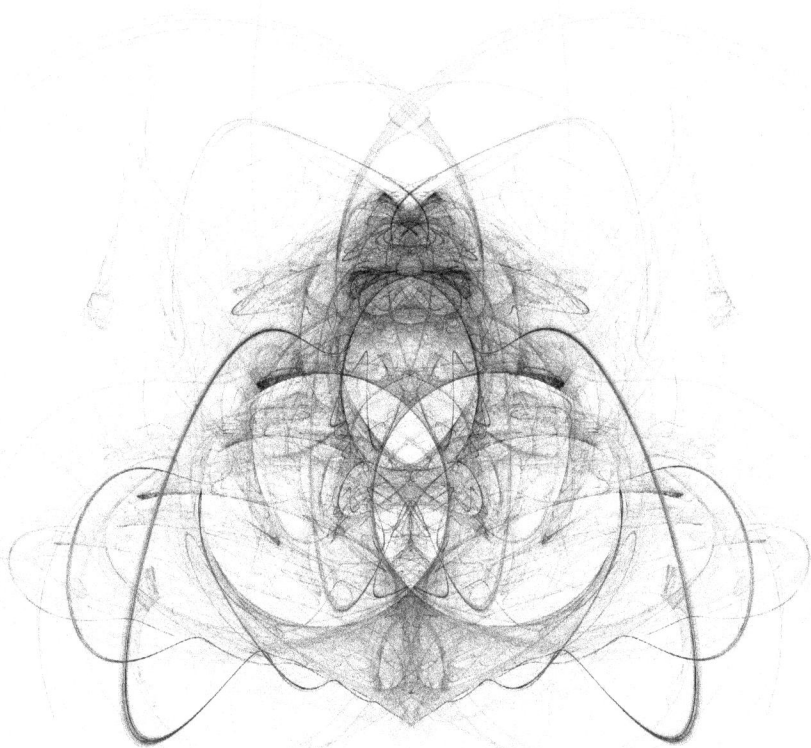

SUPER CHI

BASICS OF CHI

Chi is the life-force energy of the universe that resides in every living thing. Without chi, you could not exist, it's that simple. The more chi you have, the more energy you poses and the healthier you are. As we get older, we have less chi. We feel weaker, have less energy, and disease sets in. By expanding our chi we not only extend our life, but also our health and well-being.

Chi is like water, and water gives life. Imagine all the oceans of the world combined and available to us. We may take a cup a day, or even a bucket or a tub, but no matter what, the oceans of the world seem inexhaustible and we never run out. That is chi. It is limitless and available to all. And all may drink as much as they wish.

The ancient Chinese discovered that chi flows through our body through meridians. These meridians are like pipes, and can become clogged. This then restricts the amount of chi flowing through our body. No matter how much chi we want to flow through our bodies, our meridians restrict the flow and even limit the access in certain parts of our body. This is bad, because when our meridians are blocked off, the chi can not flow into that area of body. It becomes essentially a dead zone where disease can flourish. Aches, pains and restriction of movement also ensues, and in many cases we notice the first symptoms of an illness.

The best way to describe how our meridians get clogged is to imagine a raging river. As long as the river flows, stagnation cannot appear. That's because the water is always moving, bringing in new life as it runs its course. But tree branches or dead animals may fall into the river. And as they float down the river they may get stuck between the boulders. And as more tree branches float down, they can get entangled with other branches, and the next thing you know a dam is formed. This doesn't seem significant at first, but as the dam gets bigger it slowly diverts the river to run in different directions. Some areas may gather in small pools or swamps where the water becomes stagnant. Other areas become arid and dry as the water stops flowing in through them. The mighty river transforms into smaller streams with smaller aquatic life.   The larger the body of water, the larger the aquatic life it can support.

WHAT IS REAL HEALTH?

Most fitness enthusiasts focus on two things – our cardiovascular and muscular system. People think that good health depends on our heart, lungs, and muscles. We think that fitness is in the muscles. In other words, if you don't have six-pack abs, then you're not fit.

What they fail to take into account is that real health resides in the healthy functioning of our organs, like our kidneys, liver, gall bladder, small and big intestines, and so on. It doesn't matter if we can lift heavy weights or run marathons. If our internal organs are not functioning properly, then we're really unhealthy. And the added stress of making our bodies work harder will wear down and overheat our organs in the long run.

Many martial artists don't have slim and muscular bodies. Some of them look even fat or unfit. But they move extremely fast and are very agile. They focus more on the healthy functioning and even the correct placement of their internal organs. The reason why some of them have big bellies, is because they have learned to store chi in their Dan tien - energy center. It's like having an extra gas tank. They can be incredibly difficult to beat.

The body is made up of ELEVEN biological systems. They are the cardiovascular, digestive, endocrine, lymphatic, immune, muscular, nervous, reproductive, respiratory, skeletal, and urinary system. Each system is important and inter-dependent on each other. In other words, everything works holistically. The healthy running of each system depends on our organs and how they function. If one part of the system or organ is not functioning properly, then all eleven biological systems are thrown off. The system of the body is only as strong as its weakest link.

TWELVE PRIMARY CHANNELS AND TWO VESSELS

There are TWELVE primary channels or meridians and they correspond to the body's twelve primary energetic organs. This is a little difficult to understand. For example, the lung meridian is not only the chi that flows through the channel, but also the lungs itself. In the question of which came first – the chicken or the egg, it's the lung meridian or energy channel that existed first and then helped create the development of the lung.

In Super-Chi, if there is blockage in any of the meridians, I don't focus on the acupuncture points. Instead, I focus on certain Qigong exercises that help clear one or more meridians. For example, I may perform one Qigong exercise that focuses on the heart, spleen, and liver meridians. I then scan my client's body to get a sense where the blockage exist, because the chi is flowing along those channels.

The Qigong exercise will send chi flowing to those meridians. Remember the meridians are like pipes, and these pipes may be clogged up. Doing the Qigong movement is not going to completely unclog these blockages. It may take months or longer to accomplish. But because the chi is flowing along these channels, it will push the obstruction to the surface, so that it's easy to detect. It's like having part of the body light up or having it glow in the dark.

I then clear the energetic blockage using my healing techniques. I rescan the area to make sure it's cleared or I may repeat the Qigong exercise. When done properly, the client feels general relief, reduction of pain and tension, and more energy as the chi is able to flow. The organs associated with the meridians start functioning at healthier levels, which benefits the whole system. It's not just passively doing the Qigong exercises, but using them as diagnostic tools to bring rapid changes to the body. Otherwise you would have to see an acupuncturist or eastern medicine doctor.

Super Chi is very powerful. It is quick, painless, and very effective. I can treat all twelve meridians of the body, and when combined with Brain mapping, it becomes a very powerful system.

Lung Channel – coughing, asthma, allergies, skin problems, bronchitis, and fatigue. Blockages will show up in the front chest and upper back. I also focus on the tips of the thumbs of each hand, since this is where the lung channel starts. If there is a blockage here, it will appear at the tips of the thumbs clearing the whole channel. It's not necessary to check out each acupuncture point.

Large Intestine Channel – distended abdomen, constipation, or diarrhea. Look to the large intestine area and also the tip of each index finger.

Stomach Channel – mouth sores, nausea, or vomiting. Scan stomach and 2nd toes of each foot.

Spleen Channel – poor appetite, anemia, menstrual problems, chronic hepatitis, or fatigue. Spleen and big toes of each foot.

Heart Channel – heart palpitations or insomnia. Heart and inside tip of the little finger

Small Intestine Channel – vomiting or abdominal pain. Small intestine and tip of the little finger of each hand.

Bladder Channel – burning sensations when urinating or incontinence. Bladder and tip of each small toe.

Kidney Channel – backache, chronic ear problems, or chronic asthma. Kidneys and under each big toe.

Pericardium Channel – stress experienced as a tightening in the chest, or in a variety of breast problems. Heart and tip of the middle and ring finger

Triple Burner Channel – edema (water retention) or a stiff neck. Tip of each ring finger.

Gall Bladder Channel – bitter taste in one's mouth, nausea, or jaundice. Gall Bladder and tip of the 4th toe.

Liver Channel – high blood pressure, dizziness, pre-menstrual syndrome, muscle spasms, or eye problems. Liver and the top of each toe.

Governing Vessel and Conception Vessel – these circulate energy through all 12 channels. Tip of the coccyx and lips and eyes.

I have also found several blockages existing along the spine and neck cervical. Also in the back of the thighs. Generally, you scan the whole body because a blockage may exist everywhere, even outside of the body.

What causes these blockages in the first place?

It's estimated that 90% of all diseases are caused by excessive negative emotions. These are anger, joy, worry, grief, sadness, and fear or fright. The other 10% are genetic and environmental causes.

Anger

Connected to the liver and gall bladder meridians. Most common signs are poor vision, eye problems and brittle nails. Making poor or rash decisions. Indecision and timidity is also common.

The liver is responsible for harmonizing all emotions and overseeing the smooth flow of the entire body. Anger can easily spill and affect the spleen and stomach channels, as well lead to excessive emotional frustration or extreme and inappropriate mood changes.

Excessive Hysteria ~ Emotional High ~ Joy

Joy affects the small intestine, triple burner, and pericardium channels. Mostly it affects the head area like the tongue and facial complexion. Symptoms are muddled thinking, inappropriate laughing or crying, heart palpitations, insomnia, stiff neck, abdominal pain, and a feeling of tightness in the chest. It also causes a heavy heart, which means someone whose spirit is weak.

Worry

People who worry too much overthink things, and take little action doing things. They're not moving, and feel emotionally stuck or paralyzed. Worrying affects the stomach and spleen channels, resulting in poor digestion and stomach distention. People who worry too much usually have loss of appetite, and insomnia.

Sadness and Grief

Sadness and grief affect the lungs, large intestine, even the heart channels. Look to issues dealing with loss.

Fear and Fright

Fear and fright affect the kidney and bladder channels. This deals with water, which represents both flow and chaos. Looking to issues dealing with change and fear of chaos.

Since it deals with kidney channels and it's the kidneys that store reproductive energy, look to issues with the repressed fear of being pregnant and the responsibility of parenthood. Fear in young children creates bed-wetting issue as well.

Chapter XIX.

THE YIN YANG PARADOX

They say the body doesn't lie. And it's true. What is often overlooked is that the body determines what we can and cannot do. The body limits what we know, and don't know. In order to understand this, we have to understand the Yin/Yang Paradox.

EARS

They determine how much we learn and understand. We learn so much by listening to other people, because it offers viewpoints that differ from our own. We can't know everything, and there's always someone who knows more than we do. But, energetically speaking, when we fail to be able to listen or understand other people's opinions, then we become insular. We listen only to ourselves and to our own opinions. Because we block off all other information we become arrogant and believe our opinion is the only right opinion, despite mounting evidence to the contrary. Our Egos go on the defensive, fortifying our stance that we're right, and everyone else is wrong.

We only stay with friends who agree with us. We dismiss anyone else's opinion that contradict our own. Some people are so obtuse that they believe they can communicate with God, and not surprisingly, God listens and agrees with everything they say. People with blocked ears live in their own world. No one else understands them because no one can communicate with them. Their reasoning and logic is irrational. They have created deeply formed opinions about themselves that are unshakeable.

These deaf spots usually originate in childhood. Maybe as they were growing up, they felt people didn't listen to them, and so they figured why should they then listen to other people. Some of them may be considered slow learners, especially in school. They may get poor grades because they don't listen in class, which can lead to all sorts of problems later on in life.

Communication is another symptom of poor listening. Some of my clients don't know how to communicate or express themselves. Also reading and writing is affected. Because if you think about it, everything you read or write, you also listen to in your own voice. Sub-vocalization or moving your lips as you read is trying to make sense of what you're hearing. And if you're so focused on the sound of the words, then you're not paying attention to their meaning. It's like reading a book, but at the end of the chapter you don't know what you've read.

It's not that there's something wrong with the physiology of our ears. We may hear perfectly. Sound does not always translate into meaning. And without meaning we can't make sense of the world around us. It makes it more difficult to communicate, because we don't know how to request information we need, and have trouble hearing what is said and what it means. The tone and inflection of how people say things can display happiness, anger, sarcasm, or untruthfulness. Many of my clients have trouble telling the difference.

How do I deal with such people? Basically, I don't listen to them. Because most of what they say is wrong. And I've noticed that each time I did follow their advice, I usually ended up making bad decisions. And when I pointed this out to them, they became defensive saying they were not to blame. Just look at their lives. They're usually non-progressive and miserable. Seems their only purpose in life is to make other people as miserable as themselves. That way they're not alone, so they are eager for you to join their group.

EYES

We need to see where we're going or headed. Our vision provides us a picture of our goal that we want to achieve. Let's say you want to go from San Francisco to Los Angeles by car. You would first create a map detailing the routes including freeways to take. You could even measure the distance calculating if you drove 70 mph, how long the road trip would be.

But it's not as easy as that. Once you're on the freeway, road conditions could change. Sometimes you slow down, and sometimes you speed up, depending on traffic. Many times you'll change lanes or make pit stops to get gas or use the restroom. Weather also plays a factor. And so it's your eyes that help you adapt to changing conditions.

And that's the problem that some people have, when they set goals. They only have a vision of their end goal, thinking with plans well-laid out, things should run smoothly. It's just the changing road conditions of their journey that they need to be mindful of. As long as they keep a watchful eye and prepare for what's coming right around the corner, there will be less surprises. But often something can be staring us right in our face, and we still can't see. Why do we have blind spots?

NOSE

Our nose is in front of our face directly below our eyes. There's a jingle, "Follow your nose! It always knows!" There is actually more truth to that than we know.

The nose can lead us in the right direction, and help us choose the right people to achieve our goals. Where we point our nose is where we direct our face. And where we face, is usually where we go. The nose then directs our eyes and ears to help us focus on achieving our goals.

I knew this German restaurateur who started a very successful German restaurant. He wasn't very good in the business aspect of running his restaurant, but his one talent was picking the right people to help him run his business. It was the one talent he did have, and it saved him from bankruptcy. And same goes with picking the right investors to picking the right opportunities. You don't have to be savvy or smart. You just have to be lucky with making the right choices.

I've read dozens of books on luck. Not one of them mention smell. "Something smells fishy here! This doesn't smell right! The sweet smell of success!" The smell of fear smells sweet. I remember an old American Indian trick to tell which prisoner was guilty was to tie them over a gopher hole with their back covering the hole. They usually had two prisoners to cover two holes. They knew that gophers always created alternative escape routes just in case a snake wandered in. On the third hole they would build a fire to chase out whatever animal (could be a rabbit, a gopher, or a snake) was there. Animals are attracted to sweet scents and whichever prisoner had fear would exude that scent. The escaping animal would be claw at the back of the prisoner in order to escape the smoke, and that person was found to be the guilty party.

ARMS

We raise our arms to protect our face and chest – the most vulnerable parts of our body. We may throw punches to fight back. But if we raise our arms above our heads, then we're making ourselves totally vulnerable and defenseless. Energetically, this is what I see when people are having panic or anxiety attacks. Anxiety shows up in the solar plexus chakra, and fight shows up in the root chakra. Defense shows up in the forehead chakra, because it requires more thinking than reacting to protect ourselves.

Arms direct our hands that help us accomplish our goals. They're the workhorses of our body. Arms and hands take action and are directed by our eyes that give them feedback on how we're doing.

For example, let's say you tell the janitor to mop the floor. He hears you when you say "mop the floor", but when he does the mopping, he doesn't necessarily pay attention to his actions. He's just moving the mop back and forth in a zig zag fashion, with huge gaps in the middle – motion without direction.

If you're wondering why you haven't accomplished many of your goals, examine how you're using your arms. Just as you may not always listen with your ears or see with your eyes, you may not be able to direct your hands and your arms to do what you want them to do. Yes, you can lift your arms without thinking and those are simple tasks. The more complex tasks is figuring out the action steps to accomplish your goals. They can't be just any action steps. They have to be effective and efficient. And the more clear communication you have with your hands and arms, the more you will accomplish in your life.

HIPS AND LEGS

Hips direct where the legs will go. And legs determine how you move forward in life, or if you retreat from life, or just remain stuck where you stand.

Are you moving forward in life? Are you reaching towards your goals? If so, how fast are your legs moving? Are you moving gingerly, slowly but surely? Are you sidestepping some potholes along your way?

Are you retreating from life? Do you find yourself avoiding people or uncomfortable situations? If so, what are you afraid of? What are you running away from? What are you trying to avoid?

Do you find yourself stuck?   No matter how hard you try, you're not moving forward, but you're not moving backwards either.   You're still in the same place that you were years ago, and seem planted in one spot like a tree. Why can't you move?   Why are you not making progress?   Or maybe you're satisfied with the way things are, and if so, that's fine because it's your life.

These are the FIVE major body parts that determine how successful or limited we are in life. The blockages in each of these areas can change, depending on the issue we are challenged with. All five body parts connect and receive feedback with our brain, which is divided into seven intelligences. Information from the five major body parts constantly feeds our seven intelligences. Our brain then sends signals via the central nervous system to our five major boy parts.

Our bodies may be perfect physically. We hear well. We move well. We may not always see well, but glasses take care of that.

When I talk about blockages I'm talking about blockages that are energetic in nature. For example, if a client's ears are blocked, I see what looks like a huge cloud outside their ears. You can't see it with your physical eyes, but I can see a faint outline with my clairvoyance. If they're standing in front of me, I can pass my hands in front of their ears and feel a tingling sensation there. Sometimes the cloud is so huge that it pushes my hands back several feet, and then I know I'm dealing with a huge blockage.

It's the same with their eyes. I see a smaller but dense cloud in front of their eyes, blocking their vision. With their arms and legs it feels like there are heavy chains weighing down, or like ropes strapping them to their sides. Sometimes I feel a magnetic force pulling their arms or legs back. These are subtle sensations but with practice they can be detected. The difference with me is that I can sense my client's bodies at a distance. Years of practice have sharpened my clairvoyance.

In order to understand how we got here, we need to understand the Yin and Yang. What follows is my own interpretation.

THE YIN YANG PARADOX

Yin and Yang is a very popular Eastern symbol. It displays two circles, one black and one white, with a tail at each end. In the middle of each circle is a tiny dot – a white dot for the black circle, and a black dot for the white circle. And this is all encapsulated in a round circle.

Yin represents female, while Yang represents male. They do not represent positive and negative, because Yin and Yang have each both positive and negative aspects. That's right! Yin and Yang have both **positive and negative aspects**. When Yin becomes too large, it evolves to become Yang, and vice versa. Yin and Yang is the symbol of harmony of opposites with neither being stronger or weaker than the other. Instead, they need each other to evolve. As Yin becomes extreme, it gives in to Yang, and as Yang becomes too strong, it relinquishes control to Yin. Perfect harmony. Each borrowing from the other to evolve. Each needing the other to transform.

But ... what if this wasn't the case? What if Yin couldn't relinquish control to Yang and vice versa? What if we broke the Yin/Yang symbol apart in the middle, just at the boundary line between Yin and Yang? Then nothing would stop Yin or Yang from growing out of control. The harmony between Yin and Yang would become disharmonious. Chaos and disorder would reign! This is what I call, "the Yin/Yang Paradox."

THE YIN YANG OF THE SEVEN INTELLIGENCES

I've been studying the brain and the SEVEN intelligences for a couple of years. I've reviewed and researched them several times until I felt I understood them like the back of my hand. I've experimented with them with my clients, but always I felt something was missing.

Then one day I had a mental relapse. I had attended a mediumship class. I was never interested in talking with spirits as frankly it scares me. But I like to explore new things and decided to give it a try.

My partner was giving me a reading. At first it meant nothing to me until it dawned on me that she was channeling both my parents. I couldn't believe how this woman's first reading was so accurate. I was shocked. And then when the message of love was revealed from my mom, and it was a personal one, I almost lost it, because it brought me to my earliest memory of my mother with me. I kept fighting and resisting that this was a message from my mom. But all it did was make it worse.

It affected me all the way until I got home. I furiously did several clearings on myself throughout the night, but it had only gotten worse. I couldn't get to the core of the issue despite going through my seven intelligences.

Then it dawned on me that the brain is made up of TWO hemispheres – the right and the left. The right and left hemisphere were distinctly different from each other just like Yin and Yang. And they controlled the opposite sides of the body. Scanning the hemispheres energetically, I discovered that sometimes there were blockages either on the left or right hemisphere that were associated with each intelligence. And furthermore, that these blockages on each hemisphere corresponded to the side of the body they were connected to. Depending on which part of the body there was a blockage, I could then decipher the message the body was trying to tell me – where I was blocked and from receiving that information.

I remember in the 80's people would describe themselves as being Right-brain or Left-brain oriented. Most people wanted to be described as Right-brained, because it was associated with creativity and intuition. Being Left-brained was looked down upon, as being too analytical and less emotional.

We didn't know it at the time, but being too left or right brain made it impossible to accomplish certain tasks. It was almost impossible to solve our problems, because we kept getting the same answers over and over again. Insanity is defined when we keep doing the same things over and over again, with bad results. And no matter how many times we think it over and over, we keep getting the same answers. We can't get out of the box.

Both hemispheres see the same problem, but look at it with a different perspective. When we're too right-brain or left-brain, it's like covering one eye over the other. We see the object but not from a 3-D perspective. Energetically there's like a wall or curtain covering one hemisphere over the other. What this means is that we're getting the perspective from only one hemisphere and not the other. We need the perspective of the other hemisphere in order to help us understand and solve the problem.

When information can pass seamlessly between both hemispheres, then we're using our full brain power to the max. This synergism gets passed to our body parts which then send feedback to our hemispheres, in order to process and then command our body parts to make adjustments.

When there are blockages to our body parts sending feedback to our brain, then information becomes partial or incorrect. They become our blindspots, and it shows up in our life.

Brain mapping is deciphering the disharmony so that we can remove the blockages. It brings the Yin/Yang pieces together. The more closely connected they are, the more our life will flow.

Each brain map consists of a Yin and Yang brain map. For example, Logical, Musical, and Visual could be the Yang. And Linguistic, Musical, and Kinesthetic for the Yin. These are just examples.

There are SEVEN intelligences, but I only marked out THREE for either the Yin or Yang brain map. Why only three when there are seven intelligences? You start out with the strongest intelligence followed by 2nd strongest then 3d strongest. If you get your order right, the other 4 will automatically fall in line. You don't have to worry about them. The most important thing is to get the momentum.

The first example of Logical, Musical, and visual could be described as Yang or strong success. The 2nd example of Linguistic, Musical, and Kinesthetic could be Ying or Failure. Neither one is better than the other. We need to learn from failure in order to succeed. Too much success needs to be tempered with failure. The faster the transition between success and failure, the more it will minimize failure and help us gain greater success with proper balance.

In the first example of Logical, blockages can show up in the right or left hemisphere or both. Yin could best describe the right hemisphere, and Yang the left hemisphere. Let's say you have blockages on the right hemisphere (Yin), then the blockages will show up on the left side of the body. Then it would show that the right hemisphere with the logical side of your brain has become too enlarged and therefore overtook and suppressed the left hemisphere. Thereby you are missing crucial information from the left hemisphere, that could help you solve your problem. When the left and right hemisphere are balanced and the logical intelligence is able to get information from both, it creates a synergistic effect which is more powerful than either hemisphere separately. The two hemispheres connected harmoniously share each other's perspectives to create a third unique perspective.

Remember, with our eyes we have a vision of where we're going. But road conditions help us make adjustments with our arms and legs in controlling our car. Our ears help us get directions from our GPS or people. Our nose points us in the right direction. The shortest distance between A and B may be a straight line, but an airplane does not travel in a straight line, but is 90% in error. The airplane makes adjustments according to weather conditions and so on.

It's the harmony between the right and left hemisphere. And this shows up energetically in the body. Blockages are disharmony, and that's when we get stuck or run into problems we can't get ourselves out of. When we have harmony then we move faster, run harder, and act decisively and clearly. We begin to think with clarity, and our ability to learn exponentially increases, because we use all of our senses.

Chapter XX.

EFFERENT AND AFFERENT NERVES

Think about this for a minute. We all know people who talk and talk but don't take any action. And we know people who do stupid stunts without considering the consequences.

Some people talk a lot of game. They talk about their dreams and ambitions, and how they were going to conquer the world. It's not as if they didn't have talent or potential, because most do. Somehow life just didn't work out for them. They became a statistic and lived a normal ordinary life. Nothing wrong with that, except that they're unhappy.

And others do stupid stunts. They're reactive and impulsive. At the time, they don't consider the consequences of their actions or even the people they may hurt. They live in the moment and speak without thinking. And even though they've been sternly rebuked, they still do it over and over again. Seems like they never learn their lesson.

Now here's an exercise you can play with. Remember as a kid how you would spin around and round until you became dizzy and fell? I want you to spin in the middle of the room and have yourself timed how long you can spin. Make sure there's no furniture to crash into and that there's soft padding like carpet or pillows around you.

So? Did you last long? Or last only a few seconds before you had to stop or fell?

And once you did lose your balance, how long did it take you to recover? Did it take a while before the dizziness and lightheadedness vanished?

How you answer these questions tells me a lot about how you handle your energy. If you didn't last very long spinning, then it tells me that your system easily gets overwhelmed. And that you easily get off your balance. Spinning puts pressure on your body, and your body is very sensitive to energy. You may have big dreams, but how will you achieve success if you can't handle the pressure of implementing action to reach your goals? Or you may take action, but you haven't given it enough thought to create a strategic plan. In other words, you jump from the cliff without first taking a look at what's below. You could be diving into the ocean or hitting the ground without a parachute.

We all know people who talk and talk, but don't take any action.

And we know people who do stupid stunts without considering the consequences.

I became aware of two types of nerves – efferent and afferent nerves. Efferent nerves send signals to your brain on what to do, and then your brain send signals to your muscles to move. Afferent nerves send sensory feedback regarding how effective are your movements in accomplishing your task.

For example, let's say you see a juicy apple on the table, and you're hungry. The efferent nerves would send a signal to your brain for your arm to reach out to grab that apple. The afferent nerves would send feedback to your brain whether or not you were successful grabbing that apple. If you weren't successful, then the efferent nerves would send different commands and make adjustments to your movements. The afferent nerves would send confirmation the moment your fingers touch the apple. Mission accomplished.

When the efferent nerves are blocked, then we tend to overthink. Should we get the apple or not? Minutes can easily pass by as we debate the question. We get too much into our heads. We hesitate. We can stay stuck for eternity.

Talk but NO action.

When the afferent nerves are blocked, we do things without thinking beforehand. We commit a mindless action. It's repeating the same action over and over again, and even though it's not effective we still expect a different result each time. It's the very definition of stupidity.

Stupid acts NOT considering the consequences.

But when the efferent and afferent nerves are unblocked and flowing smoothly between each other, then it demonstrates our bodies can handle more energy. We become successful. We achieve results faster than the competition. Mistakes are minimized, and we learn our lessons quickly. There are few if any setbacks. We are constantly changing and feeling very energized.

So what blocks the efferent and afferent nerves?

The efferent and afferent nerves are the Yin and Yang of our nervous system. Efferent nerves are Yin (female), while afferent nerves are the Yang (male). When there are blockages, it means the Yin and Yang are spread apart. When they are together, our bodies can handle more energy and move more efficiently.

The first clue that I got of the Yin/Yang connection, was through my energetic scans of both myself and my clients. When the efferent nerves were blocked, I noticed there was a major blockage in my left heel while the afferent nerve blocks always seemed to stem on the right heel. The left heel and left side of the body controlled by my right hemisphere, and vice versa. The right brain deals primarily with emotion, impending doom, and fantasy images. While the left brain deals with more logic, ego, and action.

EFFERENT NERVES

Efferent nerves are blocked by high emotional states like grief or anger. People become emotionally stuck. They just keep reviewing past incidents over and over in their mind and then they plateau. They can't get over these events, and they're extremely upset over it.

Emotions overload their brain. Taking action overwhelms them. It's like they've build it up so much that it seems impossible to move forward, yet they still believe they can.

Efferent nerves work with the right hemisphere of the brain. When efferent nerves are blocked, you can be certain emotional tension is the cause. The right hemisphere deals with emotions, impending doom, and fantasy images. Impending doom makes any tasks or taking action too overwhelming to perform. It's simply too much. Fantasy images are generated when a person fantasizes how it will be when they've accomplished their dream. In their mind, their dreams become so big that they live as if in a fantasy land. They experience the same euphoria as if they are on cocaine. So the task either becomes too frightening to deal with, or they're too high to come down to earth.

Efferent nerves can also act as programs. For example, when such a person sees someone in distressed, they automatically lend them money. If someone needs a favor like painting their house or doing errands, they'll just volunteer without hesitation. They say "yes" before you even ask them.

This program was established when they were very young. As children, they were probably taught not to think of themselves, but to put family or others ahead of their needs. This program was then rewarded, affirmed or even punished if not complied with. Most of these people don't know themselves. They're confused, depressed, and very unhappy. They just live their lives for others and think that is their happiness.

I noticed a number of them as being extremely depressed and lonely. They may not have many friends. They become the target of manipulators who actively seek them out. Users pretend to be their friends in the beginning. Once they've gained their trust, the façade drops and it's all about serving them. People with blocked efferent nerves don't realize that they're being used, and may even defend the manipulator. Why? Because something deeper is at work here. It may be the first time in a long while that someone is paying any attention to them or even acting as their friend. And so they'll hold on to them, because it may be the only person that speaks with them.

Look for blockages on the left side of the body. Also an overactive heart chakra with connections to the ears. The ears deal with listening and taking direction, which influences the arms. Also an inhibited solar plexus chakra which creates an overactive forehead chakra. The solar plexus chakra deals with taking action, so if it is very small, it's difficult for the person to take action. An overactive and under-energized forehead chakra would mean a person is confused, overwhelmed, and unable to think.

AFFERENT NERVES

Afferent nerves deal with the left hemisphere. The left hemisphere deals with logic and illogic, Ego, and changing or suppressing of reality. When afferent nerves are blocked it's difficult to think logically or even think at all. Afferent nerves deals with mental and physical tension. Mostly people who can't deal with reality. When things are not working in their favor, the mental and physical stress becomes overwhelming for them, and they need to escape. Mostly addictions like drugs and gambling. Others have vices. They're running away. They can't handle stress. And they need immediate relief otherwise they'll pop. This leads to making bad decisions. This leads to dire circumstances. Blockages with afferent nerves show up on the right side of the body. Look for overactive root and solar plexus chakra. The overactive root would signify survival while the solar plexus chakra would signify impulsive or rash actions. If combined with the sex chakra then carnal desires and/or immediate gratification. Energetically the legs look as if they're sprinting or running signifying the person is in a hurry. Nose would be pointing in direction where they can satisfy their vices, and eyes would energetically be scanning the opportunities to fulfill these addictions.

The success and flow of the efferent and afferent nerves show up energetically in the ears, eyes, nose, arms/hands, and legs/feet.

EARS – deals with listening and learning. Sometimes I see the ears as big as an elephant's ear. If so that means the ears are very sensitive to what they hear. It can be connected to the heart where pleasant and rhyme tones can literally melt a person's heart and gained their trust. Or it can be connected to the root chakra where a harsh tone can make the person feel defensive or act aggressively.

EYES – deals with a vision of your goal. Also being observant and aware of what's going on as you pursue your goal so that you can make adjustments. It also tells the hands if they're doing things correctly.

People with blocked eyes energetically don't pay attention to what they're doing. And so they can commit mistake after mistake without realizing it. Because there's no feedback from the eyes or afferent nerves to the brain. Or they see what they want to see, and block the rest out.

Sometimes I see the eyes energetically watery which means they're experiencing great hurt and pain. They're truly suffering and look doe-eyed. It also signifies blurry vision so they don't see life realistically or accurately.

NOSE – because it's in front of the body it points the direction where the body will turn or go. When the nose is steady and pointing in one direction, it means there's great focus and commitment to get there. Sometimes I see energetically the nose turning back and forth which means the person is still deciding which direction they want to go.

The nose also sniffs for opportunities and the right people. And just like we can get a cold, sometimes I see the nose energetically congested. This usually deals with grief and motivates the person to resolve past transgressions or people they've hurt in the past. It's like they can't breathe right or get their life moving forward without resolving these conflicts.

ARMS AND HANDS – with arms I look at their position to the body. If the arms are raised and curved like they want to hug, then it means the person likes you. If the arms are immobile and by their sides it could mean they're waiting, no action, or if tense ready to lash out. If the arms are flailing in all directions, it demonstrates panic like "I don't know what to do!" or working mindlessly.

The hands are interesting. I look mainly if I see them clenched or relax. If the hands remain clenched energetically, then it means they're ready to fight. Sometimes they clenched and then unclench which signifies they're ready and prime but trying to relax. Unclenched fists means they're relax. Open palms means they're receptive and/or giving.

LEGS – my old gym teacher used to say, "just move your legs and your body will follow!" Legs take you places. Legs take you where you want to go. You need your legs to meet opportunity. Legs either move forward, move backwards or away (retreat out of fear and avoidance), or stayed anchored in one place. If I see the legs running, then that means the person is in a hurry. If it's kicking, then it's attacking or keeping away opportunity from approaching.

REFERENCE POINTS

In order to study anything, you need a point of reference or reference point. For example, if you're a carpenter you're point of reference would be a nail. Then you know where to direct the hammer. If you missed the nail, then you learn to angle your shots more accurately. With enough practice you'll be pounding nails without thinking.

Most people find developing their intuitive skills daunting because it's not something you can see or touch. Intuition is more of a sensation or feeling. Sometimes it's a sporadic image or a sense of knowing. That's why they always recommend you pay attention to your hunches no matter how slight they may be. It gives the mind a point of reference that it can later build on. Slowly like pounding that nail in the beginning your mind starts developing a foundation to build upon.

So these are my 3 reference points when I look at the 5 major body parts for scanning – faint, strong, and clarity.

Faint, very faint, and not detectable at all

Sometimes the signal is very faint. Faint means the signal is barely discernable but still you know it's there. Very faint means you can hear the signal but only if you concentrate silently. And finally there is "undetectable" where you can sense any signal at all.

With the ears the person doesn't want to hear what you have to say. They're blocking you out. Doesn't matter how many times you tell them, they're not willing to listen to what you have to say. Doesn't matter how much concern or worry you have for them it will fall under deaf ears. Actually they only listen to themselves and to people who agree with their view points.

With eyes, they can't see what they're doing. You could point out the mistakes they're making but they'll still think they're doing it perfectly. These people don't make progress. They stay stuck where they are. They don't improve. Many of them are very bitter feeling the world has conspired against them, and that they're being passed up for opportunities they should have gotten a long time ago. They're considered very slow.

With nose they're very naïve when dealing with people. It's like everyone is the same. They wander aimlessly in life. They have no sense where they want to go. They're like a leaf blowing in the wind.

With hands, they don't know what they're touching or doing. They have to be shown what to do all the time, and seem dependent on other people to help them out. They keep making stupid mistakes and get blamed a lot even if it's not their fault. They make very little progress, and tend to fall behind everyone else in line.

With legs, they're not sure where to go. They're like rocks in that unless someone picks up the rock and moves it, they'll still be there 10, 20, even 30 years later. They're not going anywhere soon. They're very predictable. They follow the same routine depending on the season.

Strong, very strong, and out-of-control/addiction

Strong could be one of these 3 emotions: anger, grief, and fear, but still in control. Very strong would mean ready to attack at any moment. And out-of-control/addiction means your vice has control of your mind and body. You can't stop and your whole life revolves around it.

With ears, sensitive to sounds, intonation, and words. Everything is amplified. A derogatory remark even softly said can break a person down. Messages are taken defensively even if the advice is trying to help. Imagine when an ambulance passes by. The loud siren gets your attention immediately, and you pull your car over to the side immediately.

Nose – strong acrid odor otherwise known as stink face. When you smell a strong odor, you automatically turn away. For example, Africa have periodic droughts. With the high heat sometimes animals finding the few remaining waterholes die of thirst before ever drinking the water. Their dead carcasses poison the water. Even though an antelope is dying of thirst, the smell of the foul water makes it turn its head at the last moment.

Arms/hands – I can see energetically the hands clenching and opening rapidly. There will be an attack either verbally or physically. And before the attack is done physically, there will be a verbal argument. A verbal argument doesn't mean there will be a physical attack because some people are too weak physically or don't know how to fight. But a physical attack unless the person is very relaxed is always preceded by a verbal confrontation.

Legs – always rushing or trying to get to one place as soon as possible. These people are very time-sensitive and want to achieve their goals as soon as possible. They meet deadlines. They burn candles around the clock. They don't know how to relax and take it easy. Seems like they could get a stroke any minute. They work overtime, and get other people to work overtime to meet their deadlines. Usually the strongest motivator is time is money, and they don't like to lose money.

Clarity, very clear, and crystal clear

With clarity comes strength but having strength doesn't always mean you have clarity. This is the state where you want to be. It's the peak zone where Yin and Yang flow seamlessly with each other. If it's not clear, then you either have faint or strong. The blockages will show up in the body. The 3 levels is just to determine the intensity so you know exactly what you're dealing with.

Ears – hear instructions and knows exactly what to do. Depending on clarity or crystal clear the person may need the person to repeat instructions or ask questions to clarify. It doesn't matter as the person is very reliable and knows what to do.

Eyes – very clear goal-setting and actions steps. This person is able to handle and take care of all types of problems independently and effectively. Extremely aware of what's going on and emergencies are solved before they even occur. Learns along the job, and makes very fast progress.

Nose – luck follows this person wherever they go. They know when opportunity is knocking at their feet, and they respond immediately. They can read people and know immediately if it's someone they can trust or not. They always happen to be in the right place at the right time.

Arms/hands – works very fast, efficient, and effective. They get the job done ahead of schedule. They're considered extremely talented and skilled. They rise up to the top of the ladder of success before anyone else.

Legs/feet – first ones there. Always at the right place at the right time. They're very difficult to catch up with. They never stay in one place too long because they're always moving.

Chapter XXI.

THE A, B and C'S

One of the best ways to understand a person's true nature is to observe them when they're having a crisis moment. When a person is having financial difficulty, sudden and unexpected responsibility, or a difficult problem to solve, how does this person react? What do they do? How do they handle things? Do they get upset and start yelling at everybody? Do they get physical and start throwing things or abusing people? Does it seem they act more out of immaturity rather than responsibility?

The biggest tell-tale sign that I look for is how they breathe or don't breathe. Some report tightness in their chest. Others report they feel they're having a heart attack. It can be so serious that they'll either call the ambulance or make an emergency run to the hospital to have their hearts checked out. Thankfully their heart condition is normal, but at the time they believed they were going to have a heart attack.

I'm not down-playing their hysteria. Panic attacks are serious and should never be taken lightly. Anxiety can be physically crippling, and can last for hours. But what causes such anxiety or difficulty in breathing? What I've noticed with some of my clients is that when they come across a situation they can't handle, they stop breathing.

Some stop breathing or hold their breath on the spot. Some breathe shallow, and so don't bring enough oxygen to their body. The body is thrown into a panic and the brain goes into survival. We go from being conscious to unconscious in a matter of seconds. Instead of responding, we go into being reactive.

Not breathing properly sets off a chain reaction of physical and mental tension. It feels as if you're trapped in a corner. You just want to escape. It's difficult if not impossible to think of a solution. You just want to get out! Or if it's a financial crisis – you just want it to disappear or make it happen! You may call up your friends for loans, shift responsibility to someone else to solve, or even rob a bank.

I've seen and experience this many times with my clients. The more desperate a person becomes, the more desperately they will believe anything. And that's when the person makes the worst mistakes in their life. They will persuade their victims with the most desperate pleas for help. They will tell you stories so sad it will make you cry!

Remember when I wrote that the biggest tell-tale sign was in your breathing. At first I thought this was caused by restriction around your chest that kept your lungs from expanding. Clairvoyantly it looked like a boa constrictor wrapped from the front of your chest to your upper back.   There were also energy blockages along your diaphragm. And after clearing those areas, the client was able to breathe more easily and eventually relax.

This didn't stop them from having future panic attacks, but it provided them with a great temporary relief for the moment. And so I investigated further.

There are FIVE different breath patterns:

1) paradoxical or reverse breathing,

2) hypoxic breathing or holding your breath,

3) over-breathing or hyperventilation,

4) no-haler or not inhaling or exhaling fully, and

5) code-red or the startle response which is the body's instinctive way of preparing for whatever happens next.

I discovered that when people suddenly go into survival over-drive, and they are looking for the quickest and easiest solution, they are in no-haler breathing pattern. This type of breathing causes the lungs to constrict. Most people feel it as an elephant sitting on their chest. The mind shuts down and screams to get this elephant off! This is the "disconnect".

The "disconnect" is where you go into panic mode. When you were in school, you learned your ABC's. A follows B follows C. That's irrefutable. But people experiencing a *disconnect* – their reasoning goes from A, skips B and goes to C.

A is the idea of what they want. B is the means of making it happen. C is the natural conclusion or outcome. If C doesn't meet or match A, then there's something wrong with B. C gives you the feedback of whether you meet the conditions of A. B is the means to fulfilling A. ABC – simple!

But people with the breathing pattern of "no-Haler", their reasoning process goes from ABC to A-C. For example, let's say a husband wants to take a trip to visit his family. The wife is the one responsible for paying the bills, and budgeting the family's finances. The problem is that they're on a tight budget barely keeping up with the bills. The husband insists they go on this family trip, because it's important to see his family. Even when the wife explains there's no extra money, the husband says it doesn't matter. This family trip is important, and they just have to make it happen. No Excuses! So the wife scrambles where she'll get the extra money or take out a loan. The husband just sees what he wants, and that it's going to happen - A to C. The wife who is afraid of her husband's temper just wants to get along, and so finds the means of making it happen-B. In the future, this can obviously put the family finances in jeopardy, but for the moment the sea is once again calm before the next storms comes.

This is a prime example of A-C and victim B. Both deal with the no-haler breathing pattern but differently. The difference lies with which nostril is energetically blocked. This makes a difference, as the right nostril is controlled by the left hemisphere, and vice versa. And although each hemisphere perceives the same event, it relates to it in a different perspective. The right hemisphere sees it in an emotional manner – either impending doom or fantasy, while the left hemisphere sees it in terms of Ego, deletion and changing details, and changing the outcome. A-C sees it from the left hemisphere, while B sees it from the right hemisphere. The blockages from both A-C and B also show up differently in the body, which I"ll explain in this chapter. It's just another example of Yin/Yang, and what happens when they're separated. In this case, we had an example of a couple. But there are also single people who are A-C and B.

A ~ C TYPE PEOPLE

A-C type are people who can state what they want, and then jump ahead demanding that it happens as they envision it. They don't know the means and expect or even demand of people they're involved with to make it happen. It's like the supervisor at your workplace barking out orders. They walk around and notice all the things wrong, but have no understanding or even any inclination to discover the cause of such mishaps. All they know is that they see something they don't like, and then they want it immediately fixed. They don't like to be challenged, and their position gives them the authority to act self-righteous. Yet in their defense, they feel they're only doing what's right, and should not be blamed.

The blockages show up mainly in the right nostril. It's not a physical blockage as they can breathe normally, but during times of stress and crisis the right nostril becomes more difficult to breathe into while inhaling. They go into no-haler. This creates tension in the lungs, sternum, and diaphragm. It's subtle and very unconscious. But these are the main areas I clear to get the client to immediately relax and clear.

Blockages with the right nostril are associated with mental and physical tension. The right side is the male side of the body. The masculine side shows up as anger, force, and Ego when it doesn't get its way. It bulldozes its way forward, oblivious to who it hurts or damages. The masculine side is also associated with getting things done and being fearless. That's why it needs to be tempered with the feminine side to balance it out.

Clearing the right nostril needs to be done firstly because it has a dramatic reduction on tension in the body. After the right nostril is cleared, then we can focus on the other body parts that are blocked. The right nostril, in the beginning, needs to be cleared repeatedly usually for several days. Why? Because how you breathe affects how you think and feel. Your breathing affects the functions of your entire body, even your digestion. When you can't breathe properly, you can't function. Breathing controls awareness. It controls how you think. In this case the left hemisphere becomes dominant and out-of-control.

Blockages show up mainly in the right eye and right ear. Clairvoyantly, there's a giant screen in front of the right eye. A-C type of person only see this giant screen in front of them. The picture captures what they desire most. It may even have writing on it. It floats in front of them 24/7 creating urgency and obsession. The closer the image is floating in front of their right eye, the harder it is to ignore. And so they see only what they want, and the only way to relieve themselves from this image, is to have it done.

Blockages in the right ear prevents them from listening to other people. That's why talking to them is like talking to a blank wall. A-C type of person is listening, but only to themselves. If what you're saying doesn't match what they tell themselves, then they tune it out.

Right leg or both legs look like they're running. That's why A-C act as if they're in a hurry. The legs convey the sense of urgency they feel. Nose points in the right direction, but the right eye is so blinded by the images that it doesn't see the obstacles in the way. That's why A-C charges forward like a tank rolling into whatever gets in its way. And the hands look clenched and tight, ready to fight whoever gets in their way.

When you can't handle something, you stop breathing. Then you feel the tension – the mental and physical tension. The tension reaches its peak, and you just want to escape. The left brain -your logic- is shut down, and it becomes difficult to think of a solution. You just think, "Just make it happen!". This is the disconnect. You don't connect with what you did to create it. All sense of reasoning temporarily leaves you. You don't think – you react!

The left hemisphere goes into denial of responsibility, and deletes details from your mind, that would help you solve the problem. "Let's just make it happen without regard to ABC – just A-C. You see the problem, jumping into desired a outcome without dealing with the means or how-to, because physical and mental tensions are too much to handle. You need to escape by taking the easiest route, which is not the best or correct route to take.

You need time to think thoroughly weighing the pros and cons. This needs to be done repeatedly going over more details. Unfortunately, the tension builds up to the point that we can't handle it. With repeated experience A-C becomes a mental habit that we automatically flow into without conscious thought. It then becomes part of our identity, and then we really become difficult to live with.

The solution is to remove the tension, rest, and then replenish your energy. The quickest way to clear the tension is through gentle neck rolls, nods and shoulder rolls. I know it sounds basic, but if you don't have the time to stretch or are not inclined to do yoga, five minutes will do the trick. If you can get a massage, that's even better.

Drinking water provides immediate balance and stress relief to your body. Most of us are dehydrated. After the neck rolls some people immediately fall asleep. The body needs rest. Sleep restores brain functioning. And for rejuvenation, Qigong can restore your chi or life force energy. Yes, eating organic foods helps a lot, but Qigong restores and balances your chi like no other.

B TYPE PEOPLE

B type of people breathe through their left nostril, which is influenced by their right hemisphere. The tension B people experience is emotional rather than physical and mental. And so mostly the heart chakra and the front and back solar plexus chakra (between the kidneys) are affected.

During crisis, the heart chakra becomes extremely large or overactive. When this happens the person becomes extremely sensitive and vulnerable. They feel emotional pain as if they're being tortured.   There may be no physical scars, but the emotional scars run deeper and last longer. The perpetrator can be a parent, a friend, or your partner. And the trauma can last for the rest of your life. And that's why B type people rather comply with A-C demands just to stop the suffering.

The front and back of solar plexus chakra deals with anxiety, adrenaline, and action. The heart chakra experiencing emotional pain and sensitivity creates anxiety through the solar plexus chakra. This can result in panic attacks or anxiety disorders. The back solar plexus creates adrenal fatigue over time further weakening the will of the person, making them susceptible to manipulation and control of A-C type. In other words, they feel too weak and fatigued to fight back. It's easier to give in. You've already lost the battle if you're too tired to even begin.

The emotional pain weakens you 24/7. It's very difficult to think straight. And even if you do think clearly, handling the truth in your mind is not the same as handling the truth in practical terms. The left nostril needs to be cleared so that emotional relief can come. Blockage in the left eye also needs to be repeatedly cleared, as it is blocking seeing the situation for what it is. The left eye is connected to the heart, which makes you see things emotionally. The left ear also needs to be cleared. The left ear makes you sensitive to A-C's harsh tones and words. The left ear connects to the root chakra, which emotionally and physically affects your sense of security and survival. That's why B people become co-dependent with A-C people.

Clairvoyantly, there's an energetic hook on B's nose from A-C. It's like what they do in the circus with bears. They place a ring in the bear's nose, understanding the nose is the most sensitive part of the bear. It's inhumane but it works. The bear will follow the owner wherever he goes as they're being led by the nose. It doesn't matter that the bear can easily maul the owner. The nose is like the heart chakra.

The arms of B look like puppet arms controlled by strings. I know lots of clients who just do as they're told without thinking. They're so conditioned. Getting out of this kind of relationship can be both difficult and complicated. Especially when you have children and other family members involved. The greatest deterrent is being alone.

Getting a pet makes a great companion. Making new friends opens new worlds. Focusing on a hobby creates a great sense of accomplishment and self-esteem.

A ~ C and B TYPE

A-C type of people have a "disconnect" of how the world works. Sometimes it happens, but most of the time it doesn't. They tend to live in their own world, which makes sense only to them and very few others. They live by the seat-of-their pants.

B type gets things done, but doesn't need direction on where to go. They need to identify their desires and what makes them happy. They tend to be depressed and mentally confused, as taking control is not something they're used to.

UNITING A ~ C and B

The first step is to unite A-C and B. Yin and Yang must connect together and flow seamlessly between each other. This can be accomplish through structured breathing, and creating a list of twenty things you want in your life right now.

If you pay attention, you will notice that many elderly people walk with their mouths open. They feel they need to breathe-in more, as they don't feel enough oxygen going through their body. Actually, the opposite is true. It's not that they don't have enough oxygen, but it's that their level of nitric oxide is too low.

Nitric oxide is essential in releasing oxygen into the blood stream. There are whole books on this subject, and I'll only go into it briefly. People become more reactive, the less oxygen goes into their brain. Less oxygen creates mental fog.

The first and easiest exercise to practice, is to learn to inhale and exhale through your nostrils. Breathing through your nostrils not only warms the air for your lungs, but also filters it. You also exhale more slowly creating a more calm but steady tempo. Breathing through your mouth brings in cold air and releases oxygen too quickly.

Learn to breathe not just with your diaphragm, but with your whole body. Breathe deeply down to your toes, and slowly exhale. The rhythm should be like a pendulum flowing back and forth without suspension or tension. And then after an exhale, hold your breath by pinching your nose. Hold your breath until you feel the urge to breathe again and then let go. Do not strain yourself holding your breath – that would be counterproductive. It would defeat the whole purpose of this exercise.

Just hold your breath until you feel the urge to take another breath – that's all. Then let go and breathe normally through your nose until you reach your natural pace. And then start the exercise again. Repeat about three to five times.

As you feel more comfortable holding your breath and learn to relax, you will find yourself able to hold your breath longer. This will take time, but be patient. Being able to hold your breath longer will increase your attention span. With a longer attention span you will be able to hold your thoughts longer. Instead of your thoughts fleeing from your mind, you will be able to focus and analyze them better. You won't react out of fear or impulse. You will be in control. And this will give you an advantage over the other person who breaths too rapidly.

You will start to notice things you didn't notice before. One of the first things that will improve is that you'll start thinking more logically. And then notice that most people think and say things illogically. It'll be funny. And when you confront these people with their illogic, you'll notice they don't know how to respond. Because they can't find a way out of their illogic.

The second exercise I recommend is to write twenty things you want in your life right now. Not yesterday or tomorrow, but right now. The first time you do this list you may find it difficult to think of twenty things you want now. And they have to be specific things. For example, you can't say you just want money. What specifically would you do with the money? What would you buy? If your answer is that you would pay your bills, then I would ask you "Would that make you happy or just provide relief?"

If it's a car, what model? What color? Describe the interior and options you would want. Did you choose the car because it's in fashion? Or to make yourself more important? If you're taking the car off the road, then you need a more rugged truck or SUV to handle the terrain. It can't be something you're worried about getting dirty or scratched.

Continue to refine your list, as this is important. Each time you refine your list, you're building awareness of what's really important to you. You're getting to know yourself and what really makes you happy. I've discovered that people who don't know what they want, feel mentally confused and depressed. They are the ones having the hardest time writing out their list. In the beginning they may write one or three items, before beginning to experience mental anguish. Writing these lists will bring up intense feelings, but in time this will improve.

Neck rolls and nods are simple and very effective. How many hours do you spend each day in front of your computer? You need to release tension in your neck and shoulders. Qigong is also very simple and easy to perform taking anywhere from 10-30 minutes practice. Breathing through your nose will relax you, clarify your thinking, and give you energy. And writing your list of twenty things that you want now, will both increase your personal awareness and self-identity.

PART SIX

OUR SUBTLE PATTERNS

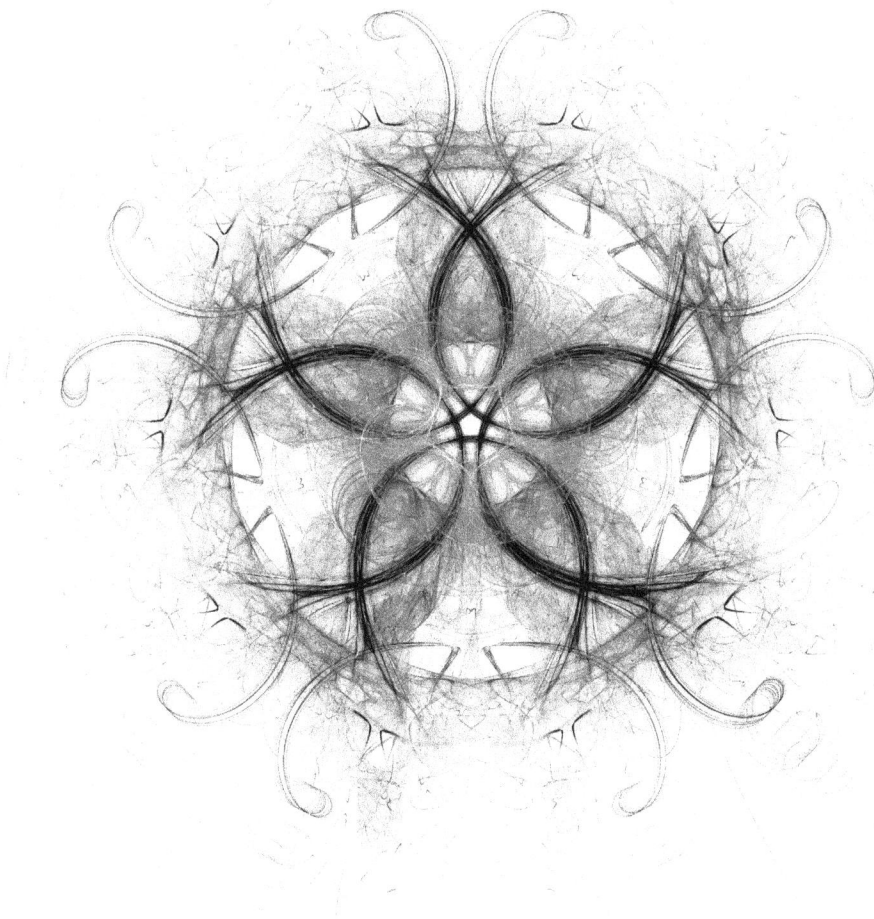

Chapter XXII.

BEHAVIORAL PATTERNS
AND TRIGGERS

Why does it seem impossible to make changes or self-improvements to ourselves? Why do we keep repeating the same habits and behaviors over and over again? We are so consistent with our habits that we're predictable. People read us. They know how we think, how we act, and our blind spots with such precision, that they also know how to manipulate and exploit us. And even when we think we know better, we fall into the same trap over and over again.

I read an article which said that conmen will scam the same victims over and over again. It's because they know their victims well. It's not that they're the most intelligent, but they notice patterns of behavior. They understand what our emotional triggers are. And during those moments the victims become unconscious. The victims go into a state of reverie, where they become flooded by a deluge of mixed emotions. It's almost a cathartic experience except there's no resolution. And some stay in this abyss of emotional soup, floating endlessly in time. They don't change. They don't progress. They try, but they don't know what to do. They search for a solution, but everything they've tried doesn't work.

I've searched endlessly for solutions. I've studied everything – NLP, hypnosis, and countless healing modalities. It's only when I studied the brain and science and started to combine it with my skills as an energetic healer, that I finally felt I understood the **structure of change**. And it made sense. What I discovered was different from anything I had studied previously.

What I learned is that change is not impossible. It can feel as if you're banging your head against the wall or that you're chained to the floor. But every lock has a key that opens it. Use the wrong key or the wrong approach, and you'll be chained forever.

First thing you need to understand is Neurology 101. Our brain is made of cells called neurons. The brain is made up of trillions of neurons. Each neuron cell has branches extending from it called dendrites. And so each neuron looks like a tree. The trunk is the neuron cell and the branches are the dendrites. Our neurons reach out to other neurons through a network of dendrites. Every time we have a thought or an emotional experience, our neurons form connections or neural pathway that create memories. From these memories we form learning experiences so that in the future we will know how to act during similar experiences.

Imagine that you walked from one village to a nearby village every day. Back and forth you walked the same way again and again. Overtime, a path develops as you step on the same rocks and plants. The ground becomes bare, and it becomes easier to recognize the same pathway. Overtime, more people (neurons) may follow the same road and each time it becomes easier and faster to follow.

There's nothing wrong with following this path. It gets you from town A to town B and back to town A. It's established, but it doesn't mean it's the best way or even the safest way. It's just a way.

But what if the road gets flooded? What if there's bandits along the road waiting to rob you? What are you going to do? What if you know of no other way to get to the next town? Then you would take your chances, and follow the same road as before, because you knew it well, and it's traditional - a habit. And to be challenged to find or use another route may be considered hierarchy.

It's the same with our habits. Our habits may be the first roads we established in our brain to go from point A to point B. It doesn't mean it was the best solution at the time, but it was all we knew during that time. In other words, we did the best we could with what we had. And once that habit of that pathway was established, it became the preferred route to take. It doesn't matter whether it's the wrong behavior, or if it brings about wrong results, it's what we do automatically. It becomes the way our brains are wired.

And it's because our brains are wired this way, we react to the same or similar experiences the same way. It's almost as if we can't help it. This can lead to repeating the same negative experiences over and over again. It's like being on a Merry-go-round. We keep revolving round and round, but we're still in the same place. We may want to get off, but it's hard to get off when the Merry-go-round keeps moving, and doesn't seem to ever stop.

It's the way our brains are wired. Our brains are shaped by our earliest childhood experiences. The things we experience, and the things we are taught lay the track roads in our mind. They basically establish how we think and act, and that is why our behavior is so automated. Our brains are wired to habits, because early on in our ancestry we couldn't survive without our survival instincts. Out in the jungle the difference between living and dying is just a matter of seconds. We don't always have time to think. We have to react, sometimes in seconds. The problem is that often our reactions are not the best responses to follow, but it's what we did in the past. And that becomes the established pattern.

When a client comes to me with a problem they're not able to resolve, I first ask them to describe the problem or experience. I don't need the whole story, otherwise the whole session will be used up. Usually a minute or two is more than sufficient. I need to get an energetic read, and when they start describing their situation to me, things start lighting up.

We could be on the phone and yet I can sense their body and body parts. I first check out if their eyes or ears blocked. Everything starts out with their eyes and ears, because it's where information enters their brain and gives them feedback. But if no information is going through, then how can they know where they're going?

Look at the parable of the five blind men touching different parts of an elephant. One blind man holding the tail described the elephant as one big rope. The other blind man touching the trunk said the elephant was like a wall. Another blind man touching the nose said the elephant was like a hose.

Another said the ears were like the leaf of a giant plant. And finally the fifth blind man said the legs of the elephant were like the trunk of the tree. All were correct, and yet all of them were wrong. It's when you combine the descriptions of all five blind men, that you can get a more complete and accurate picture.

The five blind men are the FIVE body parts of your body – eyes, ears, nose, arms, and legs. Each gives you a more complete picture of what's going on. When all five body parts are open and functioning perfectly, then you're functioning with great mental clarity. When they're blocked, then you're more prone to making mistakes, feeling limited, and running around in circles. Your behavior becomes automated so much so, that you do things without thinking, even though it brings disastrous results. You can't help it. You follow the road track, even though it leads to the cliff where you each time fall off.

What precedes every behavioral pattern is a trigger. It could be a sound, smell, or something you see. But each is associated with a memory or experience.

EYES – something you see or don't want to see. Notice how children close their eyes when they don't want to see something or simply turn their heads away.

- Sometimes I see a cloud like a mask covering one's eyes. There could be a billboard in front of them, and yet they couldn't even read the writing. You'll see signs of this where they don't know where they're going, or seem to be wandering and idling around.

- Sometimes there's a big movie screen in front of a person's eyes. No matter which way they turn, this dominant image blocks their view. For example, some people create conspiracy theories to explain why they're not so successful in life or why they always have back luck. Mostly, these people feel they have no control over their lives. Look for blockages in the left hemisphere connected to arms and legs. The arms would explain that they don't know what to do, and the legs where to go for the right opportunity.

- If the movie screen appears internally in the brain, then it's usually the right brain. The right brain deals with images of impending doom or fantasy images, that they take as reality. Look for blockages in the diaphragm, disruptive breathing patterns, and tightness in the chest or upper back.

EARS – I remember my nephew when he was little and when he was scolded by his parents, he would clamp his ears with his hands while shaking his head violently back and forth.

- "I don't want to listen to what you're saying!" We tune out what we don't want to hear or can't handle. Look to breathing patterns of "No-haler", and hyperventilation. Both will create tremendous levels of anxiety and panic. It may feel as if the emotional walls are caving in, and the person will go into fight or flight.

- "I can't understand what you're saying!" No energy in the root chakra, low energy or depression, blockages along the spine, and overactive forehead chakra. The Ajna chakra that is dealing with will and focus, looks blown apart. You will know it, because the client is trying their best to understand, but all efforts are futile. They have a look of panic and despair like a deer in headlights. Long pauses in breathing where breath is held. Similar to when a gambler places a large bet and holds their breath. It's like through sheer force of will, you can influence the outcome of the cards.

- "I can't hear what you're saying!" It feels like an out-of-body experience. Your body is here, but your soul is not. Your mind simply floated away, and you're not present. This happens mostly during school, when you're listening to either a boring lecture or can't understand the subject.

Because you have to sit there in your chair sometimes for hours, your mind wanders away to more pleasant pastures.

NOSE – children evaluate things through the air. They're enticed with the aromas they smell. Smell is how they mapped out the world, and so all memories are associated with smell. A dog knows when his owner is coming home, because they can smell them. A dog smells the particles of air and how it differs during the morning when their master leaves for work, and during the evening when they return.

- "Do you have a nose for direction?" Some people know just where to go. This has to do with the magnetic points on the earth.

- We map out our entire world through scent, and each scent carries a vibrational signature. "The sweet smell of success" or "Something smells fishy here." We are attracted to some scents and repulsed by others. What smells good to us may not smell good to others and vice versa. Scents are connected to memories and the emotions associated with them. My point is that we may be attracting the wrong people into our life, because of how they smell. It's not that we want to be attracted to these sort of people, but that we've developed a neural pathway in our brain that we're most familiar with. People, things, and circumstances smell a certain way. They all carry a vibrational signature that either attracts us or repels us. We are led by our nose.

- Our nose is connected to our legs and feet, because they lead us to our destination. Clairvoyantly the toes look to me like bloodhounds, smelling the ground and where they point, the legs follow. And they get their direction from the nose, which looks for familiar scents.

- Scents are strongly connected to either pleasant memories, or trauma. If it is an unresolved trauma, then the subconscious mind will seek out people and circumstances, as a way of bringing it up to a person's attention, in order to resolve it. It's the same with success and prosperity. You can smell if something smells like opportunity.

- Smell is the strongest motivating force. We are literally drawn to certain people and events. Look to scanning the adrenals for over-activation. The more activated the adrenals, the greater the arousal for excitement. The magnetic vortex in the second-sex chakra will also be activated. The legs and feet will look as if they're running, and the rate of breathing will be more rapid.

ARMS AND HANDS – the arms and hands deal with spatial awareness and orientation. When we want something, we reach out and grab it. If we really like it then we don't let go.

- We explore through our hands and touch. We learn through our hands and touch. Touching and using our hands send massive amounts of information to our brain, and our brains grow exponentially because of it. Clairvoyantly, the fingers look as if they're sniffing, licking, and feeling everything about the task or object. The fingers have little brains, and they're learning. That's why doing activities with our hands, especially activities developing ambidexterity, increase brain functioning.

- Look for hand-eye coordination. If there is a lack of hand-eye coordination the blockages will appear energetically in the left or right eye. Blockages in the left eye deal with emotions, and the right eye deals with changes and action. There could also be an energetic cloud covering both eyes, so even though a person can see physically well, their brains are not able to process the visual information.

LEGS AND FEET – Children run for fun. They run to their parents or people they love. And they also run away from things that frighten them.

- Legs determine where you go. Blockages in the legs show up mostly in the hips. The hips direct where the body will follow. The hips are also connected to the root chakra, an indicator of safety and security. It will avoid anything the subconscious perceives as danger. But if the person is drawn to danger, then look at blockages in the musical section of the brain. Musical intelligence deals with discerning the truth, and if something doesn't sound right, then the person can't do it. But when musical intelligence is blocked, then the person is prone to believing the lie, and doing things even though they know it is not right to do them.

- Some people have a knack for walking in the wrong place at the wrong time. You could say that bad luck follows you, but it was you who walked into that situation or place. Clairvoyantly, the nose looks like it's actively searching, extending from a few feet to several miles. The toes have little noses checking if the place smells right. The toes and nose coordinate together and it's what we're attracted to, for good or bad. That's why some people seem to always be in the right place at the time, while others in the wrong place at the wrong time.

There are three main things that keep people from changing: 1) the reptilian brain, 2) unresolved trauma, and 3) fears that are masking an even deeper fear.

REPTILIAN BRAIN

The reptilian brain is the oldest portion of our brain. It's our lizard brain that works on instinct and automatic behavior. For example, practice catching a ball, and soon it becomes second nature. The reptilian brain can automatically adjust to the speed, velocity, and distance of the ball being hurled at you, no matter the environment. It makes those calculations in micro-seconds. All done without thinking.

When you're under stress, it reacts instinctively. It goes into the first patterns or behavior wired into your brain. And these first patterns were wired during childhood. So even though we are adults, we may still act as children.

It's like water. Water seeks the easiest path, and the easiest path is usually the first path we established. The more stressed we become, the more we jump automatically into old patterns or routines. That's why we are so easy to predict and get taken advantage of. Like catching the ball without thinking, we follow the same behavior without thinking. It doesn't matter that this behavior leads to dire circumstances. When we're stressed, we feel unsafe. We just want to escape to the nearest exit.

The mind will avoid anything it perceives as unsafe. Anything the mind perceives as risky, it won't do. The mind will shut down the body, and the body will stop sending feedback to the brain. Our mental clarity gets increasingly reduced, until we're just reactive. It's a downward spiral that can continue as we get older. That is why people get crazier as they get older.

THE SUBCONSCIOUS

The subconscious is also based on safety and well-being. One of its main functions is to make sure we are always safe. The subconscious mind cannot discern the difference between something real or imagined, and will obsess about anything that poses as a threat.

We will be attracted to experience the same early childhood traumas in our adult life. That's why children who were sexually molested often become prostitutes. Men who didn't have close relationships with their mothers, have a difficult time bonding with the opposite sex.

The subconscious mind will attract to us similar circumstances as a way of bringing it to our attention, so that we can finally resolve it. You know the adage, "You can't run away from your problems". The greater the trauma, the more you will be led by your nose to those same situations. In some cases, it can be trans-generational like the adage, "The sins of the father are passed to the son" or "The apple doesn't fall far from the tree."

A FEAR OR INSECURITY MASKING ANOTHER FEAR OR INSECURITY

This was the biggest discovery I made, and I believe the biggest deterrent to change. Some issues are just too difficult to even touch. Some issues go against all rationale. For example, my teacher talked about a case where this woman was dying of cancer. The first healing treatments looked promising, and she was getting better. When the woman realized she was healing, she immediately stopped all healing treatments. When asked why, she responded that for the first time in her marriage her husband was showing real genuine care and concern. She had never been visited by so many friends and relatives telling her how much they loved her. She then admitted that if she got better, then she risked losing everyones love. Death was a small price to pay for receiving the attention she so desperately craved.

What we think is our real fear or insecurity may not be so. What we think is the real reason for avoiding things, may not be the actual reason, because even when we resolve it, nothing changes. We may have slayed the dragon, but we haven't slayed the beast.

It's like going to a Halloween party. We put on a mask to hide our identity. But sometimes when we remove the first mask, there is a second mask underneath to prevent our face from being seen. What we tell people as our reason sounds good, but is not our real intention. It's just a façade within a façade.

Our actions and behavior are just a mask, hiding our real intentions. Its job is to distract us from knowing the real truth that we're keeping secret. And we protect it with all our might, because its revelation exposes our deepest vulnerability.

It's the insecurity that we've been avoiding all our life. It was born out of our deepest despair and survival. It manipulates us, and is exploited by the people who know us the best – usually family. And we will go to great lengths to avoid dealing with it. Even the mere clue that we're coming close to it, will send us running scared.

Because of this, it is the deepest and earliest program wired into our brain. It has been running so long that we associate it as "our identity." But that's an illusion. It's not our identity. It's what we project to people, and people associate it with us. Some people have a stake in helping maintain this self-identity, so that they can continue to exploit us for their personal gain.

But it can be cleared. The first step is clearing the body and mind of tension. The body is the repository of all the tension we feel from our negative outcomes.

Clear the body parts of tension, so that it can feed the brain with proper feedback. We learn through our body, because our body tests reality. Restore the body's chi with proper nutrition, exercise, such as yoga and Qigong), and get proper rest. This is just the first part, and what most wellness programs do. Learn about the second and third part in the next two chapters.

Chapter XXIII.

BLOCKAGES

The brain is fed by the body. The body gives feedback to the brain and gives it information, so that the brain can understand how it's executing its orders to the body. For example, picking up a glass of water. The eyes give feedback to the brain on how far the glass of water is. The hand touches the glass. The fingers grip the glass. Through your grip, the fingers know how hard to grip the glass and carry it to your mouth. All of this is relayed to the brain in nano-seconds. We take it for granted, because it's a simple chore we do every day.

If the table where the glass of water is sitting on is far, then we walk towards the table with our legs - we are moving toward opportunity. Once we're close enough, then we extend our arms to reach for the glass - activity for accomplishment. Our breathing provides the oxygen and energy to do our tasks - awareness and being present. Our ears detect and alert us if anyone is close by. Maybe someone is sounding the alarm that it's their glass of water or that It shouldn't be touched - we are learning from others and our environment. Finally, through depth perception, our eyes help us gauge the distance of the glass of water from us - observation and feedback. And when we drink from the glass of water, we know our task is accomplished. The brain is satisfied, and our body's thirst feels quenched.

Okay. If life was this easy, nothing would be complicated.

So let's complicate some things.

You see the glass of water sitting on the table. Even though you are thirsty, you hesitate because you're afraid you'll be caught drinking someone else's water. Maybe that glass of water was meant for someone else or you weren't supposed to touch it.

You may see someone sitting across the table from that glass of water. Suddenly your attention is not on that glass of water, but on that person. You're looking at them, and they're starting back at you. A thousand things may be going through your mind, and you're not exactly sure what that person is thinking of. A thousand scenarios may be flooding your mind at the moment, most of them negative, but you're not sure which one is true.

The simple solution would be, to ask if you can drink the glass of water or if it's theirs. You hear the response of this person in your head, even though you didn't ask them the question. The response you hear in your mind is negative or you hear yourself telling yourself negative messages, why you shouldn't touch that glass of water.

Your breathing becomes labored or you sense slight hyperventilation. You don't notice it because your heart seems to skip a beat. Your breathing affects your heart rate, which affects your respiration rate. Your body may feel slightly hot and tense at the moment.

Your arms want to reach out for that glass of water, but somehow they don't seem to obey. Usually your arms coordinate with your legs and you just walk over and reach for it, but this time is different. Even if the glass of water was two feet away from you, you'll still find it hard to reach for, as your mind is telling you not to.

Finally you turn around and walk in the opposite direction. Your thirst is overcome by the need to retreat and get away. You're in fight or flight mode. The more distance you can put between that glass of water and the person sitting across the table, the sooner relief will come.

Once you're at a safe distance, you start relaxing. The negative self-talk and the negative visual images in your mind start to die down. Your muscles begin to relax, and breathing becomes easier with each step you take. You begin to regain full control over your body, and your mind starts thinking of alternatives, where and how you can quench your thirst.

This scenario may seem overdramatic to some people, and others they may connect with it. But let's say you don't connect or get my point. Is this any different than someone returning back to college after twenty years, and questioning their ability to learn new subject or memorize new things? Or starting a new business that has the potential of making you a lot of money, except that you may have to put your house and savings as collateral? How about looking for a new partner and relationship after being married for twenty years and freshly divorced? Do you question your dating skills? Do you worry how you may be looking older, and not as attractive as before?

Picking up a glass of water may be a simple and easy task. Our mind and the mixed messages we give it, get relayed back to our body. And our body works under direct messages, not mixed.

A mixed message is like a tug-of-war between two teams. A mixed message is composed of : "Should I, or shouldn't I? "

This is what I call "confusion" or "inner conflicts". Each body part is confused about what to do. Or to add to the confusion, the body part shuts down, refusing to give information to the brain. Without this information, the brain will be unable to make decisions or may make incomplete or incorrect decisions.

Frustration, anger, and disappointment build up while creating a major mental block. It's like building a wall. As time passes along, this wall becomes thicker and stronger, making it more impossible to climb over. This deviates us from our path or prevents us from accomplishing certain tasks. We may even need to take a detour that is out of the way. Instead of going through the Panama Canal, we have to travel 8,000 miles around the tip of South America.

In order to understand how to clear this confusion or inner conflicts, we have to understand how our brain works. We need to understand the Seven Intelligences in great detail, and the differences between the left and right hemisphere. Because although each hemisphere gets the same information, how it processes and perceives this information is different and unique. The hemispheres are like conjoined twins. Each twin has its own separate personality, likes and dislikes. They do have to move together, but they have separate opinions. And when they disagree or if one twin wants to go left, while the other wants to go right, they end up nowhere. The brain is like that. There must be total congruence between the left and right hemisphere, as there must be congruence between the right and left sides of the body. Feedback and information must flow from the body to the brain, so that the brain has complete information and is able to relay the correct commands to the body, in order to achieve results. Harmony, abundant energy, and mental clarity is also the by-product.

So let's look into the hemisphere.

BLOCKAGES in the left hemisphere of the brain are associated with memory, ego, and illogic.

MEMORY

Let us imagine the left brain is the Producer being given a documentary (memory) to be released in movie theaters. The documentary has already been filmed in real-time, or as events took place. What you see is what you get.

But as a Producer you're responsible for making sure that the documentary will make money at the box office. You're responsible for the audience liking the movie, and if it sells well, then maybe it'll be up for a nomination.

The problem is that the documentary is boring or not to the producer's liking. And so he brings the footage into the editing room, and they cut out certain scenes in the documentary that seem to be a waste of time. Maybe there's not enough drama or exciting scenes and so he calls in a new director to add new scenes, maybe a couple of fight scenes and some interesting dialogue between characters.

But the ending doesn't stand out. So the producer changes the ending. Like any good story we need it to build to a climax, and then have a good resolution to help release tension and make the audience feel good.

What ends up is a movie, not a documentary. Reality is sometimes boring and too long. Not enough twists and turns. The good guy always has to triumph over evil. But as long as it is what the audience (self) wants, we're happy.

EGO

"I'm never wrong!" "It's not my fault." "Don't blame Me!"

Most people who are charged with crimes plead innocent because there's always a chance that they might get away with it. And if they admit that they're guilty, then you have something to stick them with, and the punishment will be swift and direct.

Even if the crime or mistake was small, people still don't like to admit it. Because when you admit your mistakes no matter how small, you suddenly judged. Maybe the other person thinks you're stupid for making that mistake. Instead of honoring you for admitting and taking responsibility for that mistake, they hang it over your head each time they see you. Sadly, it's not the person who admits their mistakes, but the person who knows how to get away with it, that often moves ahead.

It's almost like protecting your child. No one likes to hear how bad their child is. In this case, our Ego is our inner child. And Mother Bear will protect her cubs when they feel they're in danger.

ILLOGIC

Reasons, excuses, and rationalizing

logic – the ability to reason correctly

illogic – the ability to reason incorrectly

People make up different versions of the truth. Some still argue that the earth is flat and not round. And they can back it up with a plethora of evidence. Some of it is even compelling.

The Earth is round!

When I come across people who don't make sense, I tend to avoid them and not listen to them. I tend to not argue with them. And most of all, I tend to not believe them. Why? Because they're not thinking correctly. And that means that everything they say or most of it is wrong.

People who are illogical tend to make a lot of mistakes in their lives. They tend to be stuck or not making progress. They're like rocks that if you place a rock on the ground and no move it, chances are it'll be in the exact same place you left it ten years or even a hundred years later.

People who are illogical are hard to talk with. They don't listen to anyone else no matter how clear and articulate you are. No matter how persuasive your argument is, they'll dismiss it. It's because energetically their ears are blocked. They can't hear you, because they've tuned you out.

So if their ears are blocked, then who do they listen to? Themselves! They listen to their own inner dialogue. Some talk to imaginary friends or even God. Not a surprise, but God agrees to everything they say to themselves.

The ears need to be energetically open, so that new information from the world and people can pass through. Then the critical mind can decide whether to accept it or not. The world is a reality with its own set of rules and boundaries. In order to live successfully in this world, we need to know those rules and what those boundaries are. Otherwise we'll get in trouble. A child needs to be taught by his parents what is right and wrong, otherwise the child can be destructive and not function when he grows up.

If a child grows up not listening and learning from their elders, then it won't listen as an adult. They will function with a logic that doesn't always fit with reality or this world. They will make up their own reality and it will make sense only to them. They will live in their own world with its own rules and boundaries. Other people may not understand their reality because it doesn't make sense, and they can't read minds. Trying to reason with them is futile, because unless it's something they agree with, they dismiss you.

It's also hard for illogical people to change, because doing so means they'll have to alter their reality. One tell-tale sign is, that you'll find them laughing at their own jokes.

We have now described the left hemisphere. Blockages will show up in one or more of the Seven Intelligences. These are the descriptions of how they may appear.

Intrapersonal – they are able to generate lots of ideas, this is why their logic is right. They tend to think and talk fast. Most of their ideas don't make sense, and so they're hoping to confuse you or that one of their ideas will stick.

Interpersonal – they use their interpersonal skills to their advantage. Because they have great social skills, they're very persuasive. They also know how to demean, shame, and manipulate you.

Linguistic – people with linguistic skills know how to talk. They can throw words as if they're throwing knives at your body. They may not be physical wounds, but mental and emotion scars are more lethal and longer-lasting.

Logical – people with the ability to reason or think clearly. They may sound persuasive, and they usually believe in what they're saying. But that doesn't make them right.

Musical – they have a tendency to believe their own lies and not the truth. Everything that they do is wrong or they make constant mistakes. And the more mistakes they make, the more reasons they have why things went wrong, and it's not their fault.

Kinesthetic – their bodies are always so tense. They are never relaxed or feeling comfortable. Look for low energy or lethargy. Some of them like to spend time in the gym, because it's the only place where they can let go of steam, but once away from the gym, they're in constant anxiety. They also are ready to fight verbally, physically or both.

Visual – they see images in their own movie with them as the star, the hero, but never the villain. They wear a suit of Teflon so nothing sticks to them. They're invulnerable, and perfect in their eyes.

Blockages in the right brain are associated with CGI (computer-graphic images) and Impending Doom

Computer-Graphic images or CGI – nowadays in the movies you can create computer generated images of anything you want. The limit is your imagination, and that's the key word. It doesn't mean the images have any connection to reality. I consider images in the right brain akin to dreaming or dreams. The thing is, you only dream at night. But if you dream during the day, then it's called imagination. And like dreams, these images are embellishments or fantasies of what you would like to create in your life.

Between the right and left hemisphere sometimes lies a veil or a curtain separating the two. Whole-brain learning and thinking is not just when you use both sides of your brain, but also when each hemisphere can communicate with the other. The more rapidly you can do this, the more processing is generated. But when a person is thinking predominantly with one hemisphere, then that hemisphere tends to take over most of the person's thinking. In this case, the right hemisphere can generate fantasy images that the person can be quite addicted to and even obsessed with.

This happens a lot nowadays, especially with online dating. You meet someone online, but they live in a foreign country so it's not like you can hop in your car and meet with them. They have an interesting profile, usually worldly, successful, and rich. They post pictures of themselves at work, at play, working out, and so on. They're very attractive. The one thing in common is, that these are all images that the right brain gravitates to, and creates fantasies or dreaming.

Because that person is faraway and you want to meet them but can't, the right brain fills in that void, by creating a fantasy experience in your mind. Energetically, I see a cloud in front of my client's face on the left eye. Their minds look blank and off to a distance. It looks as if they're floating, because their feet don't touch the ground, and the arms lay by their side. They're living in another world. You can almost see a giant movie screen in front of their face, while they're smiling and laughing at this imaginary relationship they have with this person. You know they're in this space, because they can't help but talk about this person and this imaginary relationship. But for them it's very real, and it's very serious.

You almost don't want to be this voice of reason, because doing so would pop their fantasy bubble that is not real. They don't know enough about the person, and most likely haven't met them in person. But if they do, then they've generated so much CGI that will stay there, until the reality of knowing the person personally, sets in.

Impending Doom – possible catastrophes, doom and gloom predictions, conspiracy theories, end-of-the-world scenarios

Impending doom is like CGI, but instead of being more of fantasy images, the images are filled with horror, disaster, and death. The images are so scary and real, that it can paralyze a person with fright. It's like being in your own horror-fiction movie. Like CGI, impending doom can structure the way you think, feel, and act.

And at some point, the tension becomes so much, that you must act on it in order to relieve some of the tension generated in your body and mind. It can't go on forever without ending soon. That's why you see a lot of so-called prophets make predictions when the world is going to end, and it's usually during their life time. It's never a hundred years from now or after they die, because then you don't have to worry. Nope, it has to be coming soon, because the word is "**Impending Doom**" and not "**Future Doom!**"

Impending doom puts people in 24-hr survival. They'll be in one or more of the five stages of survival – fight, flight, frozen, fainting, or laughing-it-off. Ever notice that evil villains tend to have that evil laugh?

Fight – constantly agitated, negative, and argumentative

Flight – running away, sometimes to faraway locations to escape

Frozen – given up on life, because what does it matter if disaster going to happen

Fainting – can't function in this world, don't know what to do

Laugh-It-Off – "I'm taking over the World!"

Intrapersonal – if it's CGI, they'll tend to have stories of how they'll meet that person or make their dreams come true. They have all sorts of ideas of how they'll make it happen, and how it'll be. Some of them will happily share their fantasies with you.

If it's impending doom, then they'll have a list of escape routes. You may find them at the library or trolling through the internet, gathering more information and resources, just in case.

Interpersonal – if it's CGI, they've told all their friends of their dreams or of this person. They're usually very nice and sociable and many people feel close to them. This gives them the opportunity to ask for loans, because they've probably spent most of their money making their fantasies come true.

If it's impending doom, then they will gather people or join groups that believe in their causes. They want to feel safe and be supported. They can't stand alone or be a one-man army.

Linguistic – if it's CGI, they're very persuasive, and they sound optimistic. Because they seem to be so happy, you want to be happy too. And so you may want to join them and help them make their dream come true, so that you can be part of the action.

If it's impending doom, they may be in an orator position like a preacher or a speech maker. Maybe they write books on the subject and have a following.

Logical – if it's CGI, and it's a person they're in love with, then they'll express how they've found their perfect soul mate. They'll explain why they're so happy, and how the sacrifices they'll make to be with this person are all worth it. But all the reasons will be based on love.

If it's impending doom, then they'll explain all the signs showing up in the world to prove, that what they believe is really coming true. But they'll see the signs everywhere they look and connect dots where there are no dots to connect.

Musical – CGI you'll find them in imaginary self-talk, where they'll hear all the wonderful things they want to hear. And they will repeat them like recordings. Like a broken record their self-talk will never get to the end, but will repeat again to the beginning. In that way, the fantasy never ends or has an ending point.

Impending Doom – same thing as the above but negative and scary.

Simply, blockages in either hemisphere are distortions of what's true. The problem is that you can be 90% wrong, and only 10% right but you'll focus on the 10% that is right and dismiss the rest.

In order to accommodate these distortions, certain parts of the body will either shut-off, or not relay the information to your brain. That's why people can stay in the same pattern for years without changing, and not know about it. Everything seems normal, because they're blocking information that would tell them otherwise.

Until it's too late. The body will try to warn the mind through aches and pains at first. The body will also try to get the mind's attention, and if that doesn't work, then a stronger message of disease will occur. It's hard to decipher these messages, because it's a language we're unfamiliar with.

But through detecting the blockages in the hemispheres and scanning the blockages in the body, we can see the connection and remove these blocks, so that clear communication exists through the brain and body. That's why I created Brain Mapping.

PART SEVEN

THE MULTIPLE~SELVES SYSTEM

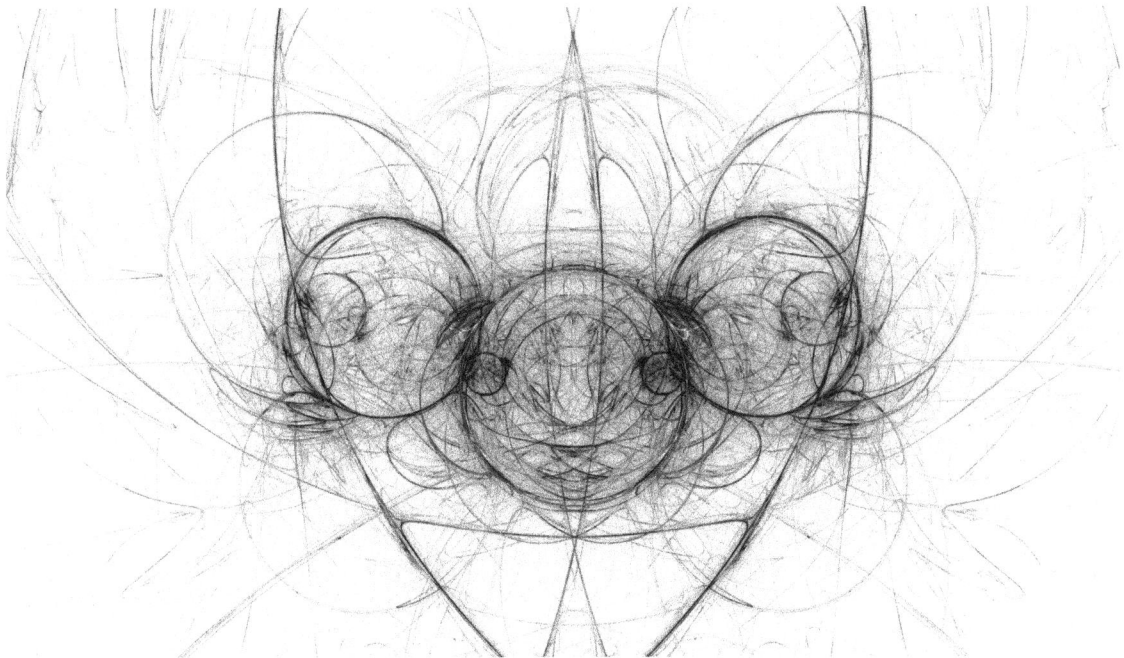

Chapter XXIV.

THE MULTIPLE-SELVES HEALING SYSTEM

Long ago I started reading a book about the 5-elements and how it related to emotional trauma. The theory was, that residing in each of us lies a Guardian. Whenever we experienced emotional trauma that we couldn't handle at the time, the Guardian would store these inner conflicts in different parts of our body. This was done so that every time we experienced trauma, we wouldn't shut down. This wise Guardian would store these negative memories in our bodies for safe keepings o that at a later time, we could resolve them.

But as the years went by, we've forgotten about these past problems and went on with our life. It was never the Guardian's intention to forget our past, and so over the years, the Guardian continued to stuff our negative memories into our body parts, until eventually there was no more room. As our arms and legs were filling up we started to numb ourselves, because the tension in these areas became painful. We quickly learned that if we stoped breathing into these body parts, then we would feel them less. But it also meant that these body parts became dead in a way, as they stopped feeding our brains.

As more misinformation was being sent to our hemispheres, our thinking process became corrupt. We began making wrong decisions in our life. It became harder to learn new things, and our ability to remember started to fail. Our mental clarity was rapidly diminishing.

Nowadays we have smart pills and brain programs to help keep our brains sharp and active. I don't use any of those. I was trained in a different way. At the time I didn't know that this would make me smarter. I just wanted to clear my emotional issues, and keep them from affecting my life. But it makes sense that our emotions cloud our judgement. Not that I'm trying to ignore them. Instead, I try to address them, so that I don't repeatedly traumatize myself by reliving them. And the first part requires me to clear away these bodily tensions, where the Guardian has stored all my painful emotions.

I then connect the dots to which hemisphere they're connected to. This rapidly clears up my thinking. My mental clarity increases, because I'm less triggered. Each time I get triggered, it's like my mind focuses on something from the past and I'm distracted from what's happening in the present. Each time I get triggered, I experience a flood of old memories and past emotions, many of them I don't understand or remember. It could be an event when I was five years old or younger, but I don't remember it. But my body does, and automatically I'm transported back to that time.

It's really puzzling. As I've learned to quiet myself within, I became aware of old audio tapes being replayed 24/7. Old audio tapes where my mom scolded me as a child are replayed over and over, like a broken record. I see mental movies of my childhood – some imagined and some real – they are playing as if I'm in an old movie house, that I can't escape from. My body would not know they're not happening in real-time, and react as if it was. Sometimes it would affect my moods, and I would react negatively to people. But there's no reason or basis for it. I was reacting to ghosts from my past. I think we all do. And slowly it starts breaking us down.

I remember my great friend, Sylvan, who was a mental health practitioner. One day he gave me a tour of the facility where he worked. The patients there looked like ordinary people I see in my neighborhood, except they were walking around like zombies, probably due to their medication.

Sylvan told me that at one time they were my neighbors, and they led ordinary but uneventful lives. Then one day they couldn't function normally, and they had to be institutionalized. The mind can only take so much before it cracks. If the mind doesn't crack, then it's the body through disease. It was a scary thought, but it reminded me of the Guardian in Chinese philosophy. Now everything made sense.

I know my mom had a very difficult childhood. She raised me with the same iron-hand rule that her parents raised her with. It wasn't her fault. It was just the way children were brought up during that time, as it was passed down through the generations. My mom confided in me her childhood nightmares, and how they still haunted her to her last dying day. I couldn't help her because my mom was too close to me, but it did help me to understand and forgive her. And from then on, we set the inspiration to finally end this generational curse.

In the 80's I came across a book about a new type of therapy. It was based on Freud's model that there were THREE major parts of ourselves – the ID, EGO, and SUPER EGO. Some say Freud borrowed this from the Hawaiian philosophy of Huna. But in this therapy, three chairs were placed in front of a patient. Each chair represented a different aspect of their inner child. One chair represented themselves when they were a child, another as an adult, and the third as a parent. The client would state the issue they were working through and sit in one of the three chairs, and give the perspective of each of their three personalities. They would ask the viewpoint of themselves as either a child, adult, or parent. The feedback they received gave them different perspectives, and together helped them to understand themselves more completely.

The multiple-selves system is far more advanced, faster, and thorough. It contends that there aren't just three parts of ourselves that need addressing, but unlimited numbers. This is what makes resolving our emotional issues so complicated and yet so fascinating at the same time.

The multiple-selves could be at varying ages, each reviewing the same issue from that stage of their life. They could also have a dozen mixed emotions from each age, but each separate and valid in its own right. For example, an event can be viewed from a five-year old perspective. Some of your multiple-selves are angry, vengeful, sad, happy, and even joyful. Some are feeling weak while others are feeling strong. That's why resolving our issues is so complicated. Sometimes we feel we've resolved them, only to later have them haunt us again.

Let's say we have 30 multiple-selves connected to a single trauma. It's like having 30 different personalities, all arguing with each other, because their view points of the issue are so contrasting. The healing is done energetically, they are placed in a bee hive where I'm using my honey bee technique energetically.

The honey bee technique is simply imagining that the multiple-selves are in the center of a bee hive. They're surrounded with the buzzing sound of the bees, which has a healing and calming effect. I then invite the multiple-selves to enter the center of the hive. I present each multiple-selves with TWO questions – "What do you need", and "How can I make you happy?" My higher self then showers them with images that address these TWO questions. That's it.

As these multiple-selves get what they need and become happy, they start melding with other multiple-selves, because they are a part of each other. 30 multiple-selves become 20, and as they continue to meld, they become stronger until they finally form one energetic self. If left alone, the process can take 2-3 days, and by that time the client feels as if the issue has disappeared. If I witness the process myself, it can take 15-30 mins. It goes faster because I'm not only witnessing the process, but giving the client feedback of what I see. But some clients don't have the time and so they just want it to be automatically resolved for them.

The multiple-selves healing system is done purely on an intuitive level. At the time of this writing, it has evolved over 20 years of practice. It was the first modality that I ever created. It came about, when I attended a workshop, "Crystal Past-Life Regression." It was the first time I attended a workshop of that kind, and I was a bit curious.

All I remember was, that I was laying on the floor with several crystals placed on top of me. There was a script read out loud, and at the end, the teacher tapped a "C" tuning fork. I was automatically transported to a past life where I was a very powerful Egyptian healer. I remember my teacher saying that whatever you were in a past life that you can download those same abilities and skills. This would explain child prodigies displaying amazing talent and mastery at such a young age.

Later I returned home from the retreat and was working with a client. During our session I started seeing little children in my mind's eye, and they were relaying messages to me. At first I wasn't sure what to make of it but as I audited these messages to my client she remarked that they were her childhood secrets only she knew as a child.

Then something magically happened. I noticed these little children were working and playing with one another. At first I thought I could direct them to the issues my client needed work on, but straightforward they said it was none of my business. They wanted to be left alone, and needed no direction from me. it was the most important lesson I learned because there was no way I could understand all aspects of my client's issue, but her multiple-selves knew. I learned from then on that I was just the facilitator, and not the healer. My job was to set up the right environment that was supportive for them, and then let them do their business. It was really that simple. From then on the system has continued to evolved and get better.

But the multiple-selves is only done in the end. It's imperative that the body and brain hemispheres be cleared first. Otherwise these blockages will act as anchor points, and the residual energy will manifest again re-infecting the multiple-selves. With the body and brain patterns cleared, there is less resistance and the healing is streamlined.

I believe that every illness whether mental or physical is a result of emotional disturbance. This is the heart of what I call, "Compass Energetics".

Chapter XXV.

THE 5 PRINCIPLE MOTIVATIONS

They say that in order to understand someone, you need to understand their needs and wants. Sounds simple, but for me, it's not that simple. In each of us there exist unseen forces that influence, limit us, and drive us to make unwise decisions.

These unseen forces that control us are what I call our "motivations" or "lack of motivations". And there are FIVE types. If you understand these FIVE types, then not only will you better understand yourself, but you will understand what makes other people tick.

LACK OF MOTIVATION

1. You lack interest in starting a project.

2. You may feel the task is beyond you. You lack the skills, confidence, and ability to get the project done.

3. You don't have the energy to finish the project once you've started or can't get started at all, because you're always too tired.

Lack of interest in the project - that depends on which of the SEVEN Intelligences are the strongest in you

* **Intrapersonal** – this person requires a lot of solitary space or alone time. Feels more comfortable with books than with people. You'll find this person more comfortable in a library, either public or their own personal library, or trolling through the internet. They're very creative and innovative, as they combine different sources of related or unrelated information and piece them together like a jigsaw puzzle. These people like to work on projects on their own. They need a lot of privacy. They don't like to be disturbed as they're spending their time doing a lot of deep thinking.

- **Interpersonal** – as much as intrapersonal people are comfortable with books, interpersonal people prefer the company of people. They're approachable, friendly, and have greet social skills. They know lots of people and are very active in social media like Facebook. Actually Facebook seems to be made for them as they're great networkers. They have a rolodex of people they know, to help them figure any out problem, or if they need assistance with something. They function best in groups, and hate doing things alone.

- **Linguistic** – they need to write everything down. They function best when they can read the material. In that way, they can review as many times needed to get a clear understanding. Some of them like to talk things out loud or have someone listen to them, as they recant all they've learned. This helps them clear their minds, and as they express themselves, they listen to what they're saying and gain new insights. They need people to act as their sounding board. If there isn't anyone around, they will journal it.

- **Logical** – these people won't be interested in any project, unless it makes sense to them. If they're presented with a project and there's no rhythm or rhyme to it, then they won't do it. Because for them it's meaningless and stupid. The way to entice them is with projects that appeal to their intellectual capacity. They strive on mental challenges.

- **Musical** – they need to hear the truth of a project, otherwise they won't do it. They need to know it's important and align themselves with a worthy project like saving the planet and so on. They need to feel their efforts have a purpose, and that it's the right thing to do. If it doesn't feel right or it's a lie, then they won't align themselves with it.

- **Kinesthetic** – kinesthetic people like movement. They always need to move their body. The worst thing you can do to them is enclose them in a small space or office. They best function outside or in different locations other than their homes. They can function in a coffee shop, because it's a different location than what they're used to. They can be around people, because people move, and they like movement. Anything that restricts their movement in any way will make them go nuts. They need projects that demand physical action. Projects dealing with the physical body, like learning anatomy or working out, because they look at it as their own body.

- **Visual** – visual people need maps, drawings, or pictures. They need to have clear and precise mental images of the project, where they can project it to the future and be guided. These mental images keep them motivated when all hope seems lost.

SELF-DOUBTS AND LACK OF CONFIDENCE

Some people feel they are not up to the task or that it's too much for them to handle. They may cite lack of experience, getting easily frustrated and wanting to give up, or just not being able to handle the small details.

Energetically there are blockages in the eyes and ears. Because of blockages in the ears it is very difficult for them to listen to other people's advice or instruction. You can talk to them till you're blue in the face, and they still won't hear you. That's because they listen to their own self-talk which is usually very negative.

Their eyes are energetically blocked. Clairvoyantly I see huge movie screens either in front of their face or behind their eyeballs. These movie screens play movies of impending doom or why things won't work. This rules their lives, and they believe it in with all sincerity, to be true and forthcoming. And these movies are played 24/7.

I'm feeling too tired! I don't have the energy to begin anything!
Just leave me alone!

If you leave a rock on the side of the road and no one moves it, it'll still be there. Some people are like rocks in that they stay the same as they grow older.

Their root chakra, which is the chakra that controls physical vitality, is depleted. The Mein meng which controls the adrenals and blood pressure is very overactive and can be very dangerous. Look also at the back heart chakra, which is located in the middle of the upper back, and controls the lungs. When the back heart chakra is blocked, it means you're not breathing properly. And this will stop you dead in your tracks. It doesn't matter what you're doing or if you're in the middle of a project. You will suddenly feel fatigue and a need to go somewhere in order to rest.

The most detrimental belief that has kept people unmotivated is "there isn't enough time or space to get these things done!"   Time is relative. Sometimes you may feel there's too little time and so why start. Other times you may feel you don't have enough room to grow, because you have too many obligations.

The most successful people I know feel they have enough time, and so no matter how long it takes, they'll still keep at it. They make sure they have all the space they need to complete their projects, and that's because they don't let things or even people get in their way.

A WALL OF RESENTMENT AND RAGE

When you don't feel you have control over your life or that you are not allowed to make your own decisions, there can be a wall of resentment and rage inside you. This wall imprisons you and constricts your movements like a boa constrictor.

There's an inner war between your thoughts and your emotions. This results in too much overthinking, and very little action. You'll see it in the solar plexus which will be depleted, and the forehead chakra which will be overactive. In this manner, the mind is overruling the body with too many mixed commands, like go left, no, go right. The body only takes straight commands that are clear and concise. When the mind is jumbled, the body doesn't know what to do.

And finally, look at depleted dopamine levels in the brain. When dopamine levels are low, depression usually sets in.

THE EGO MOTIVATION

- "If I do this for you, what's my reward or what's in it for me?"
- Prestige! Image! And Power!
- "I need people's love!" "Respect is everything!"

So what's in it for me?"

There has to be an incentive or a reward, usually monetary, otherwise why should I do this? It's pretty self-explanatory. A lot of people are enticed by rewards or promises of getting rich. That's why they usually get involved in sales, where you have the daily pressure of meeting quotas.

It's a daily grind that burns people out. It's no different than dangling a carrot on a stick in front of a mule. At first it may work, but soon the mule catches on, and no longer chases the carrot.

People think that having nice things will make them happy, but that happiness is short-lived until the next big thing comes along. It doesn't last. It makes things easier, but over time, everything begins to smell old. Studies have shown that people working for incentives burn out quicker than any other group.

Power, prestige, and personal image

As long as you fill the voids of your life with material and external possessions, you'll never be happy. You'll always be miserable. Nothing lasts. But the price of having nice things you can ill afford, will rapidly deplete you of other benefits.

The need for power is the need to control others. It can only work as long as people are submitting to your authority. It's a power game of ruthless intimidation and manipulation. You gain power through fear. But once these people rebel, they are no longer in your control. The karma is that you will feel powerless.

Energetically, people who like power have a very small heart. Their heart chakras are very small, and their solar plexus chakra are very overactive. Basically, when a person is angry, they don't care about you. It doesn't matter what the relationship is or how close you are to them. When they're angry, they are essentially trying to hurt you in the most vulnerable manner. That's why partners cheat, because it's the most devastating way to hurt a person's ego. And a person who needs to learn anger management will always hurt you.

Clairvoyantly, the people who are easily intimidated by these kinds of people, have energetically enlarged ears. The ears connect to the root chakra which is connected to survival. I always use the example of a deer standing in the middle of a forest. If you stand in front of it but make no movement, it'll think that you're a tree or something harmless. It's because you're making no threatening moves. But once you make the slightest sound, the deer will stamper off to escape. Nature has provided this survival response, because it may be the one tip-off to escape. It's no different when you hear the siren of an ambulance or fire truck. Or when a baby cries out because it's hungry. We stop whatever we're doing, and for a moment feel disoriented. Our ears are very sensitive to sound and intonation. It literally rattles the body. And if done on a regular basis, intonation can trigger PTSD to the point that we become dysfunctional.

Unfortunately, it's difficult to clear this out, especially if you're living with a person who craves power and likes to intimidate. They like power because it feeds the entity possessing them. The entity is there, feeding off this person's weaknesses, but in exchange it gives them the feeling of being powerful. But it's a false illusion, as the power is not their own, but borrowed from the entity itself.

Removing these entities is a simple process, but it does take practice. And it needs to be done on a regular basis ,otherwise they will return. They will return because the person has their own mental scars, where they were intimidated by someone else, when they were much younger. And so it transfers from one generation to another, until the one of the next generations resolves it.

The THREE trappings

1. Buying the latest and newest toys

2. Looking to enhance one's image or status.

3. Looking for compliments and praise

Buying the latest and newest toys – is very common especially with young people. The need to buy the latest gadgets and most expensive cars are status symbols of wealth and power. It drives many people to earn more money. But it's a never-ending cycle of constantly being in debt. It's a money monster that's never satiated.

Looking to enhance one's image or status – Respect. Some people have all the power and money in the world, but they don't have respect or love from their community. Many rich people then go into philanthropic projects to redeem themselves like Andrew Carnegie and Bill Gates.

Looking for praise and compliments – How many times have you bought a new dress or a new watch hoping someone will compliment you on your appearance? Sometimes you receive it, and sometimes you don't.

The one critical factor in all this is, that you're at the mercy of the world giving you or not giving you what you want. Power can be taken away when someone stands up to you or leaves you. All material possessions get old and dusty. And anyone can withhold compliments and praise. You are at the mercy of how the world chooses to treat you.

"I have no choice but to do this."

1. I suffer from low self-worth. I suffer from feelings of guilt, shame, and disappointment in myself.

2. I don't have a choice. I feel pressure to do it, otherwise there will be consequences to pay.

3. I'm in a controlling relationship. I have to live by someone else's rules.

4. My word is my word. If I say I'm going to do it, then I will.

Most of this stuff is what you tell yourself you can't do. It's internal negative dialogue. Clairvoyantly, it sometimes looks like a big heavy cloud, either on the left or right ear. It's like a record player whispering in your ears 24/7. Usually they're old recordings of both your parents, telling you what you can and can't do. Sometimes they're tapes of intimidation and putdowns that you're replaying to yourself, but you're unaware. The next time you feel yourself stopped from doing something, listen quietly inside. It's either you telling yourself that you shouldn't do it, or a repeated message from someone else telling you what to do.

Look at both musical and logical intelligence blocks in both hemispheres. Musical because you're tending to believe the lie rather the truth, and so are doing things that you know are not right. This would explain why you feel you're imposed to do things you don't necessarily want to do or believe is the right thing to do.

Look at logical blocks because usually you're going by someone else's reasoning rather than your own. Maybe what they're saying is not right or correct, but you haven't given yourself time to think about it. And when you do you may find that you have more logical sense than they do.

Everybody suffers from low self-worth from time to time.

We've all done things that we're ashamed of. What's interesting is that we seem to attract the same situations that brought us guilt, shame, and disappointment. It's a pattern that we seem to follow or follow us, and there's a reason for it.

We're haunted by our mistakes form the past because our subconscious mind brings it up to our conscious mind. If we're not constantly thinking about our past, then it seems it's what we're attracting to ourselves or finding ourselves in the same situation. It's like our past follows us wherever we go.

We can't run away from our past. Part of it is self-judgement. There is no harsher critic then ourselves. We need to forgive ourselves. Everyone makes mistakes. That's why they put erasers on top of pencils. Nothing is permanent.

Our higher minds is also to blame. They communicate with the higher minds of other people, and actually tell them how they should treat us. Sounds like a betrayal, but it's to help us learn certain lessons in life. If we don't learn these lessons, than we're bound to repeat them. It's like playing with fire. If you don't learn to stay away from fire, and respect it, than one day you may find your clothes on fire.

Clairvoyantly, low self-esteem can also be a "disconnect" between our eyes and our arms. Our arms is about taking action, but our eyes give feedback to our brains on how we're doing. If we don't pay attention to how we're doing things, then we won't be aware that we're making mistakes or not.

I know this doesn't seem possible because how could our eyes not see what we're doing. I remember watching a chef competition where a young chef was given a simple task of a cutting sirloin into 8 oz. steaks. Instead of cutting them into 8 oz. steaks he was slicing them in 1 oz. slices. Even when this was pointed out to him, he refused to believe he was doing it wrong. Before given the task, he was interviewed and he commented how everybody thought he was slow.

I looked at him clairvoyantly to see what going on with him. One of his ears was open to instruction, but the other one was closed to hearing criticism. Even though he was standing next to the cutting board, both his legs looked like they were running which explained why he was rushing through the job. Both his arms were also moving fast influenced by the legs so he wasn't a lazy worker. But his eyes weren't giving the visual information to his brain of what 8 oz. steaks look like. His eyes were clouded with large images of trying to impress the judges and his peers, and so he really wasn't paying attention to the task at hand. Breathing from both nostrils were irregular and fast – in other words hyperventilation.

"I don't have a choice.
I feel pressure to do it, otherwise there will be consequences to pay."

Check for blockages in the right hemisphere because it deals with "Impending Doom!"

"I do it because I want to do it.
No one is forcing me to do it.
I do it with passion and drive."

This is the highest level of integration and coordination between mind and body. All the body parts (eyes, ears, nostrils, arms, and legs) are open and in direct communication with both hemispheres. Information is fed to both hemispheres and all 7 intelligences where commands are sent back to your body parts.

So how do you achieve this? It starts out with doing things through your choice. You need to make your own choices without pressure or stigma. No one can force you to do things unless it's by your own independence and freedom.

The 2nd criterion is having a strong purpose or mission for doing it. You have to believe in what you're doing, and what you're doing serves the better good of humanity. Nothing is more noble then that.

And the 3rd criterion is the more you practice, the better you get. Becoming better takes on a life all its own. As mastery brings more ease, it becomes playful.

Chapter XXVI.

AURA VARIATIONS

When you drop a pebble in the middle of a pond, it sends a cascade of concentric circles ever widening from its center. This wave of circles reaches the far edges of the pond, disturbing everything both on the surface of the pond and below it. For good or bad, the ripple effect returns back to its origin, like salmon returning to spawn to the place it was born.

The type of pebbles you are dropping in your pond will determine what type of ripples and waves you are causing. Each wave functions like karma where there is cause and effect. And whatever you send out in the universe eventually returns back to you.

Imagine for a moment that every pebble you drop is a thought. And the ripple effect are the emotions in reaction to that thought. If you project positive and loving thoughts, then happiness and contentment will be your reward. If you project angry thoughts, then you will attract negative people and circumstances. If you project fear and insecurity, then you will have low self-esteem and people will take advantage of you.

Now imagine the pond is your aura. It could be teeming with lots of fish and lilies, or it could be filled with snakes and frogs. You can tell if the pond is fragrant with the scent of flowers, or the smell of death and decay from a distance. These are all significant tell-tale signs, because the state of your aura is what you attract into your life.

When I work with clients, I see a vibrational point emanating from the center of their heart, passing through their aura and to the environment around them. It's like a homecoming signal alerting and influencing things around them, and bringing forth both positive and negative forces. Like a magnet, it attracts. Most people are unaware of the frequencies they attract. They are like ships navigating the seas of life, without someone steering the rudder, yet they seem to reach the same destination consistently. Perhaps it's just luck or the vibrational waves they are unconsciously charting.

THE THREE MAJOR MOTIVATIONS

Affiliation – friendship and family are most important.

Lack of affiliation – less concerned with friendship or another person's feelings and needs.

Power – the need to control or have people submit to them and their demands

Powerlessness - feeling powerless, allowing others to control and manipulate them due to low self-esteem. Also, not able to think clearly or think for one's self, more than willing to take directions and allow others to think for them (co-dependency).

Achievement – by all means necessary to achieve objective. If they have to be charming to gain trust, then they will be their best friend or send love bombs if they're in a relationship. A certain degree of mental awareness is required to observe what the person's wants and desires are. By fulfilling what they want and desire most with the objective, they will in the end help others accomplish whatever their goals are.

Lack of achievement – not able to reach one's goals in life, much less know what they are. Like a ship drifting in the ocean with no sail. Just allowing the currents of life to take them wherever, without a destination.

LOVE AND FEAR

There are two basic emotions – love and fear. These two emotions form the very basis of all vibrations. They are antagonistic to each other. In other words, one cannot exist while the other is present. For example, anger springs forth from fear that the other person or thing has control over you. It springs forth when you feel you're no longer in control and feel vulnerable.

When a person is angry with you, they momentarily forget how much they love or care for you. Anger is very destructive, because when one is angry, all they want to do is hurt the other person. And this leads to destructive choices. If they are in an intimate relationship and are angry with their partner, then the easiest and swiftest way to hurt them is betrayal. If it's a business partner, they will swindle them out of their money. And if it's someone they really hate, they may inflict physical harm or even murder.

Most people are really unaware of what type of vibrations they are sending out. They seem oblivious and often cite themselves as victims. But through doing countless readings and healings, I can honestly say that nothing happens by accident. And past transgressions will follow you, no matter how long ago they occurred. It's like when a person smokes for ten years and yet for the last twenty years they stopped. The person believes that after twenty years of non-smoking they are in the clear and that their lungs have healed sufficiently, but that is not the case. Twenty years may have slowed down the progression of lung disease, but the consequences of their years of smoking still exist. That's why later in their advanced age, they may suffer severe health complications, as a result of previously smoking for ten years.

So why is it that you may have changed on the inside, but you seem to attract the same negative circumstances into your life? It's your aura. The pebbles you dropped years ago are still manifesting the same type of waves. You would think that because you've changed, you are dropping different pebbles and sending out different waves to counteract the waves you sent out earlier.

Not exactly.

Unless you're really aware of yourself – your habits, thoughts, and emotions – then you don't have an honest assessment of where you are at, and what you need to change. The world around you is a mirror of what you create. Either you see what you're creating or you don't.

That is the reason why I created the body parts assessment system. If your ears are energetically blocked, then you're not willing or able to hear outside opinions. If your ears are blocked, then the only voice you hear is your own, telling the same lies or untruths over and over again. You won't accept outside opinions, because that might challenge what you fervently believe, and that will be a blow to your ego. The point is this: the voices you hear in your head may not be your own, but the voices of your parents or friends, advising you what to do long ago. That may have been okay at the time, but times have changed, and you need to upgrade this programming.

If your eyes are blocked, then you are not able to see what's happening in the present. You may or may not able to observe what's going on, are therefore you may not be able to make correct assessments of what to do. Images run us. Sometimes these images are in front of us like a movie screen. There is a reason why the audience in a movie theatre sits in the dark and the movie screen is so large - in order to amplify our visceral perceptions. And sometimes the images are in our inner mind that only we can see and understand. It's the way our brain works, but we need to compare what's happening in the real world to our inner images, so that we can make changes to what we see and believe.

Blockages in our nostrils or breathing has the greatest effect, because our thinking automatically shuts down, if we're not receiving enough oxygen. Our energy can drop substantially, so we feel sleepy or unable to concentrate. Not having enough oxygen, even by a small margin, puts us in a state of survival. Short and frequent breaths disrupt our thinking process, while people who have longer breaths have longer and more complex thoughts. That alone is a game changer. For example, people who have math anxiety go into hyperventilation. It's unconscious. It's quick. And it makes it impossible to think properly.

These THREE main blockages affect our arms and legs energetically. Because it's our ears, eyes, and nostrils that effect what actions we take, and where we go. This is known as the command center. It's where instructions are given. But the signals from our brain go beyond our limbs and body. They are projected like radio signals, interacting with the signals everyone else is also projecting. When two signals of similar frequency come into contact with each other, then these two signals develop a magnetic attraction to each other. It's like two dogs sniffing one another trying to tell if they are friends or foes. "Are you aggressive or friendly? Can we hang together in a pack or not?" The aura operates in this manner, independently. When you first meet someone, are you not also checking them out? The clothes they wear, how they move and how they talk are all tell-tale signs of who they are. But even as you are walking towards each other, both your auras are sharing and communicating information. People who are psychic are able to read others they don't know by tuning to their aura, even while quite a distance away. It's just a matter of practice.

Following are three basic types of auras.

LOVING AURA

Main motivation – Affiliation with balance of Spirituality

Intelligence blocks - None

This aura is extremely large. It's feels warm and comforting like sitting below the sun. A simple smile radiates happiness even from a photograph. In turn, people are drawn to people with loving auras like magnets, literally. That's because love has the highest vibration of them all. Love is the vibration of the universe.

Kindness, respect, and communication comprises the loving aura. Never make an insulting or judgmental comment, even if you think you're right.

Patience and understanding goes a lot further. Compliments and praise are the key. Just be nice!

The heart chakra of a person with a loving aura is obviously highly energized. When the heart chakra is energized, it means that the person doesn't worry much, feels a great deal of contentment, and peace of mind. It's also slightly overactive, meaning there is some concern for the well-being of the other person, but not overly much. The forehead chakra is also clear and not overactive, so there's not too much overthinking going on. The root chakra is not overactive, meaning the person is not in survival mode.

The main motivation is affiliation, but it's balanced with Spirituality. The person is not overly concerned with money, materialism, or prestige. They enjoy being happy with one's self while surrounded with people they love and who love them in return. Connections with people are very important to them. Stress is almost non-existent as they occupy themselves with hobbies that they enjoy. Most are elderly or in retirement. They basically have gone through various stages early on in their life and now they can relax.

But Spirituality can be achieved through:

1. Making your own choices without someone telling you what to do or persuading you to do something you don't want to do. Making your own independent choices is the single most empowering thing you can do for yourself. Yes, you will make mistakes and it may cost you in terms of money, time and resources. But you will learn from your mistakes and gain confidence. More importantly, you will improve your decision-making - mental clarity.

2. Find a cause you believe in, and is beneficial to other people. You have to align your actions with good values. This will give you a purpose.

3. Develop competence. You may not be perfect in the beginning, but you will get better. And as you get better, then what you practice becomes art.

VICTIM AURA

Main Motivation – Affiliation without the balance of Spirituality

Intelligence Blocks – Musical and Visual

When the Musical intelligence of a person is strong, then they are difficult to deceive or manipulate. They can not commit acts that they believe are wrong or do not feel right.

When the Musical intelligence is weak or blocked, then the person is prone to believe someone's lies or manipulations more so than the truth. That is why, when friends try to warn them, the person with a victim aura will instead defend the person or partner that is causing them distress. Their ears will be energetically blocked from hearing their friend's advice. In other words, they won't believe anything you say.

Their visual intelligence is blocked, especially in the right hemisphere which deals with fantasy images. Look for blockages in the left eye, where they're maintaining visual images of this person. If it's a male partner, then they're Prince Charming. If a female, then they're Beauty Queens. It doesn't matter that it has no relation to reality – beauty is in the eyes of the beholder.

Overactive chakras – Heart, Forehead, Back heart, Meng Mein with depleted Root chakra

Overactive chakras are depleted of energy. But when demand on these chakras are in a state of emergency, then they take over the personality of the person.

Overactive heart chakra person becomes overly sensitive to people's needs and moods. They literally feel what other people are going through. If they are sad, they feel the sadness as their own, and it hurts. If someone is angry with them, they really feel it, even though no words are spoken. If words are spoken, then it is ten time worse. In order to stop feeling all these painful vibrations, they do their best to appease their friends. Anything to stop feeling the emotional pain that is directed towards them.

Overactive forehead chakra – too many thoughts are crowding their mind - overthinking. They can't think clearly, feel confused and overwhelmed. This makes it difficult to make decisions, and so it's easier to leave the decision making to someone else which may not be to always to their benefit.

Back-heart chakra is located on the upper back, between the lungs. This chakra controls breathing, and when blocked, it feels as if you're not getting enough oxygen. You feel tired and it is hard to concentrate. You may take more rest, breaks or even naps. Breathing issues cause anxiety and even panic attacks. Let's put it this way, if you walk slowly, you'll probably make it a few blocks. But if you had to run, you'll collapse before you reach the finish line. When someone is putting pressure on you, it feels as if you're running. And when you go unconscious, you're less aware of what's being said to you or what's going on.

Meng mein with depleted root chakra. The root chakra is located at your tail bone, and the Meng mein is a chakra located between your kidneys and adrenals. The Meng mein deals with your high or low blood pressure. This is very dangerous to your health.

When the root chakra is depleted you have less energy, including life force for your body to function properly. Your chakras then become less energized, except for the heart chakra. But the body has to keep functioning, and so it uses the reserve energy in your kidneys and adrenals. This is not healthy for your body, as it can cause serious health issues. This can go on for years or even decades.

Most Empaths have victim auras. Their main motivation is affiliation, but it's not balanced with Spirituality. Without Spirituality, the heart chakra over-expands without limitations, making them overly sensitive to people's moods and feelings. Like a vacuum cleaner, they pick up vibrations of others around them, especially negative people.

The characteristics of the heart chakra are to love, heal, and take care of people. That's why they're attracted to people who need fixing. The more messed-up a person is, the more they feel an obligation to help them. They may even marry them. It doesn't mean they will have a happy life, but a life of servitude.

People with victim auras don't believe they are deserving of love and affection, and so they give and give with the hope of receiving something. Usually they end up depleted. As long as their partners and friends can still get something from them, they will continue to drain them. And if they can't give anymore, then they will wait for a later date when they've recovered, and the cycle begins all over again.

Choice has usually been taken away from them. Their partners keep them on a very short leash. They constantly monitor them, keeping tabs on their comings and goings and checking constantly on what they're thinking. This is to make sure they stay in place.

People with victim auras are controlled by guilt and shame. They worry about the other person before themselves, and feel responsible and tied to them. What keeps them from walking away from their partners are two factors: they are so depleted of energy that it's hard for them to move away or take action, and their minds are focused on the hardships their partners will go through if they walk away.

Clairvoyantly, the heart chakra is extremely overactive. You can feel the aura of the heart chakra, which can be as large as the person's body with feelers extending several feet away. This is followed by the forehead chakra, also overactive but not as much as the heart chakra. This is why the person is extremely empathic. The forehead chakra controls thinking and thoughts. It also controls the prefrontal cortex. When the forehead chakra is overactive, then it means that the person is overthinking or too confused to think straight.

In addition, the person will find it difficult to breathe. There will be blockages in both the sternum, lungs, nostrils as well as the Back Heart chakra located in the top center of the back, and the Mein meng chakra located between the kidneys. There is major blockages in both kidneys and adrenals, which would explain why the person is constantly fatigued. With no energy to think and being overly sensitive to other people's emotions, it's no wonder it's a victim aura.

It's not easy to heal. People with a victim aura are plague with anxiety and panic attacks. The protocol is to first clear these anxieties by clearing blockages along the sternum, to help them breathe more easily. This needs to be counterbalanced with sending them mass amounts of chi energy to replenish them. Blockages along the spine need to be cleared, so that the chi can rise upwards from the root chakra to the top of the head. This is critically important, as it supplies the forehead chakra with energy.

I've studied numerous emotional clearing modalities. Some of them work fantastically. But the one thing they are all missing is, that while the client may have emotional relief, their chi or their root chakra remains depleted. They are still in the same vulnerable state as before. Their thinking patterns that have gotten them into the state of the victim aura are still the same. By energizing their root chakra or directly energizing their brain, they will regain some mental clarity. Next time they are faced with the same situation, they will be able to look at things with fresh eyes. They will start to notice things they were not able to notice before. They will finally start to see and hear things that their friends have been warning them about, and with these new observations they can begin making better choices.

Two Most Powerful Techniques
to Combat Victim Aura Syndrome

ONE: Practice neutrality. Disengage from your emotions, and say to yourself, "For right now, I don't have to do anything." The attitude is, "I won't do any harm to anybody, but at the same time I will not allow anybody to harm me."

Get in touch with your intuition. People have a wrong concept of what they think intuition is. Intuition is not emotional – it's neutral. Intuition is like the GPS on your car. The commands of a GPS are simple and direct – "Turn left or turn right" if you miss a turn, then it simply says to make a u-turn at the next corner. It's not "TURN LEFT RIGHT NOW!" that's your heart chakra screaming. Your intuition is neutral and says things in a matter-of-fact voice. Your intuition doesn't put you down or make you feel bad.

TWO: When the heart chakra is overactive, clairvoyantly there is a large vortex over the chakra. This vortex is usually as big as the person, but it can be larger. The larger it is, the more it will absorb negative vibrations from other people.

Simply imagine your fingertips closing down on this vortex, making it smaller and smaller until closed. Imagine grasping your fingertips on the outside perimeter of this vortex, (it doesn't matter how large it is) and bringing your fingers together to a single point. That's it. You can do this several times, if you feel the vortex opening up.

In a few minutes, you'll notice yourself calming down emotionally.

Of all the Seven chakras, the Heart chakra is the only one that doesn't depend on the root chakra to get energized. I discovered it by accident while working with a client. This went against what I was taught by my teachers. I was taught that the root chakra is responsible for energizing the remaining six chakras.

But in numerous scans over the years I've discovered that the root chakra can be depleted, and so the rest of the chakras should be depleted as well, but not the heart chakra.

I wondered why.

I noticed a pattern, as it turned out, the clients with the biggest heart chakras were also the nicest people. And because they were so nice with others, people sent them loving thoughts and compliments. This was what was energizing their heart chakra.

Sounds good, but it wasn't. With no other energy source available, the heart chakra became dependent on people sending them loving thoughts. In time, it became the means for them to function day-to-day. Maybe because they were searching for love and someone to care for them. Some people need love like they need to drink water.

Overtime, the heart chakra suppresses the forehead and the solar plexus chakra. With the forehead chakra suppressed, they're not able to think properly. With the solar plexus chakra, they don't have boundaries which allows the heart chakra to constantly feed itself. Things don't always work as planed. You attract good people as well as bad people. It doesn't matter, since the heart chakra doesn't discern, because the forehead chakra is suppressed. This can lead to a lifetime of servitude to other people.

ANGRY AURAS

Main Motivation – Achievement then Power.

Achievement – the strangest thing is that people with angry auras don't appear to be angry at first. They appear charming. That's because their goal is to win you over. They want you to like them. They are very focused on their self-image and that's why they look good. In nature the most colorful insects are often also the most deadly.

Their objective is to find someone who will take care of them, put them on a pedestal and treat their wants and needs like they are their top priority, while feeling no need for reciprocity. If you're looking for a friend, they'll be your best friend in the world. If it's a romantic relationship, they'll throw love bombs until your defenses are destroyed, and they totally have you. They will study you and learn your weaknesses.   And they can be very persistent, despite your rejections. They will wear you down until they achieve their single-minded objective. They only get angry with you when you're not playing their game.

Power – once they have achieved their objective with you, the game changes - switches toward Power and Control. And that's when you see the true nature of the beast.

SIX SIGNS TO WATCH FOR

1. It's very difficult to say "No" to their constant demands. They disempoweryou by preventing you from making your own choices.

2. They will bring up your past over and over again in order to shame and make you feel guilty. This is to distract you from what's going on in the present, and have you perpetually stuck in the past. You won't be able to think straight, and your self-esteem will be at an all-time low. They will use your own negative emotions to weaken you, and keep you from thinking straight. Their agenda is to break your spirit, by using your insecurities against you. Once they do, they can get what they want from you.

3. If you protest and fight back, they will accuse you of being crazy. They are never wrong, and are blameless. They have the ability to turn your words against you and start making you doubt yourself. You'll stop thinking for yourself and lose your mind. You'll be reduced to being a robot that takes orders and doesn't question it. Because every time you do, you will fear they will get angry with you. You've been intimidated to the point of submission, and not know it. It's easier to not fight back, and just get along.

4. They are true masters of changing the subject, and deflecting blame from themselves. They're like Teflon – nothing sticks to them. They'll do this every time you bring up the same issues. They want you to make you forget these issues. If you stand your ground, then their next strategy is to walk away.

5. They leave a trail of broken promises and tears. They'll say anything to make you happy, and to get you off their case. But they'll never deliver. They'll only deliver if it benefits them, and that's all. Your interests come second in line.

6. They like to feel important, and that they know what's best for you. They always have an idea for everything in your life, and wish you would consult them more often. But their ideas more often than not, lead to bad results. And when confronted, they deflect blame and even responsibility. A common tactic is to say it was your choice. And their bad ideas keep coming, because they have short-term memories of what they said to you before.

IT'S ABOUT CONTROL, NOT LOVE

Power is about controlling you, and making you submit to their will. If you thought they loved you, they'll suddenly turn and become heartless. And you will be miserable! The funny thing is, your friends and your family will not believe you, because they've projected such a wonderful impression on them.

You think that it is your fault, because of their change of personality. You think that's why they stoped loving you. When anger is present, there is no love. Love and understanding are not always the right solutions. You think that love will make them stop hurting you. At first it will, but later they get used to it and become immune.

You have to understand that before they met you or if they were your close family member or even parent, they came from a place of great pain. It is the story of their lives that they can't get away from, and it haunts their waking dreams on a daily basis.

They're damaged. Clairvoyantly, there is an image of their inner child huddled in a fetal position. The memories of their early childhood are still present, where they are subjected to the same emotional and physical abuse they experienced. They're miserable. Their definition of displaying love is to display anger and meanness, because that's was what taught to them. It's twisted. It's difficult for them to display gentleness and express feelings. They don't know how. They want retribution for what was done to them.

Anger creates tension, and tension either needs to be released or expressed. You cannot sustainably hold this tension very long. It becomes too unbearable. And that's where the manipulation and mind games emerge. They're hurting others because they themselves have been hurt.

Anger directly impacts the aura. Clairvoyantly it looks like spikes jutting from their body. These spikes are designed to keep themselves emotionally distanced from people. These spikes are very sensitive, not so much to other people's auras, but to the angry person behind them. In other words, they're very sensitive and it feels as though they're constantly getting hurt. That's why they can be so cold and callous – it's the numbness they've developed from the pain.

Overactive chakras

forehead, solar plexus, sex chakra, & root chakra.

Forehead chakra – the more often you get angry, the less intelligent you become. You stop thinking, and become more reactive. And as you get older, you begin to act crazy.

Solar plexus chakra – deals more with your base emotions like anxiety, anger, envy, and jealousy. If you know how to scan the subtle energy, you can survey how many blockages exist there. The more blockages, the more this person is prone to anger. If it's in the back solar plexus, then it's resentment and they're more prone to passive aggression. They also tend to be more selfish and self-serving.

Sex chakra – overly concerned with their personal needs, desires, and image. That's why they look so good. They wear fancy clothes, drive fancy cars, and appear very charming. Everybody loves them except the ones who are really involved with them. They see their true colors.

Root chakra – they're always in survival mode. They're nice until you cross them. It's all about them and what they want. They're nice to you as long as you're serving them, but once you stop, they feel as if you betrayed them.

I call narcissist strategies "fishing lures" or just "lures" for short. It's like when a fisherman baits a hook to attract fish. One nibble is all it takes before they reel you in. They may try to be friendly to you, but what they're really looking for, is to get your defensive guard down so that you'll be again on friendly terms with them. It's because they know who you are, and that you have a big heart. They know that you're always willing to help or give and that's what they're counting on. Then it goes back to the same pattern where you're doing them favors, because they always seem to be in trouble. And you're the only one that's available and willing to help them. That's what they're counting on. Because no one else is willing to help them. Few people are willing to help, and that's why they look for empaths like yourself – because you're a rarity.

Clairvoyantly, there's a vortex in front of the heart chakra and it's constantly pumping the heart full of emotional pain and anxiety. It's very hard to think clearly doing this phase because you're feeling so emotional.

Intelligence blocks

Logical

The blockages will be on the left hemisphere, connected to the logical portion of the brain. The left hemisphere deals with logic, reasoning, and Ego. The left hemisphere will delete from memory certain facts that it deems threatening to the Ego, in order to hold the person blameless. It will even invent false memories, so that they are the victim and not the perpetrator.

This is dangerous because it messes with their sense of reality. They will start to believe their own lies. The karma is that they will forever be imprisoned in their miseries and will never find happiness. People they love will stay away from them.

That's why people with angry auras are difficult to reason with. They won't listen to you no matter how legitimate your arguments are. Their logic is not logical, but it's illogical. It makes no sense. Yet they come up with creative, sometimes even ingenious reasons why it does. And that's why they have so many problems – problems they'll never solve because they're illogical in the first place.

One Attracts the Other

People with angry auras look at people with big hearts -Victim auras- as vulnerable prey. They smell them like the way a sharks smells blood in the water. They send out what I call "fishing lures" or "lures" to attract them. And then when they bite down, they're caught like a fish. They're slowly reeled in where they'll be cooked for tonight's dinner.

Chapter XXVII

YOUR LIFE IS SHAPED BY YOUR EARLIEST TRAUMA

EXPANSION VERSUS CONTRACTION

There is an electrical field around the brain that expands and contracts, depending on what you're thinking. When you're thinking positively and confidently, this energy expands. When you're more negative and angry, this energy contracts.

This electrical field is the attractor that manifests things in your life both positively and negatively. When this field is expanded, it sends a beacon signal that pulls in people, resources, and opportunity to you. When it contracts, it's like your field pulls away from everyone around you, and you become isolated.

Positive/Positive - when the electrical field around the brain expands and is positive, the person's values are in alignment with their actions. This is a person with a very lucky aura. They're able to manifest their deepest desires with resources and opportunities paving their way. This is because their values are in alignment with their actions. Their life is filled with a deeper purpose in mind, which is to serve humanity.

Positive/Negative – This is where Evil appears as something positive. On the surface, this person is successful, rich, and even charismatic. But their means for achieving these aims are criminal and nefarious.

They can operate for years, even decades, and not get caught. The reason is that they're very intelligent and know how to protect themselves. Unless you're part of their inner circle, you would never know who you're really dealing with. And this is how they get the masses to follow them.

Negative/Positive – The energy of the brain is not so expansive on the outside, but is immense inside. This is because the person has created an inner world that is isolated from the outside world. There are 2 types:

1. People living in a fantasy world – it could be a time when the world was more innocent and they're living in a still-frozen moment that never changes. Usually it refers to something in childhood, where they feel it missing or they want to recreate. Either way they're very protective and guard its fragile existence.

2. Scientist like Sir Isaac Newton are negative/positives because they need to isolate themselves from the world in order to devote themselves to their study. It's not necessarily a bad thing, as this is sometimes necessary to make great accomplishments.

Negative/Negative – People who have isolated themselves in groups of like mindedness or are by themselves. Together they have formed cults who shun the world, so that they can live their own lifestyle and ideologies. These ideologies are based on fear and hate.

LOGICAL vs. ILLOGICAL THINKING

Logical thinking – in order to reach success, you need to learn how to solve problems. And in order to solve problems, you have to have good logical skills. One way of doing this is by reading, and constantly learning new things.

The basic formula of logic is that A follows B which leads to C. If you follow this formula, then your results should be consistent and successful. If you're not achieving the results you desire, then there's something amiss with the steps you're taking.

The biggest problem I see with logical people is that they keep on following the same formula, even though it doesn't work anymore. It may have worked in the beginning, but it may not be working now. Why?

Because conditions change. Markets change. People's tastes and desires change. And the world keeps revolving. And when logical people don't adapt, they become illogical.

Illogical thinking - The majority of our problems are caused by our illogical thinking. Because when we're not getting the results we want, we are unhappy. The problem is people who think illogically don't know that they do. They embrace their illogic tightly and defend it with reasoning, that only make sense to them and not to others. They even try to impose their illogical views on other people, and dismiss all arguments to the contrary. Anyone can make the most obscene reasons sound logical.

The hardest illogic is the ones called, "blind spots." Because the person doesn't even know that they're stuck in an illogical pattern, that brings no happiness or success. They just keep walking blindly into the same brick wall, no matter how many times their forehead get bruised.

I have seen people staunchly defend their views to the last nail. Yet they complain how things don't work in their life, and how miserable they are. They take no responsibility for their lives, while idly watching it pass them by. You can't advise them because their ears are energetically closed. They are addicted to their Ego as they are addicted to their drama.

In order to resolve these issues, you first need a map of the roads that you've been traveling. For me, there is no better map than the chakras themselves. Following is not a definitive guide to the chakras – you can get books on that anywhere, but more like a quick-guide to help you understand yourself better.

When you think of your issue, scan each of your chakras to see which are blocked, and then read the following descriptions of them. Then use the body scan system like your eyes, ears, and especially nostrils, to see which are blocked or not giving feedback to your brain. These will give you important clues.

CHAKRA MAP

1. ROOT CHAKRA – security, survival, and trust issues. You can't move forward if you feel insecure or unsafe. You will avoid and retreat where you feel safe. If you try to move forward despite your fear, your senses and body parts will shut down preventing you from moving forward. You cannot fight what your subconscious mind deems a threat to your safety, whether imaginary or real.

2. SEX CHAKRA – addictions, materialism, and desires. Closely connected to the root chakra, so if a person has survival issues then it will be associated with the sex chakra. All their issues will have a desperate life or death attachment, like they have to attain this at all cost. In other words, they won't feel complete, satisfied, or happy unless they get what they want. And this will be used to justify the means of them getting it. And they will believe under the circumstances that they were right, because they feel they had no other choice.

3. SOLAR PLEXUS CHAKRA – blockages in the solar plexus chakra usually means inability to take action. I didn't say the person didn't want to take action. Just that they find it difficult to follow-up with any action steps. And it can be followed with the moment they feel ready to take action, that their energy drops and they feel suddenly tired.

4. HEART CHAKRA – feeling too much empathy from other people. Sometimes it's real and sometimes it's an overblown reaction to what you think the person is feeling or going through. Sometimes it's feeling so much emotional pain that it's anxiety-producing debilitation. In other words, almost impossible to function or experiencing shut-down.

5. THROAT CHAKRA – when the throat chakra is blocked, it's because the person was rebuked for telling the truth when they were a child. This ends up either the person staying quiet or telling lies. If it's staying quiet, then the person feels all bottled up and not feeling safe to express themselves in the world. If it's telling lies, then there's a pervasive lack of taking responsibility and learning from their mistakes.

6. FOREHEAD CHAKRA – too much overthinking. Overthinking due to feeling confused and unclear. This confusion leads to overcrowding your mind with thoughts, and then you feel overwhelmed because there's too many things you want to do, but you don't know where to start. You can't start because you're feeling too confused. And when you're feeling too confused and overwhelmed, this leads to depression. And depression is internal suppressed anger, feeling that you're stuck in the same place and not moving anywhere.

7. CROWN CHAKRA – emotional issues or emotional instability. It can also be the portal where entities enter a person's field of energy. Easily damaged through drugs and alcohol.

8. NAVEL CHAKRA – source of low vitality when depleted. Can be used to energize all other chakras, and so is invaluable.

9. SPLEEN CHAKRA – when this chakra is depleted, people lack initiative or find it difficult to start projects. People think it's a sign of laziness, but actually it's a lack of energy. Because once this chakra is energized, people start projects they've been putting off.

10. MEIN MENG CHAKRA – located in-between both kidneys. Each time this chakra is blocked, I've noticed I feel stuck. It's a subtle feeling that most of the time I'm not consciously aware of. It's like a Grandfather clock that rewinds itself through the swing of the pendulum. When the pendulum stops swinging, the clock stops.

One explanation is that the Mein meng chakra is above the root chakra, and it distributes your energy through the rest of your body and chakras. When the Mein meng is blocked, it usually means the root chakra is depleted of energy, and so you use your reserve energy which are your adrenals. But even so, my experiments have shown even energizing the root chakra is almost impossible when the Mein meng is blocked. As soon as I energize the root chakra, the energy flows right out. This makes the Mein meng chakra one of two highly critical chakras to unblock.

11. BACKHEART CHAKRA – located in the middle of the upper back. This chakra highly influences your lungs and your ability to breathe.

The backheart chakra is the most critical chakra that I look at, when a person is in a repeated pattern of being stuck or failing. The backheart chakra controls:

- When you suddenly stop breathing due to stress, anxiety, or fear, the backheart chakra is blocked

- One or both nostrils can be blocked severely limiting how much oxygen you inhale, thereby lowering your energy level

- The pattern of your breathing determines attention level, flow and interruption of your thoughts, and ability to think and concentrate.

- Mental awareness is the key to success in all endeavors – it's not just memorization. With mental awareness, you can learn ten times faster than without.

When I work with a client, I ask them to bring up one issue in their mind, and only one issue that they want to work on. As they're thinking about it, the blocks in their chakras lit up. If they suddenly change, and think of another issue, then the readings of the chakras will not be consistent.

I go through all ELEVEN chakras fairly quickly. If a chakra is energized, then I skip to the next chakra. If it's energized, then it's unlikely that it's blocked. If the next chakra is depleted or overactive, which actually indicates a vortex over the chakra, then the chakra is not functioning properly. Usually it means that it is blocked.

When the client's chakras are blocked, I do a body reading. I scan which body parts are blocked, like for example their eyes and ears, and so on. This reveals a lot of information on how information or lack of information is being fed to their brain. Reading the left and right hemispheres also gives me information as to which of the Seven Intelligences are blocked.

All of this gives me a very accurate picture of what's going on with a client. I'm able to give a reading to my client that's both specific and insightful, and many have commented that this was the most accurate reading they've received. There's no second guessing. Everything follows a logical and sequential pathway. Of course I get flash-intuitive images, but they are easy to interpret, because of the strong foundation I follow.

When you are able to clarify an issue for a client, it takes them out of their confusion and overwhelmed state of mind. Suddenly it's like turning on a light switch in a dark room. They can see the objects they've been bumping into. Armored with fresh insights, they begin to open up and the pieces of the puzzle start coming together. Their problems, which seemed insurmountable at first, are now manageable. Suddenly their anxiety level is reducing, and they feel more empowered.

CLEARING YOUR BLOCKS

I've studied every form of energy healing there is. I've extensively studied clearing the chakras and auras. I've even studied Western psychology and applied their therapeutic models. And I still didn't feel I found the answers I wanted.

It was only when I began to study the latest in brain research that I found my answer. You see, everything emanates from the brain. All your thoughts, emotions, and habits. The key was figuring out how thoughts appear energetically in the brain. If I could understand that, then I would have clues how to change our thought process and reprogram it. The system took me years to develop, and became what is now formally named, "Compass Energetics".

CONCLUSION

I never thought that my life's calling was being a healer. It's funny how a sudden turn-of-events can radically change the course of your life. My purpose in writing this book was to honor my parents for the sacrifices they made for me. I never knew that the journey provides its own rewards.

Writing this book has been the most rewarding experience for me as a healer, and researcher. Through the support and encouragement of my editor, Sabrina Mesko, I finally achieved my dream of writing a book. Otherwise, my ideas would have been lost to time.

I am always discovering new things. Now I have a record and a platform where I can continue building a strong foundation and share my knowledge and discoveries with inquisitive readers like you.

It's taken me one whole year to finish writing this book. I have never accomplished anything so gratifying or rewarding in my life. Soon after completion, I thought I would take a long hiatus and just relax for a while. Nothing could be further from the truth. Within a week I called Sabrina, and said I was ready to start my second book. I had some ideas on what it would be about, but like any good adventure, I never know how it will turn out until the end. I will present new material as it is being developed and researched. I don't know what new discoveries I will make, but it will be exciting to find out.

I am enthused to reveal, that the new material promises a powerful and effective new modality with exciting new insights into energetic healing. I look forward to sharing with you my latest discoveries. Until then, I wish you great fortune in discovering your own personal journey.

Pura Vida!

ABOUT THE AUTHOR

Jeffrey Miraflor has studied extensively with Master Choa Kok Sui and the Pranic Healing System, Sabrina Mesko's Mudra Mastery courses, OptimaLearning, Theta healing, crystal healing, BrainGym, and numerous healing modalities. He has also studied Western psychology, neurology, and other sciences. His unique gift is that he's able to combine both Western and Eastern science together by seeing clairvoyantly what happens to the energetic body as they are performed. Like a scientist he's able to perform energetic experiments moving variables around to see how they interact with the energetic body and the effect they have. This has led to new concepts and innovative techniques.

Visit his website at:
wwwCompassEnergetics.com